Articulating Aliens

CONSTRUCTING THE MIGRANT IN AMERICAN DISCOURSE

BY HOLLY SEVIER

Keywords: immigration, nationalism, popular culture, migrant subjectivity,
media analysis, discourse analysis, discursive crossover

DEDICATION

This book is dedicated to my grandmother, Moreen Leroy, and to all those who ignore the conditions of the possible.

CONTENTS

LIST OF FIGURES

LIST OF ILLUSTRATIONS

Ernesto Yerena. *obeygiant.*

Image 18: Screenshot of *Best Friend* campaign commercial. 2010. Sharron Angle.

Image 19: Trump. 2018 @realDonaldTrump. 5:44pm - 5 July.

Image 20: Trump. 2018 @realDonaldTrump. 6:44am - 23 April.

Image 21: Sand Dune Fence. nd. US Department of Homeland Security.

Image 22: Web meme. 2015. Bachmann fabricated as being quoted on *Fox News.*

Image 23: Build the Wall Trump 2020 Kit. 2019. *TrumpStoreAmerica.*

ACKNOWEDGEMENTS

This work sprang from a challenge to think beyond national definitions. It led me on a journey of ideas from "We the People" of 1787 to Trump's proposed border wall. My analysis prompted me to think about two things: the successive collectives of alien others who are restricted and excluded from the US; and the myriad ways that discourses interact to code particular desired and undesired national subjects. These studies resulted in a PhD in sociology and the following work that is in large part a reprint of my 2019 doctoral thesis.

I am grateful to Sang-hyoun Pahk for encouraging me that no idea is beyond examination. I am also glad for the contributions of my PhD committee: Nandita Sharma, Michael J. Shapiro, David Johnson, Katherine Irwin, and Nevzat Soguk. There is no way I could have done this without the love and support of my family. Raymond, Ray, and Toby, in particular, all deserve a prize for putting up with me pausing and recording bits of random television.

PREFACE

The idea of nations is perhaps most perfectly expressed in the ubiquitous schoolroom globe. Each nation is organized in a patchwork of pastel hues, the oceans in-between a uniformity of blue. The countries are separate, but not unique. Here a pink one, there another. Africa with so many patches it is a wonder they don't need more colors to keep the countries apart. Australia so large and undivided it is a one-color continent. Oceans and rivers separate some countries, yet others separated as if by an invisible hand, lines so straight a ruler could have drawn them. This promising vision of the world is static: each pastel country simply one uniform part of a color-coordinated whole. There are seemingly no disputed borders, no illegal aliens, no internal divisions.

On critical inspection, though, this pastel globe vision conceals more than it reveals. The world is divided through violent struggle; borders are maintained through massive and myriad means; the lines on the map separate families and divide communities; the globe is not static but rather ripe with movement. A country, it turns out, is not just a country, it is a nation-state—a specific form of state power deeply concerned with—and reliant on—ideas of the 'nation', of its rightful 'national' subject, and of a hermetically sealed border to separate those who 'belong' from those who do not[1].

This work examines articulations between diverse types of alien discourses in the US and focuses on the political and material effects of these articulations for those produced as migrant. In analyzing rhetoric about the alien, I use a Foucaultian approach to discourse analysis. Discourse in this sense signifies what is said or shown within a specific socio-historical and political context that leads to specific political and material outcomes. Leaning on the critical theoretical concepts of ideology (Marx 1845) and hegemony (Gramsci 1971), I explain how the figure of the alien is socially constructed (Berger and Luckmann 1966). This analytic approach emphasizes that discourses emerge out of structures of power and reproduce power relations.

Through a genealogical analysis, I trace the historically specific contours of the discourse that produces the migrant subjectivity. This figure first appears as the 'alien' of the 1790 Naturalization Act and throughout this study I illuminate a number of key shifts in the discourse to highlight changing problematizations in the migrant subjectivity from 1790 to today. Drawing from a necessarily large and diverse font of media—from campfire songs of the gold rush to Trump's tweets —I show how historical ideas, problematizations, and 'solutions' concerning the migrant inform and impact the contemporary discourse as well as lend legitimacy to proposed solutions.

One of the ways the migrant subjectivity is problematized, I argue, is when the language used to produce the 'alien' migrant does so in a way that purposefully invokes the 'alien species' discourse and the space aliens discourse. This occurs routinely, for example, when Trump tweets that migrants, "infest our Country" (@realDonaldTrump 19 June 2018), or when Reagan refers to an, "illegal alien invasion" (Reagan 1977). I term this process discursive crossover and in developing this theory I add new nuance to Kristeva's (1986) notion of intertextuality by considering how *unrelated* discourses have the potentiality to inform each other. This theorizing draws from—and extends —two further concepts: Fine and Christoforides' idea of metaphorical linkage (1991), and Deleuze's idea of the attendant character (1981).

This study argues for three consequences of discursive crossover: that it forms an ontology that reifies ideas about 'difference' and 'belonging'; that it promotes widespread ideologies about the migrant as a figure to be feared; and that intentional crossovers between such discourses lends support to the contemporary understanding of immigration-as-crisis. In short, fear of the alien Other supports the social construction of the immigration crisis and legitimates efforts to 'build the wall'.

This study is politically significant at a time when the US deploys increasingly inhumane tactics against migrants (particularly those labeled illegal or alien), prepares to augment its wall across the southern border, and works to permanently prohibit the entry of people deemed 'dangerous' (e.g. the 'Muslim ban'[2]). Through this work I hope to open pathways of possibility for an alternative imagining of global human mobility.

Assuming the National

The idea of the nation is so normative that to imagine an alternative reality seems beyond us. Such thinking in the social sciences is referred to as methodological nationalism (Wimmer and Glick Schiller 2003). Across sociology, economics, history, as well as in other fields, scholars assume that nation-states are a given. Societies are analyzed as groups of people contained within nation-states (Urry 2000). Comparative studies are conducted between nation-states, and history is conceived as the history of one nation-state or another, or as the relations between different nation-states. Like nationalism itself, methodological nationalism homogenizes people into one uniform unit, like the globe that imagines nation-states in one uniform color. In this kind of thinking, society is equated with the nation-state, so that we have American politics, say, or the British way of doing things. Membership in this imagined community of the nation (Anderson 1983) is tied to labels like 'citizen'; membership is also tied to specific rights and obligations. As

John Urry (2000) notes: "This societal structuring has been bound up with notions of what it is to be a member or citizen of a given national society and of the particular societally guaranteed rights and duties of citizenship" (2000:2). The challenge facing theorists of the nation-state, according to Andreas Wimmer and Nina Glick Schiller, is "to avoid both extreme fluidism and the bounds of nationalist thought" (2003:576). We must avoid looking at migrants as either the marginalized exception or some kind of global prototype (2003:600), but also avoid an analysis that naturalizes the world as divided into discreet national units.

In this work I strive to accept Wimmer and Glick Schiller's maxim, but also to reveal the conditions of possibility for a world where the movement of people—particularly the movement of the global poor and those fleeing persecution—is not condemned. In order to achieve this, I explore historical and contemporary discourses that construct and problematize the migrant subjectivity. I trace the changing problematizations of the alien migrant from the first invocation in the 1790 Naturalization Act to contemporary iterations that allow for increasingly aggressive state practices such as family separation and indefinite detention. I argue that a common result of such discourses is to consolidate socially constructed boundaries. Such multifarious processes of boundary making help to define both the world system of nation-states (Nevins 2010:4), as well as to define collective figurative identities that are imagined as either belonging or out-of-place within each nation-state. Whether it is the cartographic color codes that separate one nation-state from another, or the idea of a nation-state as a homogenous pastel whole, boundary making involves ideologies and practices of spatial belonging that construct and privilege certain bodies while alienating others.

Subjects of the Nation

Key to the success of nationalism are representational

practices that produce and reproduce collective subjectivities. Such practices operate as diffuse modes of power that construct both the legal and figurative subjects of the nation[3]. Chief among these subjectivities is the citizen, a legal state category as well as an everyday term that positions citizens as the just and rightful inhabitants of the nation-state. Co-constituted against this subjectivity is the alien; both a derogatory label as well as the official state category for un-naturalized people in the US from the Naturalization Act of 1790 to the present day.

In contemporary political practice, while use of the term *alien* is seen as contentious and many state agencies and media outlets refuse to use it, politicians such as Trump or Supreme Court Justice Alito regularly and emphatically refer to migrants as aliens (Egelko 2018). It should be noted, however, that calling someone an alien—even when uttered by powerful figures like a president or a judge—is not the same as applying a state category to a person. State categories are powerful technologies of rule that administer subjectivities to individuals and can have significant political and material effects in terms of rights. The official designation alien, for example, when administered to resident migrants as a state category with its associated 'green card' and 'alien number', establishes a migrant's eligibility for employment, and gives them the right to exit and enter the US without a visa.

But the moniker *alien* is not always used as an official state category; it is also deployed as a derogatory label in order to evoke a very specific kind of *figurative* subject. The key question this work asks is what kind of figurative subject is the migrant? It is a problematized subject, for sure, but what kind of socio-economic and historical conditions lead to this problematized understanding? And how does this subjectivity transform over time? In particular, what are the political and material ramifications for the migrant subjectivity when the space alien discourse and the alien species discourse interact with the alien migrant discourse? How is the migrant subjectivity administered, and through what modes of power? And what is the relationship between the construction and administration of the migrant subjectivity and the construction and administration of the US as a nation-state?

The migrant is represented in both historical and contemporary discourse as a transgressional figure who threatens to out-compete the national, an 'outsider' figure whose very existence is constructed as a violation of the norm. In this manner, the migrant is produced as the internal enemy (Stoler 1995) of the nation-state; a figure who is often inside the physical boundaries of the nation and who is often represented in discourse as a deviant intruder. Such ideas emerge in discourse and are reflected in statutes that turn the alien and citizen into legal categories.

Roxanne Lynn Doty (2003) contends that a symbolic internal boundary is produced by the alien subjectivity. Application of *alien* as either a derogatory label or an official state category produces a sort of symbolic internal border that follows the migrant—as well as a person merely suspected of being such—however far they attempt to move from the physical border. Notes Doty, "the border itself is often a flow, moving along with those whose identities have been marked with odious terms such as 'illegal alien'" (2003:33). In other words, such identity-marking mobilizes the power of the material border and disperses it so that the border itself becomes mobile.

Subjectifying labels when accepted as commonsense can be conceived of as powerful technologies of rule that conceal their material and political utility. In this manner it makes 'sense' to hear a person being called an alien on the news, for example. As a result, we neglect to critically question such notions and ask whose interests are being served through such commonsense understandings. Use of such labels can thereby be seen as, "techniques and tactics of domination" (Foucault 2003:34), or practices that subjugate mobile bodies by turning them into objects of 'knowledge' (Foucault 1995:28). I posit that the extra-legal use of the label alien steers the immigration discourse towards crisis mode, lends support for immigration restriction and exclusion, and bolsters plans for a prophylactic border wall. Analyzing the details of the immigration discourse and the construction of the migrant subjectivity is thereby essential for understanding the kind of discursive work that such subject-making does for the imagined community of the nation.

Subjectivities are an important part of political practice that work to differentiate people based on a range of intersecting ideas. In *Race, Nation, Class: Ambiguous Identities* (1991) Étienne Balibar and Immanuel Wallerstein analyze these articulations as they explore the contemporary nature of racism, and show how ideas about race, nation, and class coalesce to produce varying subjectivities. Noting how ideas of nationalism are at once homogenizing and ambiguous (1991:54), Balibar posits that racism emerges out of nationalism (1991:53), and, "in articulating itself to nationalism, it is, in its difference, necessary to nationalism" (1991:50). The discourse of racism, in other words, is beneficial to the discourse on nationalism. It refers to it, articulates with it, strengthens it, and in these articulations supports the nation project, as well as 'the people' that it is being ruled for, and those who are seen as excluded.

The discourses on race and nation evidence what Balibar calls ideological symmetry (1991:45), meaning that not only do they articulate and 'speak' to each other, but also that there is a sort of parallel logic at work. As I undertake a review of the theories concerning ideas of race and nation in chapter two, I draw on the work of Balibar and Wallerstein not just to focus on subjectivity constructions as they do, but also for thinking about the power effects that can result when discourses articulate. In particular, I question whether the discourse on immigration transmutes racism and nationalism into a more sayable form. In other words, if discourse is what can be said within the realm of the possible—and if we are at a historical moment in which overt racisms and nationalisms cannot be uttered without serious consequences—then does immigration provide the discourse that is readily sayable in order to marginalize, restrict, or exclude those constructed as migrant?

Analyzing the emergence and proliferation of such categorizations and articulations—tracing the changing nature of the discourse over time and noting any significant developments in the discourse—is essential to understanding our contemporary predicament with regards to immigration, one in which the migrant is so feared that even migrant children can be separated from their parents and imprisoned as part of a strategy of deterrence at the border.

Alienated Workers

Central to the success of the nation-state is the ideology of nationalism that constructs some workers as alien and constructs others as citizen. In the mid-1860s—just as a commissioner of immigration is established under the US Department of State (US Congress 1864)—the discourse on the alien migrant begins to proliferate. Increasingly, it is the citizen who is valorized as 'belonging' in the US, and increasingly, it is the citizen-worker who is seen as the rightful heir to the jobs and prosperity of the nation. The alien-worker thereby becomes doubly alienated; both from the nation that has constructed them as alien, and from their own selves by the sale of their labor-power (Marx 1867/1997:403). Such people, in other words, are constructed through the system of immigration that subjectifies them as alien as little more than dehumanized components in a capitalist world economy.

The alien-worker is the ultimate human commodity, and the ideological nature of the alien-worker subject conceals that they provide a cheap supply of labor that is often essential for the material success of the nation-state. From a Marxian perspective, this ideology conceals its economic base, and also conceals its utility to the owners of the means of production. Writing about coded terms in discourse, Norman Fairclough (1995) notes that ideologies and ideological practices become, "disassociated...from the particular social base, and the particular interests, which generated them…seen to be common-sensical and based in the nature of things or people, rather than in the interests of classes or other groupings" (1995:35). In other words, the ideology of the alien-worker produces their cheapness as commonsense.

The commodified alien-worker is also supported as such by immigration policies and practices that deny them legal rights. Such policies and practices ensure a continuing and profitable supply of inexpensive and powerless labor. In large part because of their vulnerable status as migrant, such people are rendered among the most powerless and thus highly exploitable workers in the US. This status means that if they complain to their employers, for example, they can be fired with impunity (Sassen 1988:42). What adds to their alienation and commodification, Sassen finds, are situations where any claims on permanent residence are severely restricted (1988:51). Through processes of restriction and exclusion, the alien-worker becomes the 'illegal alien'; vulnerable and exploitable, just another commodity of the nation-state that renders them Other. Use of illegal alien may also be functional in that it produces a boundary to solidarity between the illegal worker, the authorized immigrant worker, and the citizen worker (Doty 2003:41).

Such a Marxian understanding of power is grounded in economic process, by which the division of labor is seen as the salient explanation of power differences, with ideology being understood as a consciousness-producing force. For Marx, the ruling material force in society is also the ruling force for the production of ideas (1845:10) meaning that ideological notions that are produced and reproduced through discourse serve material functions. The alien migrant can be seen as an ideological figure because its utility to the 'national economy' is concealed within its construction as an illegal. In the contemporary US, for example, it could be argued that the social production of the illegal alien is essential for the maintenance of a capitalist reserve army of labor, to use Marx's terminology (*Capital*

1867:444), a reserve army that is necessary for the economic vitality of the nation. When we talk about the ideology of the illegal alien, then, we talk in part about constructed identities tied to economic process.

But while a focus on economic process may illuminate how a system of immigration restriction and exclusion proves useful for business interests (see Portes and Walton 1981, or Sassen 1988, for example), such an approach veers away from the politics of representation. For it is not the *actual* humans we are studying; rather this work seeks to unearth the regimes of practice that construct the migrant as a *figurative* subject. Accordingly, the focus is on how the migrant subjectivity has been constituted and problematized over time. The key question to ask, then, is what particular socio-economic and historical conditions lead to the emergence and transformation of what kinds of problematized migrant subjectivities?

Discourse Analysis

This study employs discourse analysis as a method to understand commonsense representations of the migrant subject. Commonsense discourses—everyday ideas and artifacts that shape dominant understandings of reality—are where hegemonic visions of the world are given form. Discourses do not just represent ideas; they are productive of such ideas, and tactically so.

By way of introduction, discourse is used in this study in a broad sense, not just to indicate what is said or shown, but also to understand what *can* be said. Discourse analysis is used to understand systematic sets of thoughts and actions. Like the concepts of ideology, hegemony, and social constructionism, the practice of discourse analysis encourages us to look beneath the surface. "Discourse analytic methods facilitate the examination of the various mechanisms at work in texts" (Doty 1993:305). Mechanisms at work can be textual ones that give writing form, commonly employed metaphors or labels that denigrate migrants, for example. At work in a discourse can also be visual elements such as stereotypical images or symbolic clues that lace together an artifact such as a TV news story. Such textual and visual mechanisms percolate from manifest discourses that purport to reveal the 'truth' down to common-sense beliefs. No discourse is free from the socio-structural conditions out of which it emerges. Each is imbued with the ideological beliefs, values, and practices of the creator(s), the reader(s), as well as the institutions and culture of the wider society.

Popular mass media artifacts like cartoons or tweets may seem inconsequential, yet they are anything but. Perhaps it is the very casual nature of popular culture—a nature that defies serious reflection—that gives it its power. For instance, it wasn't until I emigrated to the US that I first saw a map where England wasn't in the middle. It provoked a profound shift in perspective. Not that I believed England was the center of the world but seeing something familiar suddenly out of place awoke me to the ideological nature of my beliefs. It is the ability of such popular culture artifacts to produce and reproduce ideologies that needs examining.

It is this sense of an idea that has amassed a taken-for-granted popularity that we need to explore. In order to do so we can employ Antonio Gramsci's (1971) concept of hegemony: the process by which ruling class understandings of reality come to dominate. Hegemony is originally conceived of as the direct rule or dominance of one group of another, but when reimagined by Gramsci—a journalist and communist politician who wrote from inside an Italian jail in the late 1920s and early 30s—it came to mean a whole system of domination where the political, social, and cultural lean on each other for their power. Gramsci's view of hegemony adds to Marx's (1845) conceptualization of ideology where a dominant and often illusory truth obviates both the position of the creator and the creator's political intent. Both concepts show us the processes by which ruling class understandings of reality come to dominate. Both point to the material privilege enjoyed by a powerful few that affect their ability to shape what people come to know as truth or 'reality'.

In this manner, and relatedly, where the concepts of ideology and hegemony stress unequal power relations, the idea of social constructionism (Berger and Luckmann 1966) urges us to examine the socio-historical relationships that underpin things that are thought of as 'known'. Socially constructed realities differ from place to place, and from one historical period to the next. The processes by which such realities are created, imbued with meaning, and shared or claimed as our own are necessarily affected by the social conditions of the worlds in which we live. What social constructionism prompts us to analyze is not the nature of reality itself; rather it points to the social relationships that surround the creation, understanding, and sharing of particular ways of knowing what is—and is not—a reality. Social constructionism, instead of assuming that some sort of pre-discursive reality exists, points to social relationships that underpin the social organization of truth, particularly truths that become hegemonic and so commonsense or normative. Together, the critical theories on ideology and hegemony along with an understanding of social constructionism are the set of conceptual tools with which I analyze the discourse on the migrant.

An analysis of the discourse on the migrant shows that the way knowledge about the migrant is constructed and propagated—as well as the way such knowledge attains the status of commonsense—is informed by the materiality of social relations. As Dorothy E. Smith (1990) notes, although knowledge may take an objectified form, presented as independent of power as well as independent of, "the presences and activities of subjects" (1990:66), it is still very much a product of social organization (1990:61). Thus, knowledge production is not only reflective of existing social relations, its construction contributes to the *reproduction* of social relations. In the discourse on immigration, for example, the migrant is structured as a particular kind of deviant figure, one who is central to commonsense understandings that immigration is a 'problem' for nations. What we 'know' about the migrant is structured by the subordinate social position of the migrant within the nation-state. But what we know is also structured by the utility to the nation-state of making the migrant a problematized subjectivity.

If hegemonic discourses were watertight in their construction and promotion of unequal power structures, change would be an impossibility; neither would there be room for counter discourses to exist within the same culture. However, it is one of the enduring features of hegemony—and one of the endearing features of popular culture—that antithetical discourses do exist, albeit in a marginal way. As Foucault notes: "Where there is power, there is resistance" (1978/1990:95). Yet sites of alterity are also part of the discourse, "never in a position or exteriority in relation to power" (ibid). Throughout this study, therefore, I give room to explore the counter-discourse. Sometimes this is found in works of satire and I analyze whether satire functions to expose hegemonic portrayals of migrants or whether satirical discourses add to the propagation of such portrayals. Satire is described by Robert C. Elliot (2019) as, "[an] artistic form, chiefly literary and dramatic, in which human or individual vices, follies, abuses, or shortcomings are held up to censure by means of ridicule…caricature, or other methods, sometimes with an intent to inspire social reform". But as Judith Butler (1997) notes on the related art of parody: "Parody requires a certain ability to identify, approximate, and draw near; it engages an intimacy with the position it appropriates that troubles the voice… such that the audience or the reader does not quite know where it is you stand, whether you have gone over to the other side" (1997:266). Satire and parody are part of the counter-discourse, but in engaging with the dominant discourse there is a real risk that the satirist perpetuates the hegemony rather than challenging it.

Social problems only come to be defined as such when a person or group identifies them in that way. In other words, they exist, "through the enterprise of groups or individuals who create them" (Spector and Kitsuse 1977:161). Such problems may emerge following single significant events, especially if there are vivid illustrations or images that accompany such events. Cobb and Elder (1993) describe such events as "triggering devices" (as noted in Johnson-Cartee 2005:59). Fishman (1978), writing about themes in crime, highlights the order that results from combining disparate events into a recognizable social problem: "A news theme is a unifying concept... Calling these things 'unrest' imposes order on the events reported. Audience members are meant to see the events as unified, as instances of a single theme" (1978:534). The mass media is therefore an important vehicle for defining situations for the media consumer, shaping events into themes, and themes into problems, and shaping the manner in which such problems should be both debated and solved. In other words, the mass media construct our present 'reality' of immigration-as-crisis. Notes Surette, "the media is a major force in society and is a primary engine in the social construction of reality" (1998:xi).

Media organizations are socially constructed systems that themselves construct versions of reality for our consumption. Those constructions are patterned and produce patterned responses that mold people's experiences of reality. In selecting and defining immigration as a problem, therefore, the media play a central role in shaping social attitudes towards issues, manipulating the salience of people's fears, and influencing the responses that affect public policy-making decisions. As David Altheide (2002) points out in *Creating Fear*: "Although they are not the sole factors in the creation of a social problem, the media play a pivotal and strong role in defining and legitimizing the problem as well as promoting official interventions, policies, and programs" (2002:146). It is critical, therefore, to pay close attention to the manner in which the media select, define, and frame migrants as problems and as symptomatic of a crisis.

Discursive Crossover

One way that this crisis is constructed, I argue, is when the alien migrant discourse becomes connected with the seemingly disparate discourses on alien species and space aliens. This occurs through a process that I term discursive crossover. For example, there are unwanted animal and plant species who are described using the alien label and given anthropomorphic motives of 'invasion' and 'infiltration'; and likewise, there are the space aliens who are the sinister and duplicitous antagonists of many a science fiction narrative. When such discourses are purposefully connected—when migration is referred to as a swarm, for example, or when migrants are described as alien invaders—I argue that the result is to produce the migrant subjectivity not only as problematized, but also as demonstrably dangerous to the nation-state and 'its people'.

This study argues that discursive crossover between the three alien discourses forges significant negative transformations to the human migrant subjectivity as well as promoting material responses that are appropriate to this magnified threat. I contend that beginning in the mid nineteenth century —just as there is a precipitous and exponential growth in the global movement of goods and peoples—there is a new discursive focus on belonging, and, likewise, a dramatic new emphasis on incursions by the out-of-place in particular national spaces. Accordingly, by 1847, the word *alien* is now also used to define a plant or animal, "brought from another country or district and subsequently naturalized; not native" (*OED* 2012, alien, adj. 1.b.b). Just like with the understanding of *alien* in the immigration discourse, the meaning of *alien* in the realm of flora and fauna acts as an ontology reinforcing ideas of nation, national difference, autochthony, and naturalization, and reifying the idea that geography acts as a marker of difference. There is also the implicit suggestion in such a discourse of the need for anti-miscegenation, this time for preventing the mixture of alien species in order to protect 'native' or national ones. The process of discursive crossover allows us to understand how the alien species discourse impacts upon the alien migrant discourse, allowing ideas—but also fears and material 'solutions'—to transfer readily from one discourse to another.

By the late 1870s, just as the discourse on the so-called 'new immigration' from places like Ireland and Germany approaches crisis mode, the problematizing discourse on alien fauna and flora intensifies. Such species are increasingly seen as threatening, overly competitive or overly fertile, and as invasive or dangerous to 'native' or species and environments. Such species are often labeled with a national label (such as Mexican marijuana, or the English sparrow), and as Fine and Christoforides (1991) show, when the discourse on out-of-place animals is metaphorically linked to the discourse on problematized immigrants[4], it makes sense of the human migrant problematization. But rather than just focusing on the process by which problems become defined as Fine and Christoforides do, my theory of discursive crossover broadens its reach to show the political and material *outcomes* of particular subjectivity constructions when ostensibly or even radically different discourses articulate.

The space alien discourse, for example, at first glance bears very little in common to the human migrant discourse other than the link provided by the moniker *alien*. However, I argue that the space alien discourse is routinely invoked to articulate with the human migrant discourse in order to promote the idea that human migrants are a threat. I further argue that the repetitive framing of human migration as an 'alien invasion' by a succession of presidents and others, forges consent for military-style solutions. This is because the language and ideas employed in the discourse on space aliens are often indistinguishable from the language and ideas used in the discourse on alien people. Such entities are not just represented as out-of-place (or from 'outer' space), but also as aggressive competitors who invade, contaminate, and threaten the 'natural' habitat of the nation, and who intend to plunder 'national' resources. The space alien discourse, in other words, when purposefully articulated to the human alien discourse, tells us something about the essential nature of *all* aliens. And that nature is threat.

Historically, from the inception of the figure of the space alien in narratives going back to Lucian's second century *True History* (~160-190), the alien is a menacing character. Seen as warring and invasive, destructive and deceitful, the space alien is almost invariably portrayed as having one eye on resources and the other on a takeover of power. And then by the turn of the twentieth century when H. G. Wells writes his masterpiece *War of the Worlds* (1898), we have both the space alien who invades the urban metropolis and causes panic and death, and also the deadly red weed that has traveled unwittingly from Mars and now brings down the formidable Martian enemy with its voracious unchecked growth. In 1894 the planet Mars has been unusually close to Earth, leading to much observation and speculation as to who or what might possibly live there. This is also a time of increased scientific understanding of epidemic diseases such as cholera and the bubonic plague. International Sanitary Conferences are conducted in both 1894 and 1897 that lead to new restrictions on movement and the quarantine of both ships and passengers deemed to be at risk (Bulmus 2012:146). And so, in *War of the Worlds* we see represented for the first time these conjoined fears of unrestricted movement and invasive species all tied up in a vivid story of alien invasion, panic, and deadly destruction. And at the root of this crisis is the alien.

From the turn of the nineteenth century and increasingly throughout it, I contend, the moniker *alien* cannot be used of people without invoking attendant sets of ideas related to alien species and space aliens. Whether this crossover is invoked intentionally or incidentally, the effect is the same: to raise the conditions of possibility for crisis. And so when Trump tweets that a migrant 'caravan' at the southern border threatens, "an invasion of our Country" (@realDonaldTrump 29 Oct 2018), or says that migrants, "infest our country" (19 June 2018), the chief effect of such crossovers is to augment the negative and problematized nature of the human migrant subjectivity, and to transform the discourse into a fear narrative. In this manner, the idea of immigration-as-crisis is produced as commonsense, and the proposed 'solutions' are seen as valid. I return to this concept at length in chapter four to delineate the varying ways that crossover between the three alien discourses affects the migrant subjectivity, suffice to say here that discursive crossover reifies ideas of autochthony, nativity, and belonging, as well as invasion, contamination, and crisis for *all kinds of alien*.

Materials Selection

This study analyzes the hegemonic discourse on the migrant as found in a broad array of media. This includes television and print news, legal statutes, government press releases, political speeches, films, novels, popular songs, road signs, protest signs, street festivals, web memes, social media broadcasts (e.g., tweets), illustrations, artwork, and cartoons. The aim of analyzing across disparate genres—from the formal edicts of government down to the everyday terms used by Border Patrol agents—is to gain a broad picture of how the migrant subjectivity is produced and reproduced in discourse.

I focus on discourses in which migrants are termed aliens and pay particular attention to the processes of labeling and stereotyping, as well as to ideas of race and nation that inform many such articulations. In a sense, selections are opportunistic, "picked up by chance", to quote Bridget Anderson (2013:8-9) whose influential book *Us and Them: The Dangerous Politics of Immigration Control* relies on a similar technique. Where Anderson's selections are largely from middle market tabloid newspapers such as the *Daily Mail*, and are specific to the

UK, I approach discourse analysis from a broader stance, regarding the whole gamut of media in the US from historical cartoons to contemporary tweets, and from White House press releases to everyday figures of speech. The central time period under analysis is from the Naturalization Act of 1790 to today.

I have collected materials related to this topic for over seven years (2012-2019). I organize materials by theme, as well as by media type, in order to facilitate access to what has become a large 24-volume compendium of media and historical documents related to problematized migration in the US. The sources are diverse in genre, style, and content. I read widely, spend a fair amount of time wandering social media and trawling the Internet, and watch television and films that appeal to me as well as to my immediate family. I subscribe to multiple popular magazines such as *GQ*, *Wired*, *Vanity Fair*, and *US Weekly*, as well as more academic mass media publications. I have access to the *New York Times* database TimesMachine that includes searchable articles from 1851 to present, and that historically often include reports from newspapers across the US.

Approaching the mass media broadly and taking a long historical view enables me to analyze changing problematizations of the migrant subjectivity, analyze through what modes of power the migrant subjectivity is administered, and focus on the power effects of such discursive formations. Taken as a body of materials what surfaces are systematic sets of thoughts and actions, coherent pictures of, "the reality of everyday life" (Berger and Luckmann 1966:21). Discourse analysis is supported in this study by the genealogical method that Foucault outlines in *Language, Counter-Memory, Practice* (1977). Such an approach does not privilege one source of knowledge over another, but rather seeks to uncover varying knowledge forms from across the spectrum, and so draw from a necessarily large fount of source material.

Genealogies attend to the knowledge transmitted in cultural artifacts as well as to ideas, values, feelings, assumptions, and instincts (Foucault 1984:80). Genealogies attend to what is said in the discourse, as well as what is omitted (1984:76). What is essential for a genealogical approach is to analyze why a particular discourse emerges or is deployed at a particular time, the form it takes at that particular time, and what the material and political effects are, particularly for the subjectivities produced and reproduced in the process. The purpose of using a genealogical approach is to form a historically contextualized picture of the whole web of discourse on the topic, including an analysis that situates the emergence of the migrant subject within its historical framework, in order that we can, "constitute a historical knowledge of struggles and…make use of that knowledge in contemporary tactics" (ibid). In other words, I am not just using a genealogical approach to historicize the changing problematizations of the migrant subjectivity; I am also using it in order to promote positive social change. A more detailed explanation of the method of discourse analysis and the limitations of such an approach form the following chapter.

HISTORICAL OVERVIEW

An introduction is warranted at this point in order to historicize the emergence of the migrant subjectivity in the US, to highlight the shifts in the discourse that are indicative of changing migrant subjectivity problematizations, and to reveal some of the contradictions implicit in the contemporary rhetoric of immigration-as-crisis in the so-called 'land of immigrants'.

Historically in the US, expansionism is the ideology upon which the so-called 'founding fathers' build their nation. Thoughts of population expansion in the imperial US align with an ideology of mercantilism, "which made the presence of a large population the key to the prosperity and power of a nation" (Federici 2014:87). Population expansionism is evident during the time of the Declaration of Independence, for example, when one of the charges laid against the British King is that, "he has endeavoured to prevent the population of these

States...refusing to pass others to encourage their migrations hither" (US 1776). Population expansionism is still evident almost 100 years later when a shortage of fighting-age men during the Civil War contributes to Lincoln signing the 1864 Act to Encourage Immigration (US Congress 1864). An increased population is deemed necessary for the success of the US, and this increased population can only come about through the arrival and acceptance of newcomers.

Ideas about the US nation and its inhabitants proliferate leading up to the signing of the Declaration of Independence in 1776. At this point in time there is no system of immigration *per se*, and no notion of immigration restriction either. Most people who enter the US during this time are simply not counted. Even when counting people becomes a state practice (part of what Foucault refers to as biopolitics), and even when the US census begins its enumerations in 1790, the counting is highly selective, with the race, nation, 'class', and gender of a person impacting whether they are counted or not.

Less than fifteen years after Congress adopts the Declaration of Independence comes the Naturalization Act of 1790. The act marks the first time in the US that we see the state categories *citizen* and *alien* appear in official documents, and significantly, the act connects ideas about the idealized national citizen subject to those of race. The act is signed by George Washington in March of 1790 and establishes a uniform path to citizenship for, "any alien, being a free white person" (US Congress 1790) who has lived lawfully in the US for at least two years. It also marks the emergence in discourse of the alien of "good character" (US Congress 1790), a person who can become naturalized as a citizen if they have, "proof to the satisfaction of such Court" (ibid). Such a representation suggests there are aliens who are *not* of good character and marks an emergence in the discourse of the legal suspicion with which the alien is treated.

Unlike contemporary ideas about immigration control, the Naturalization Act of 1790 is aimed at mitigating interior threats to the US, not on restrictionism and keeping Others out. Such resident non-citizens, under the act, are to be assuaged as a potential threat by allowing them a route to citizenship. The children of 'naturalized aliens' are also provided for in the Act, "considered as natural born citizens" (ibid). Such ideas elevate the subjectivity of the citizen as being something of value to the nation while simultaneously producing the alien subjectivity as a potential internal threat.

After the 1790 Naturalization Act come a succession of legal acts that refine definitions of the alien subject and describe an ever-growing series of infractions that make an alien ineligible for admission. The Alien and Sedition Acts of 1798, for example, cast direct suspicion on the un-naturalized alien, and grant the president the right during war or threat of invasion to make those, "not actually naturalized…liable to be apprehended, restrained, secured and removed, as alien enemies" (5th Congress, S.II, Ch. 66:577). The acts are signed by John Adams soon after he takes office in 1797 following his declaration, "to place our country in a suitable posture of defense" (in Hildreth 2012:176) and resistance to the four laws that make up the Alien and Sedition Acts is instructive.

In 1798 John Armstrong—a former major in the Continental Army and future US Secretary of War—writes a broadside against the acts, concerned that they might, "become the foundation of a system of alarm, of suspicion, of tyranny and of expense" (1798:1). Armstrong's concerns are not just that the acts might be unconstitutional, but also that the Alien law in particular, "must in its effects have a direct tendency to prevent migrations from Europe hither" (ibid). In other words, in the late eighteenth century, not only is migration seen as necessary to the future prosperity of the US, but Armstrong's opposition also reveals that the idea of regulating or restricting migration has yet to become commonsense.

But Armstrong's concerns reveal another emerging problematic: that migrants seeking asylum might be denied entrance to the US. Such people are described by Armstrong as, "born and bred under oppression" (1798:1) and accepting such people into the US is viewed during this time period—as in others—as an act of compassion. For this reason, Armstrong concludes his statement by summarizing: "Revoke your alien law, and let America long continue to be the asylum of the wretched" (ibid). However, this idea about the US as a sanctuary for the oppressed is not inviolable: asylum has been contested at key points in US history for migrants constructed as asylum seekers. A genealogical approach is of utility here because it highlights these key moments when there is a shift in how such subjectivities are invoked, administered, and dealt with at particular historical moments.

In the 1921 Quota Act, for example, no distinction is made between migrants or refugees escaping persecution, and the effects of this are deadly. During the Second World War, for example, over 900 Jewish people who have sailed from Germany on the *St. Louis* seeking refuge in the US are denied entry and forced to return to Europe. Many of them subsequently die in the Holocaust (US Holocaust Museum, nd). And under the current administration, people seeking asylum in the US are regularly turned away at the border, detained indefinitely, or denied asylum as part of a more general strategy of deterrence at the border (Blitzer 2018). And so, when we read in today's news that child migrants are being separated from their parents and locked for weeks in cages, "hungry, crying and unwashed" (Rubio and Dickerson 2019; Dickerson 2019), it seems very much as if Armstrong's 1798 predictions for alarm, suspicion, tyranny, and expense have come to fruition.

While the Alien and Sedition Acts are among the first to invoke the migrant as a problematized subjectivity, there are still no restrictions on people entering the US in the first half of the nineteenth century. Population expansion is the ongoing impetus, and so in 1864 Congress passes the Act to Encourage Immigration. This act authorizes the appointment of a Commissioner of Immigration under the auspices of the Department of State, and also affords migrants greater protection against labor extortion. The act accordingly states that migrants, "shall pledge the wages of their labor for a term not exceeding twelve months, to repay the expenses of their emigration" (US Congress 1864). The idea of immigration *restriction*, however—an idea that aligns with our contemporary understanding of immigration—does not emerge until the Page Act of 1875, almost one hundred years after the nation is invoked by the Declaration of Independence.

The Page Act marks a significant turning point in the immigration discourse, not just because it is the first law that restricts migrants from entering, but also because of the nature of the subjectivities that are invoked in the Act. Now prevented from entering the US under the Act are felons, prostitutes, coolies, and unfree subjects, "of China, Japan, or any Oriental country" (US Congress 1875). Significantly, these subjectivities are based on articulating ideas of race and nation, as well as internal and supplementary ideas of criminality, sexuality, poverty, and slavery. In chapter three, as I analyze the key shifts that occur in the discourse around the time of the passage of the Page Act and the even more restrictionist Chinese Exclusion Act of 1882, I analyze the subjectivities that such laws both produce and are also dependent upon. I focus on 'yellow peril' representations of the Chinese migrant during this time period, representations that I argue help usher in Chinese Exclusion and also provide precedent for the stereotypical and derogatory representations of migrants in the contemporary immigration discourse.

Image 1: Friendly Aliens and the British Army.
c.1914 Central London Recruiting Depot

By the first World War there emerges a distinct divergence in how migrants are represented; following a dialectic process that tends to push ideas into false binaries, the migrant is now seen as either friendly or enemy. Accordingly, we have pleading advertisements in the UK for "Friendly Aliens" to go to their Local Recruiting Office: "DO NOT HESITATE BUT COME AT ONCE AND DO YOUR DUTY TO THE COUNTRY WHERE YOU CHOOSE TO RESIDE" (Central London Recruiting Depot, circa 1914). An editorial cartoon of the same era in the *New York Herald* offers the dichotomous flip-side of the alien, depicting a gaseous Hun labeled "ENEMY ALIEN MENACE" towering ominously as it sweeps through New York City.

Image 2: The Breath of the Hun. 1918. Editorial cartoon by W.A. Rogers for the New York Herald

Even in the enlistment advertisement for "Friendly Aliens" the language is deeply problematizing. The wording of the advert suggests that some aliens are not friendly; the ad places a primacy on being British-born; and further, in stating "...THE COUNTRY WHERE YOU CHOOSE TO RESIDE", the ad constructs the flawed—but nonetheless predominant—idea of human mobility as choice. Notes Saskia Sassen-Koob: "The main explanatory model in the literature on international migrations is built on the axiom of individual choice and motivation" (1981:65). This commonsense idea of 'individual choice and motivation' ignores the oftentimes tremendous peril that migrants face—particularly those who are fleeing war or persecution. It also obviates the far-reaching power of a system of global capitalism that acts as an external force, pushing people from their ways of life, oftentimes into desperate poverty.

If the first World War marks a hardening of the alien subjectivity into either friendly or enemy, this is also the historical point at which ideas about the migrant worker shift. And once again it is ideas of race and nationality—articulating with ideas about intelligence, 'class', and gender—that inform the migrant worker subjectivity, as well as the policies and practices that shore up this subjectivity. As Massey, Durand, and Malone point out (2002), both Chinese Exclusion and the so-called Gentlemen's Agreement with Japan in 1907 have effectively removed 'Asia' as a source of labor, resulting in serious labor shortages in industries like agriculture and construction. This labor shortage intensifies during the war, just as the war simultaneously spurs a massive expansion in industry in the US. Accordingly, labor recruiters spread out into northern Mexico promising work in the US, and, even after the war ends, this practice continues. And so, while exclusion stays in place for 'Asian' workers, immigration from Mexico is heavily encouraged during the post-war years.

This post-war period marks a significant shift in the immigration discourse in the US as southern and eastern European migrants become the focus of new subjectivity problematizations. And so following the failure of a 1917 literacy test to reduce immigration to the levels hoped for by those who had instituted it, an 'experimental' quota law is enacted in 1921 titled, "An Act to Limit the Immigration of Aliens in the United States" (US Congress 1921 Session 1, Ch.8). But this law does not target all 'aliens' equally; rather it aims to limit specific populations based on articulating ideas about race and nation. Accordingly, the 1921 quota act, and those that follow, permit migrants to enter the US based on limited quotas of 'races' and 'nationalities' as determined by varying historical censuses. The use of the 1890 census in the Immigration Act of 1924 (rather than, say, the 1900 census, or the 1910 census) is seen as a concerted effort to reduce 'undesirable' immigration from southern and eastern Europe, as migration from *northern* European nations like Ireland and Germany is more numerous in the 1890 census. In this manner, the quota law simultaneously appears just and fair, while also supporting the negative racialization and ensuing restriction of people from southern and eastern Europe.

And ultimately, as the laws do restrict the entry of southern and eastern European migrants, quotas are seen—at least for a while—as successful for protecting the nation from particular kinds of migrant subjectivity. In effect, such laws and practices also produce a *national* subjectivity. Notes Adam McKeown (2008:334): "Even countries that did not adopt the quota provisions admired and emulated the use of policy to define and create national character, as well as the refined distinctions among types of immigrants, nonimmigrants and excludables".

Another mode through which the migrant subjectivity is problematized during this time frame is through the increasing use of fearful metaphors to describe migrants, as well as through the increasing use of homely metaphors to describe the nation. I return to this point in the following chapter in which I trace a genealogy of the key metaphors in the immigration discourse in order to show shifting problematizations of the migrant subjectivity. Suffice to say here that from the 1920s onwards we start to see human migrants described in fear-rousing hydraulic terminology, for example, as 'flooding' the nation. And then during this time period the nation itself starts to be described using the metaphor of *home* (quotas, for example, start to be described as a 'gate' to unrestricted immigration). And then from the 1950s onwards the metaphor of 'invasion' becomes pervasive. The effects of these metaphor deployments are threefold: to elevate the US as a nation deserving of protection; to elevate the US citizen as a desirable subjectivity; and to lend legitimacy to the idea of quotas as successful for restricting the entrance of 'undesirable' migrant subjectivities.

But the undesirable migrant subjectivity is not just willed into being by journalists and politicians using fear-rousing metaphors: it is, as Foucault might say, the result of a diffuse network of elements that work together to produce the 'truth' of the undesirable migrant. And one way that the undesirable migrant subjectivity is both understood and 'made true' during this time frame is through the procedures of inspection and categorization that are given a new impetus and domain of concern after the US Border Patrol is created in 1924.

Difficulties in deciding how to categorize people of varying 'races' and 'nationalities' might have stopped immigration officials from enacting the restrictions of the quota programs. But throughout the 1920s and at an ever-widening array of border sites, new disciplinary modes of inspection are enacted, both in order to categorize new arrivals, and in order to respond to negative ideas about migrants as a source of 'contamination'. These inspections have historical precedence in the inspection, fumigation, and disinfection of Chinese migrants by quarantine officers aboard ships in San Francisco harbor during the 1880s (see Trauner 1978). But border inspections do not just *deal* with undesirable migrants; border inspections often include the stereotypical classification of people according to visible or assumed 'differences' that in effect *produce* particular categories of migrant. And then, through the fixative process of the immigration system, these 'differences' are given the weight of state categorizations. Notes Ali Behdad (2005), "immigration inspection is the fixing of individual differences as the new modality of power" (2005:153). And after the quota acts have gone into effect, restricting southern European migration and excluding 'Asian' migration, the focus of these inspections and categorizations increasingly shifts towards the southern border with Mexico.

Migration from Mexico to the US has increased dramatically after 1900. Political and socio-economic upheaval following the Mexican Revolution spurs further out-migration, and the quota acts of the 1920s are never applied to Mexican nationals, encouraging Mexican laborers to cross the US-Mexico border in ever increasing numbers[5]. This increase in arrivals forges changes to how the migrant subjectivity is imagined and problematized, and also prompts changes to how Mexican migrants are dealt with at the border. Notes Greg Grandin (2019:164), border patrol agents, "had the power to turn what had been a routine daily or seasonal event—crossing the order —into a ritual of abuse. Hygienic inspections became more widespread and even more degrading. Migrants had their heads shaves, and they were subjected to an ever-more-arbitrary set of requirements and to the discretion of patrollers". Testament to how badly the Mexican migrant subjectivity is perceived at this point, there is very little public or political opposition to these civil rights abuses at the border. There is also a complete lack of political opposition to the ensuing forced removal of up to half a million Mexicans during the economic depression of the 1930s (see Daniels 2001:26; also, Massey, Durand, and Malone 2002:34).

New labor shortages during the Second World War result in a new labor program called the Bracero Program that permits some Mexican migrants to enter, and also prompts some employers to hire migrants without permits. This results in a growing understanding throughout the 1950s of migrants as 'illegal', and this has devastating impacts on the migrant subjectivity. Joseph Nevins (2002) provides a detailed account of the construction of the 'illegal immigrant' as an outcome of policies and practices at the border, noting that the lack of opposition to this construction relates to, "the strengthening of the social boundary between legal and illegal immigrants, and between citizens and aliens" (2002:182). And as Ali Behdad (2005) notes, the results of these constructions are twofold. First, they transform immigration inspection into a generalized mode of surveillance that imposes what he terms *visibility* and *vulnerability* on the migrant as a disciplinary mode of power (2005:154). Second, such constructions shore up national understandings. Notes Behdad (2002:11): "The figure of the 'alien' as a menacing source of sedition, discontent, insurrection, and resistance provides a differential other whose perpetual presence is necessary in order to manufacture a homogenous national identity". In other words, the diffuse modes of power that produce the alien migrant as derogatory subject-figure also shore up co-constituted ideas about the idealized national citizen subject, as well as elevating the US nation-state as an entity worthy of protection. I would argue that a further outcome of the construction of the migrant as *alien other* is to promote material responses at the border and elsewhere that are appropriate to deal with the magnified nature of this threat.

Border inspections that produce certain categories of migrant are finally codified in the 1952 Immigration and Nationality Act (also known as the McCarran-Walter Act). The act details an exhaustive list of aliens deemed 'undesirable', establishes an 'alien registration system' for those allowed passage, and marks a decisive shift in the US immigration discourse. Notes Behdad (2002:114):

> Indeed fundamental shifts such as the Chinese Exclusion Act of 1882, the quota laws of the 1920s, and the McCarran-Walter Act of 1952 have gradually transformed the ways the United States has treated its immigrants, from more lenient and receptive to more restrictive and regulatory. These critical moments constitute ruptures in the nation's discourses and policies of immigration, and as such they demystify linear histories of im-

migrant America.

The idea of the US as a 'nation of immigrants' is a powerful one, however, and has been invoked by numerous past presidents—some of whom advocate for harsher restrictions on immigration. But it is only recently that the nation of immigrants idea has come under direct attack. The idea is used by Franklin D. Roosevelt who declares in 1938: "all of us...are descended from immigrants" (21 April 1938); Roosevelt, however, is also instrumental in denying Jewish refugees asylum because of the threat they may pose. *A Nation of Immigrants* is the title of a book written by then senator John F. Kennedy in 1958 and published posthumously in 1964; in it he argues for immigration reform but notes jarringly, "Such legislation does not seek to make over the face of America. Immigrants would still be given tests for health, intelligence, morality and security" (1958/1964:80). Such language about making over, "the face of America" (ibid) is a metonym (face stands in for the nation) with racializing connotations. Kennedy's solution of 'tests' mirrors that of the 1917 Immigration Act, a central requirement of which is a literacy test for immigrants (US Congress 1917). The phrase nation of immigrants is summoned again by Bill Clinton in 1996, and by George W. Bush in 2006. Perhaps the phrase is used by such presidents to invoke a carefully scripted history, one in which the 'land of the free' has not been constructed on the wastelands of 'Indian' societies[6]. Or perhaps nation of immigrants is used by political leaders in an attempt to assuage fears of racism while simultaneously advocating for a racialized view of the nation. In 2018, however, the notion receives a direct blow as the US Citizenship and Immigration Service removes the passage "nation of immigrants" from its mission statement in favor of a statement promising efficiency and fairness in administering, "the nation's lawful immigration system" (as cited in Rezaian 2018). If the US is at one time discursively envisioned as a *nation of immigrants*, now it is more emphatically than ever a *nation of laws*. Genealogical work necessitates that we contextualize such shifts in the discourse historically, but it also provokes a focus on the political and material effects of such shifts. What does it mean for the problematized migrant subjectivity when the passage "nation of immigrants" is removed by the government agency that has been set up to provide 'service' to immigrants?

This preface operates as an introduction to some of the theories and themes that comprise the main body of this work. I have also in this preface articulated my key research questions and suggested why my research constitutes a contribution to our understanding of how discourses interact and affect each other.

Chapter one explores the method of discourse analysis, offering an explanation of what constitutes a discourse, as well as limitations of using a discourse analytical approach. In my analysis of some of the main themes and ideas in the historical and contemporary discourse on immigration in this and subsequent chapters, I focus on two key things: the historically specific social relations out of which such a discourse emerges, and the material and political effects for the subjectivities invoked in the process.

In chapter two I review key theories concerning race, the nation, and subjectivity construction. In showing how race and nation articulate to produce both the legal and figurative subjects of the nation, I contend that such articulations produce the citizen as the default or 'normal' member who 'belongs' in the nation-state and produce the alien as the deviant Other. Central to these articulations are ideas of 'difference' that reify ideas of the Other, as well as co-constitute ideas of the national subject. Such commonsense understandings can be seen as organized biopolitical knowledges reliant on articulating ideas of race and nation that work to exert control over populations.

In chapter three I employ a genealogical method to look at nineteenth century transformations to the migrant subjectivity. Extending the idea of articulating discourses, I show how newly transformed ideas of race and nation—along with internal and supplementary ideas concerning poverty, criminality, gender, and sexuality—generate new ideas and practices that restrict and exclude the mobile working poor. Starting with the rhetoric of the Know Nothings from the 1850s and looking to anti-Chinese rhetoric from the 1870s and 1880s, I argue that such discourses create the figure of the migrant as a uniquely degraded subjectivity. Such rhetoric is not just seen as useful for political parties, however; anti-immigrant rhetoric from this period is also seen as productive of consent for practices of immigration restriction and exclusion.

Chapter four investigates the construction of the migrant as a threat through what I term discursive crossover. I theorize that these are instances when the discourse on the alien migrant is connected to the ostensibly disparate discourses on invasive alien species as well as space aliens. The idea of discursive crossover extends the concept of intertextuality (Kristeva 1986) and draws on metaphorical linkage (Fine and Christoforides 1991), as well as Deleuze's idea of the attendant character (1981). One of the chief functions of discursive crossover, I argue, is to heighten the fear of alien migrants and so support the hegemony of the idea that immigration is in crisis. A further result of discursive crossover, I argue, is to produce as commonsense the 'solutions' found in aggressive state practices such as indefinite detention, militarized border control, and family separation.

The fifth chapter of this work considers the construction of immigration-as-crisis by leaning on Cohen's (1972) concept of a moral panic. Moral panics are predictably patterned discourses that present events, people, or subjects in exaggerated ways that demand exaggerated responses. Such discourses rely on stereotypical folk devils—people who are constructed as anathema to the dominant social group—and rely on claims-makers who have something material or political to gain from their positioning on the subject. Looking at contemporary representations of the collective figure of the migrant, I argue that such subject-figures are deployed in the immigration discourse as visceral illustrations of unwanted human mobility. Finally, I argue that the fearful nature of such representations operates to rally support for Trump and lend legitimacy to his plans for, "a great, great wall on our southern border" (16 June 2015).

△△△

This study comprises a historically-situated analysis of mass media discourses that define and defend the desired subjectivities of the US nation-state as well as its necessary Others—the aliens among us. Such boundary-making involves ideologies of spatial belonging that construct and privilege certain bodies (including non-human animal and plant species) and alienate others. This strategy is seen as both relational and hierarchical and emerges in regimes of practice such as the immigration system to the advantage of the privileged few. Discourses that construct ontologies of us and them are theorized as an essential part of US political practice, contributing to the hegemony of the nation-state, one with a homogenous and fixed identity that necessitates enhanced boundaries in order to counteract the immigration 'crisis'. In a contribution to theory, I argue that when diverse discourses such as the invasive species discourse and the space alien discourse are conjoined with the alien migrant discourse, the result is to amplify fear of the migrant subjectivity, to produce the idea of immigration-as-crisis, and to lend legitimacy to practices of immigration restriction and exclusion. This theorizing is done in order to show how today's immigration crisis is produced as commonsense, and in order to counteract the hegemony of such ideas.

In this study I analyze popular discourses in order to illuminate the historical roots of contemporary ideas regarding humans represented as migrant. Symbolic representations are found in many domains, but this study focuses on discourses of the everyday. Such discourses include commonplace cultural artifacts and popular media that I contend act as a cradle for commonsense beliefs about the appropriateness of mobility and belonging. What it is important to study are those discourses concerning mobility and belonging that shape understanding of the Other to the advantage of the status quo. Through such an analysis I hope to raise the conditions of possibility for migrants to be seen as people rather than problems.

1/DISCOURSE OF THE OTHER

When we read in the *Los Angeles Times*: "the immigration crisis in Europe…could be the first gush of a human tsunami that will swamp the continent" (Horsey 2015), we can speak in terms of a discourse that claims to picture reality and that produces what Foucault calls, "effects of truth" (1980:94). This piece of writing is an opinion piece in a popular and widely-respected US newspaper. It is a discursive artifact that relates to prior discursive articulations on the 'immigration crisis' and is part of a wider discourse about global human mobility. Such artifacts describe a situation—the immigration crisis—and its associated subjects—migrants—that is recognizable to the author, the editors and publisher of the *LA Times,* and its readers. Such artifacts are influenced by—and have an influence upon—discussion, framing, and understanding of the situation, its subjects, and its solutions.

Because such things are *possible* to say—publishable in a major newspaper—we can describe them as being part of a discourse that produces tactical effects. For example, when migrants are framed as about to 'swamp the continent', it is productive of a host of negative and fearful associations. These in turn lend legitimacy to the idea of immigration-as-crisis and support material and political solutions such as more restrictive immigration and enhanced border walls.

This chapter comprises an overview of discourse analysis and then uses this method to analyze a range of discursive artifacts that construct the figure of the migrant. It also attends to a number of contemporary artifacts that counter the discourse. Horsey's 2015 opinion piece quoted above is selected because it communicates some of the major commonsense themes in the contemporary mass media related to immigration. It is written 10 weeks after Trump announced his candidacy for the presidency in June of 2015 and connects what Horsey calls, "the immigration crisis in Europe" (para. 1), to the US's "challenge dealing with illegal immigration from Latin America" (para. 2). It is replete with numerous metaphors that are common in the discourse on immigration such as the hydraulic metaphor that are deployed in the discourse to rouse fear.

In this chapter I trace a genealogy of military, hydraulic, and home metaphors in order to historicize how the discourse that produces the migrant subjectivity shifts over time. I also use a television news story from *Fox News* of 2013 to illustrate how the framing of ideas in visual media structures the symbolic figure of the migrant. Two other artifacts employed in this chapter are contemporary web memes that I use to show how discursive crossover can be deployed as a tactic of subversion. All these artifacts are demonstrative of what can be thought of as 'commonsense knowledge' about global human mobility.

DISCOURSE ANALYSIS

A discourse can be thought of as sets of related statements (including visual statements) positioned within specific socio-historical and political contexts that shape specific social and material outcomes. Discourses comprise systems of thoughts and are found everywhere: in diverse forms from political speeches to everyday speech, movies, novels, press releases, TV news images, political strategies, historical monuments; even the kinds of terms used in everyday language on a particular topic are considered discourse (Wodak and Meyer 2009:3). Discourses encompass, in the words of Foucault, a, "multiplicity of objects" (1972:32).

Discourse analysis is an approach that places power differentials and the de-mystification of ideologies as central to its analysis (Jorgensen and Phillips 2002). The goal of discourse analysis is to answer the following key questions: what knowledge is being organized, how has such knowledge developed historically, and what impact does this knowledge have on broader social and material relations? In short, what are the political and material effects of particular discursive formations?

Discourse is not just what is said (or shown); it is a form of social practice that is both reflective of the social world and tactically constitutive of the social world. Wodak and Meyer (2009), elaborate: "discursive differences are negotiated; they are governed by differences in power...texts are often sites of struggle in that they show traces of differing discourses and ideologies contending and struggling for dominance" (2009:10). A discourse, in other words, can be conceived of as an interactive domain that is productive of certain types of knowledge that is materially useful to power. In this manner, discourses are heavily implicated in what Smith calls, "relations of ruling" (1990:14).

Discourses do not emerge in a vacuum; they are constructed knowledges that achieve meaning because of how they articulate with historical ideas and contemporary iterations. In fact, a discourse is only intelligible when it is relational, that is, it: "draw[s] from the archive of the already said, from what is already part of a system of meaning production" (Shapiro 1997:172). The word *discourse* hints at this, stemming from the Latin *discursus*, meaning "action of running off in different directions" (*Oxford English Dictionary* 2013, discourse, n., etymology).

The headline of Horsey's *LA Times* opinion piece, for example, links what it terms, "Europe's migrant crisis", to "US problems on the Mexican border" (Horsey 2015). In this manner, the crisis is at once global and local, a 'problem' of global magnitude that is nonetheless relevant to Horsey's readers the US. The two situations—Europe as having a 'migrant crisis', the US as having 'Mexican border problems'—articulate with each other, that is, they relate to each other, as well as inform upon each other. The effect of such articulations is to lend legitimacy to the idea of immigration-as-crisis in the US.

But paying attention to an amalgam of historically-specific discursive elements shows that the figure of the migrant is not solely informed by ideas about human mobility. In chapter four I show how articulating ideas of race and nation—that are informed by internal and supplementary ideas about 'class' (or, rather, poverty), criminality, gender, and sexuality—structure the migrant as the 'abnormal' or deviant figure of the nation. In chapter five I enlarge my scope to consider discursive crossover between the migrant discourse and seemingly disparate discourses about out-of-place aliens. The outcome of such interactions, I argue, is to structure the migrant subjectivity as fearful, a structuring that has profoundly negative effects.

This idea of articulating discourses builds on Julia Kristeva's (1986) concept of intertextuality in which she argues that discourses are interwoven with ideas and meanings from other discourses. Reflective of the late 1960s philosophy of post-structuralism, Kristeva sees discursive texts as embedded in a field of practice that has three dimensions: the subject that is being written about, the reader being addressed through the text, and the relationship between what is being written and what Kristeva terms, "exterior texts" (1986:36-37). This understanding in turn leans on the work of Mikhail Bakhtin (1929) who argues that meaning is created dialogically, that is, informed by its relationship to other texts. But both Kristeva and Bakhtin assume that these exterior texts are related to what is being written. I argue instead for the potential for *unrelated* texts to impact each other.

Perhaps the most useful way to understand Kristeva's concept of intertextuality is to focus on discourse as a web with many inter-related parts. Ruth Wodak (2001) takes this approach, articulating discourse as, "a complex bundle of simultaneous and sequential interrelated linguistic acts" (Reisegl and Wodak 2001:66). In later chapters I look further into this sequencing, showing how historical ideas about migrants—as well as historical 'solutions' to the 'problem' of immigration—reverberate with contemporary ideas, problematizations, and solutions. I call this process discursive echo and posit that the outcome of such historical reverberations is to reify contemporary ideas of immigration-as-crisis, as well as to lend legitimacy to immigration restriction and exclusion.

Robert S. Miola (2004) offers a broad approach to discourse that accounts for multiple forms of intertextuality. These include conscious imitations—such as intentional author cross-reference—but also allows for unconscious links evoked by the reader rather than the author. Miola excludes what he terms, "purely linguistic expressions, such as puns [or] homophones" (ibid) but notes that new types of intertextuality, "clamor for attention" (2004:23). Among these are what he terms, "onomastic intertextuality...the range of allusion, reference, or significance evoked simply by a name" (ibid). This new type of intertextuality helps us understand the productive nature of the *alien* label. When used as a label for migrants as well as for other non-human species, intertextuality means that a host of profoundly negative meanings are evoked. I return to this concept in chapter five to show how ostensibly and even radically disparate alien discourses relate and inform upon each other. Suffice to say here that such discourses interact as part of the meaning-making process.

By way of introduction, the following web memes illustrate how unrelated discourses can be connected to construct social problems and transfer fears from one arena to another. Such memes combine nationalist anti-immigration tropes with historical contact-decimation narratives to highlight the wrong done to 'Indians'. They can also be seen as a counter-discourse that attempts to subvert the hegemony of Anglo-American nation-state 'ownership'.

Image 3: Web meme collected from facebook on 07/06/2017

These discourses are not directly related; there is no system of immigration in the late 15th century when Columbus first sets foot in the Americas, nor are Indians ever thought of as migrants or refugees. But in connecting the two discourses (that of immigration, and that of Indian decimation) there is a transferal of both fear of contact and threat of the outsider from one discourse to the next.

Image 4: Web meme collected from facebook on 09/20/2017

Now these memes are found on facebook and can be thought of as a minor part of the discourse on immigration since, first of all, they are web memes with limited reach and political influence, and second, they are more to do with the discourse on Indians in North America than they are to do with immigration[7]. The question to ask is what are the routine discursive formations that rouse a sense of danger or threat in the discourse on migration? These are pertinent questions because the character of a discourse that iterates a social problem relates to the kinds of responses that are deployed. Notes Bridget Anderson: "The particular ways in which migrants are portrayed offer insights into the nature of popular anxieties about the foreigner as invasive other and clues as to the political responses that can help to counter these anxieties" (2017:8). In other words, discursive formations can be mined in order to study how the problematized migrant subjectivity is constructed, as well as the process by which political and material solutions are made commonsense.

Ideology in Discourse

Discourses produce commonsense knowledge that can be conceived of as ideological when two things are obscured: the underlying social relations and the effects of power accrued from such ideas being accepted as commonsense. For a deeper understanding of the relationship between ideological discourses and underlying social relations, we can look to the work of Karl Marx and Friedrich Engels in *The German Ideology* (1845). They write: "The ideas of the ruling class are in every epoch the ruling ideas, i.e. the class which is the ruling *material* force of society, is at the same time its ruling *intellectual* force" (1845/2010:59). In other words, the class that controls material production shapes cultural production. A result of this is what Marx and Engels term, "rule of concepts" [8] (1845/2010:23). What the reader 'knows', in other words, is directed by the ideas of the ruling class, and supports the dominant material class.

Intellectuals in a particular society—journalists, for example—produce knowledge but this production process can never be neutral. Not only are the most powerful media outlets for-profit enterprises whose products are affected by the values and interests of owners, advertisers, internal corporate culture and structure, their reportage is also shaped by what sells, i.e. the values and interests that are dominant in particular historical periods. Journalists produce knowledge in order to fulfill the obligations of their jobs and to engage their readers. However, since journalists are often educated and privileged members of a society who have strong ties with business and cultural leaders, their interests are most likely aligned with those of the dominant material class. The ideas they promote can therefore be seen as what Marx and Engels term, "ideological reflexes and echoes" (1845/2000:36), that is, reflexes and echoes of dominant material processes.

The idea that global human mobility is an "immigration crisis" (Horsey 2015, para. 1), for example, is shaped by people positioned to make such claims (Spector & Kitsuse 1977:161). David Horsey—the journalist quoted in the opening paragraph of this chapter—is educated, privileged, and respected enough that his voice is recognized as 'opinion' in the commercial media institution that is the *LA Times*. What Horsey writes is affected by his own values and interests as well as by those around him. His opinion piece would not have been published had it strongly contradicted the values and interests of his editors, managers, the owners of the newspaper, or the advertisers who pay to exhibit their messages. What Horsey writes is thereby constrained by social, historical, and political context, as well as by other material constraints related to the mass media industry. And what he writes has both political and material effects. When President Trump, for example, addresses the nation in a speech titled, "On the Crisis at the Border" (8 Jan 2019), he is building on the widely circulated and already established idea that there *is* a crisis. Horsey does not invent the idea of the "immigration crisis" (para. 1), but in using this iteration—and in presenting it as commonsense rather than as something to be questioned—he supports the ideology. The question to ask is how do such ideologies work to support ruling relations?

Dorothy E. Smith (1990) finds ideological 'knowledges' to have a power effect on social and material processes. For Smith, such processes are understood as diffuse: "that total complex of activities, differentiated into many spheres, by which our kind of society is ruled, managed, and administered" (1990:14). What Smith argues for, in other words, is an understanding of how knowledge is socially organized in ways that are strategic to the exercise of ruling relations. Smith notes that discourses work to effect commonsense knowledge, that is, "objectify knowing as knowledge" (1990:200). Like the Marxian approach upon which it builds—and which it stretches—Smith's approach focuses on the process of knowledge construction as embedded in social relations. Like Marx and Engels, Smith also attends to the actualities of people's daily existences. Discourses are seen as structuring knowledge, and so structuring experiences, but, Smith argues, they do so in a manner that is divorced from actual, everyday lived experiences. Women's experiences, for example, become subdued in the discourse, both silenced by the voices of 'experts' or 'authorities', as well as silenced by the commonsense generated through gendered social relations. Because of this, Smith argues, women's consciousness becomes bifurcated between the work they do, and the external order that their work contributes to (1990:19). In this bifurcation, Smith argues, women experience alienation from themselves[9].

Hegemony in Discourse

For Antonio Gramsci (1971), ideological discourses are considered hegemonic when they are accepted with what he terms, "'spontaneous' consent" (1971:145). When Horsey, for example, writes about "the immigration problem in the US" (Horsey 2015), he is repeating a commonsense stance that situates certain people crossing national borders as migrants and that positions such migrants as 'problematic'. Such hegemonic formations are influential in part because they assume this commonsense stance, that is, they do not appear to be affected by—or productive of—social or material relations. Marx and Engels argue that this is essential to the continuance of rule. Each ruling class has to present its ideas as, "the only rational, universally valid ones" (1845/2010:60) in order to, "carry through its aim" (ibid), that is, in order to perpetuate its dominance. A result of this universalization of experience is to normalize inequalities that are based in class struggle, and, once again, to alienate the subjects wrought in the process.

According to Gramsci, hegemony operates as the indirect exercise of power by the dominant group (1971:145) and operates as a complement to the direct exercise of power by the state and courts. A society's intellectuals—their priests, teachers, writers—are seen as 'deputies' of the state working at the sociocultural level in a population to effect consent to their will. In other words, to gain acceptance of dominant ideologies as commonsense, as well as to promote the interests of the ruling class and state as their own interests. Coercive power (of the state and courts, for example) and consensual power (as effected through discourse) go hand in hand in order to give regimes the influence they need to exercise power. Notes Gramsci: "one should not count only on the material force which power gives in order to exercise an effective leadership" (1971:215). Consent to power is also needed. Hegemony is seen as an intensely interconnected set of processes that work to inculcate the masses with the ideas of the dominant ruling class.

Hegemony exceeds the concept of ideology in its Marxian sense by enlarging its focus from dominant ideas being the product of a particular class interest, to dominant ideas being part of a whole process organized by governing values and beliefs. We can understand these dominant values and beliefs to be culture, used in the broad sense employed by Raymond Williams in *Marxism and Literature* (1977). Williams conceives of culture as a complex and variable two-fold concept, as, "a noun of 'inner' process, specialized to its presumed agencies in 'intellectual life' and 'the arts'... also a noun of general process, specialized to its presumed configurations in 'whole ways of life'" (1977:17). Culture is something that is both created by intellectual and aesthetic practitioners and something that is lived or experienced. Hegemony, then, implies that the social relations of domination and subordination are produced and experienced in the 'whole way of life' of the individual. When a particular discourse attains the status of hegemony, it has detached from its material foundations and has entered the lifeworld-encompassing realm of culture—perhaps something akin to the *Lebenswelt* of Berger and Luckmann (1966). It still conceals the socioeconomic relations underlying the discourse, and the benefits that dominant members of society accrue from such a discourse, but as it presents as entirely commonsensical—as something 'we all know'.

Hegemony is an effective concept to help understand how political and cultural institutions are connected through ruling class power and how two different modes of social control—coercive and consensual—operate side by side. But hegemonic discourses are not forced upon us; to be hegemonic, we must 'know' such discourses make commonsense. In the words of Stuart Hall (1982), hegemony is achieved, "by means of winning the active consent of those classes and groups who were subordinated within it" (1982:81). In this understanding of hegemony, subordinated peoples accept ideologies and actively engage in preserving them through accepting such ideas as commonsense or simply 'the truth'.

FRAMING THROUGH METAPHOR

The manner in which ideas or subjects are discursively presented has very real consequences for the ideas and subjects being constructed in such a way. Building on Goffman's (1974) concept of frame analysis, David Altheide (2000) posits that framing—or what he calls, "the definition of the situation" (2000:1)—is where commonsense knowledge and material outcomes intersect. Notes Altheide: "if people define things as real, they are real in their consequences" (2000:2). I argue that the use of alarming and antagonistic metaphors produces a fearful migrant subjectivity, and further, that this has devastating outcomes. The consequences of such metaphoric framing are to make visceral the threat of the migrant, to make commonsense the idea of immigration-as-crisis, and to produce consent for increasingly aggressive and dehumanizing 'solutions'.

In George Lakoff's classic work *Metaphors We Live By* (1980), Lakoff explains that the metaphor is a figure of speech that pervades both thought and action. Notes Lakoff: "The essence of metaphor is understanding and experiencing one kind of thing in terms of another" (1980:5). Much of the time, however, metaphoric expressions are not even noticed as being metaphorical (1980:27). Regardless, they are seen by Lakoff as essential to structuring how we think about things, how we experience things, and how we understand them. In other words, metaphors are not just ways of expressing ideas: they connect ideas and in doing so are *constitutive* of ideas. This is especially important to note when we are looking at how metaphors become vehicles for constructing problems. Notes Gerald O'Brien: "problems are framed in large part through the employment of metaphors" (2003:33). Or as Bridget Anderson (2017:15) states in her analysis of press coverage of people termed migrant:

> They [metaphors] are a crucial element in the structuring of our conceptual systems, providing cognitive frames that make issues understandable. They bridge the gap between logic and emotion, exposing and shaping our feelings and responses and acting as both expression and legitimation.

So not only do metaphors help produce a visceral reaction to issues, they also lend legitimacy to ensuing responses.

A common metaphor in the discourse on migration is the metaphor of *home* for the nation, and by focusing on the shifts in how this metaphor is used, we can get a good overall picture of how both the immigration discourse and the migrant subjectivity has shifted over time. *Home* is frequently used to emphasize personal belonging to the nation (as in a 'home country', or 'homeland'), and is also used to provoke ideas of protectionism through the related metaphor of a door or gate. While the term homeland is in use from the early 1600s to describe varying geographic places (*OED* 2011), the related metaphor of a door or gate emerges in the US immigration discourse at a specific point in time—the early 1920s when quota systems are being introduced.

The following cartoon (image 5) shows how a metaphorical quota gate is imagined as working to restrict the entrance of 'undesirable' migrants. Drawn by Hallahan for the Providence *Evening Bulletin* in 1921, the cartoon depicts the commanding presence of Uncle Sam inserting a quota-tagged "GATE" into a large funnel that acts as a bridge between Europe and the US. Stuffed into the European end of the funnel are hordes of people bearing improvised luggage, with a cloud looming over their heads. On the fairer shores of the US, a small but orderly number of people have been allowed to enter.

THE ONLY WAY TO HANDLE IT.

Image 5: "The Only Way to Handle It." Cartoon by Hallahan for the Providence Evening Bulletin, 1921

The cartoon is titled "The Only Way to Handle It", suggesting the quota gate is an effective tool to restrict disorderly mass immigration to the US. The representation of an over-sized Uncle Sam holding both the laws of the land and the quota gate, lends legitimacy to the idea that government *should* step in to protect the nation-state from unrestricted immigration. Such metaphors make commonsense of the idea of gates, doors, and walls as effective measures to combat mass migration. They also make visceral the idea of the nation-state as a personal property that warrants both legal and physical protection. Three years after this cartoon appears, the US Border Patrol is created, and the Uncle Sam of this image is supplanted by a real life federal Border Patrol agent. Just as the gate metaphor makes visceral the idea of the nation-state as a home, it also makes commonsense the idea that the 'homeland' should be protected by federal agents, as well as by structures of enclosure.

Related to the metaphor of home for nation, the metaphor of the *open door* is used both to constitute a visceral negative reaction to immigration, and also to produce consent for immigration restriction and exclusion. So, when Trump tweets in 2014 that: "Mexico is allowing many thousands to go thru their country & to our very stupid *open door*" (@realDonaldTrump 2014, emphasis added), he is linking ideas of the nation to that of a personal property, both of which have 'doors' that should be kept closed for safety. A contemporary Instagram post (@_thecatbus 2019) in response to a post about immigration, illustrates this ideology, once again using the metaphor of home:

> Tell me sir, do you have walls in your house? Do you lock your doors at night? Do you see who's there before you let someone in? I care about the American citizens of this country just like I do with the family in my house. I want a locked door and walls just like any other country has.

In this post, the metaphor of home for country is used to make the issue of unauthorized migration understandable to the reader. It suggests that the US is alone in having an 'unlocked door and no walls'. The use of the home metaphor also lends legitimacy to the emotional nature of the writer's response.

A second way we can trace changing problematizations of the migrant subjectivity is to historicize the use of military metaphors in the immigration discourse. The term *invasion*, for example, is first used in the period leading up to the Chinese Exclusion Act of 1882 in order to frame unwanted Chinese migration as a danger to the US nation and its 'people'[10]. From the early 1950s until the arrival of the recent 'caravans', however, the term invasion is used almost exclusively to describe the appearance of Mexican laborers in the US. The term invasion is used pervasively from this time period onwards to link what is framed as poor southern border security with a supposed national security threat. Such metaphors conceal the economic and political conditions that lead to mass migration, as well as the fact that the appearance of undocumented Mexican laborers in the 1940s and 1950s is largely driven by state-sponsored immigration practices. Such metaphorical framing, in other words, not only highlights the shifts in the discourse, it also heralds the ruptures in material practice. This is because metaphors have the potential to frame not only the 'problem', but also the 'solution'. And so following the 'invasion' of Chinese laborers in the 1880s comes Chinese Exclusion; and following the 'invasions' of Mexican laborers in the 1950s comes a series of military-style 'Operations' at the border to 'round up' Mexicans and other people framed as 'undesirable'.

A brief historical detour is warranted at this point to highlight the changes in immigration policy and enforcement practices that result in this shift in the Mexican migrant subjectivity from seasonal laborer to invading alien.

Labor shortages in the US during the Second World War lead the Roosevelt administration to negotiate a treaty called the Bracero Program that encourages 168,000 farm workers to be recruited from Mexico (in Massey, Durand, and Malone 2002:36). As with all named programs and operations in US immigration policy, the naming of this program in itself is extraordinarily revealing. *Bracero* derives from the Spanish word *brazo* meaning *arm*, and while the translation is roughly 'farm hands', it is hard to ignore the effects of this metonymic framing: to detach the labor from the actual human to whom the limbs belong. Or, in other words, to produce the labor while reducing the laborer. And while this happens on a metonymic naming level, it also affects the lives of the actual people involved. As Massey, Durand, and Malone point out (2002:105): "Throughout the twentieth century the United States has arranged to import Mexican workers while pretending not to…politicians and public officials have persistently sought ways of accepting Mexicans as workers while limiting their claims as human beings". Calling them 'hands' or aliens—rather than receiving them and perceiving them as entire human beings—is just one way that farm workers are dehumanized through discourse and immigration policy. And although the Bracero guest-worker program is extended a number of times throughout the 1940s and 50s, the labor supply still proves insufficient and so US farmers and agricultural interests increasingly hire undocumented workers to make up for this shortfall.

Adverse reaction to the growth in undocumented laborers in the US in this time period is augmented by the widespread use of antagonistic metaphors to frame the situation. In a widely circulated letter written in 1953 by Assistant Attorney General J. Lee Rankin, for example, Rankin refers to unauthorized migration as an, "invasion on wages, standards of living, and our own domestic agricultural workers" (as reprinted in the Congressional Record of 1954:8129). Later in his letter, Ranking connects this 'invasion' of laborers as a threat to the nation, noting (ibid):

> [F]or each apprehension three Mexican aliens cross the border and either return undetected or infiltrate into our northern industrial areas…the great majority are 'braceros' who seek only seasonal employment, but it is apparent that this border is also an easy avenue of entry into our country for almost any number of Communists or foreign agents.

This discursive formation maximizes the threatening nature of the undocumented worker in three ways. First such workers are labeled "Mexican aliens" (perhaps a precursor to today's 'illegal aliens' moniker); second, they move "undetected" or threaten to "infiltrate"; and finally, their appearance is perceived by Rankin as an indication that the southern border is vulnerable to a breach by enemy agents.

The use of these dramatic and antagonistic metaphors increases as tensions associated with the Cold War escalate throughout the 1950s. These discursive formations have the effect of shifting ideas of the migrant subjectivity from seasonal Mexican laborer to potential enemy invader, and I argue that this shift lends legitimacy to practices of increasing restriction and exclusion. For example, in testimony from December 1953, the acting commissioner of the Immigration and Naturalization Service, warns Congress that, "the 'mass invasion' of illegal aliens 'flooding the Southwest' [is] beyond the control of the U.S. border patrol" (in CQ Almanac 1954). Such discursive formations rely on military and hydraulic metaphors (invade, infiltrate, flood). In the manner of discursive crossover, the idea of an *invasion of aliens* also evokes the idea of a space alien invasion (I return to this topic in chapter five, suffice to say here that the space alien invasion genre also becomes hugely popular during this time frame).

All of these discursive formations that frame the migrant subjectivity as a military-grade threat during the early 1950s forge consent for future military-grade 'controls' or 'solutions'. And this is exactly what happens. In June 1954, some 800 officers are deployed to the El Centro Sector of the border in Southern California to mark the beginning of the US Border Patrol's tellingly named "Operation Wetback" (US CBP 2018a). If there is any doubt who these discursive formations and state practices are really targeting, this racist naming of a military-style 'operation' after the assumed 'wet back' appearance of undocumented workers who have crossed the Rio Grande gives us the answer: Mexican aliens.

Further escalation in the Cold War conjoined with the new 'drug war' of the Reagan years leads to what Timothy Dunn (1996) refers to as the militarization of border and immigration enforcement. This is accompanied by an increase in the use of military metaphor in the immigration discourse, as well as an increase in links being made between southern border incursions and weak national security. The effect of these ideological shifts is to transform the migrant subjectivity from potential enemy invader to invading foreign terrorist. During the late 1980s, for example, President Reagan links border security to national security by suggesting that foreign terrorists can simply drive over the border (in Massey , Durand, and Malone 2002:87). And then in the early 1990s, a persistent economic recession as well as a number of high-profile stories about Haitian refugees and ships carrying unauthorized Chinese migrants, helps to fuel further anti-immigrant sentiment (in Nevins 2002:109).

Making 'sense' of these events in the summer of 1993, President Clinton speaks at a press conference to warn about, "those who would enter our country to terrorize Americans" (in Nevins 2002:110), and ends by promising to, "make it tougher for illegal aliens to get into our country" (ibid). Following Clinton's dire warnings about 'terrorizing illegal aliens' are a new series of military-style operations at the southern border. A two-week offensive named "Operation Blockade" is launched in November of 1993 (although it is later named "Operation Hold the Line" in order to lessen the offense to the Mexican government). Hundreds of extra border patrol agents are deployed to patrol the El Paso region of the border, in what Joseph Nevins describes as, "a highly visible show of force" (2002:111), and inspections are stepped up at official ports of entry. Migrants get deterred by this new security theatre and apprehensions in the EL Paso region drop to 90 percent of previous levels (ibid). The effect of framing such practices as military-style operations—as well as the appearance and assumed efficacy of the practices themselves—stimulates much positive publicity in the media. The consequences of this are to reinforce the idea that increased militarization of the border is an appropriate 'solution' to the 'illegal aliens' that Clinton warns are about to enter our country to 'terrorize Americans'.

But fear about immigration only intensifies throughout the early nineties, both as the economic recession continues, and as California grapples with Proposition 187 that seeks to deny education, health, and social services to unauthorized immigrants. And so finally, in 1994, "Operation Gatekeeper" is deployed, a military-style operation whose name echoes discursively with the quota gates of the 1920s. All of these changes in practice can be seen as a response to changes in how the migrant subjectivity is represented during this time period. The effect of such representations is to reify the threat of the migrant, but also to effect a change in how the border between Mexico and the US is imagined. These changes, notes Nevins, turn the border from a, "zone of transition within which the peoples and places have much in common, to a boundary that represents a stark linear demarcation between a strongly differentiated 'us' and 'them'—both territorially and socially" (2002:114). In other words, the use of military metaphor to frame the situation—and the ensuing militarization of the border—does not just shore up the physical boundary between two nation-states, it also shores up the subjectivity boundaries.

The militarization of the border that has its roots in the Cold War, and that is supported by the increased use of military metaphor and terminology throughout the twentieth century, intensifies once more following the September 11th terrorist attacks in 2001. Now Clinton's warnings about terrorizing aliens seem to have come to fruition[11]. As part of the official response to the attacks, President Bush signs the Homeland Security Act that creates the Department of Homeland Security (DHS) whose mission statement is to, "safeguard the American people, our homeland, and our values" (US DHS 2016). This statement promotes ideas of a homogenous 'American people' who belong to 'our homeland' that needs safeguarding from threats to 'our values'. In this example we can see how the metaphor of home is deployed in order to provoke a visceral reaction to threats against the nation-state, and so to lend legitimacy to a new and wide-reaching federal agency.

A final metaphor that is prominent in both historical and contemporary iterations about migrants is the hydraulic metaphor, and I contend that its use to describe human movement produces the idea that migrants threaten to overwhelm or 'drown' the nation. The notion that immigrants are a "human tide" (Horsey 2015, para. 1), for example, or a "human tsunami" (para. 2), who "rush" (ibid), and "gush" (ibid) and who will "swamp a continent" (ibid), is an argument rife with hydraulic metaphor that frames migrants as dangerous to the entire nation. Such hydraulic metaphors construct and perpetuate migrants (always plural) as moving in an unstoppable flow, just as migration assumes a plurality, rather than the more individualized migrations (Sutcliffe 2001).

If we trace the emergence of the hydraulic metaphor in the immigration discourse, however, it is interesting to note that its early uses do not have a negative connotation. A genealogy of the hydraulic metaphor shows that as immigration becomes increasingly problematized, so the hydraulic metaphor is used in increasingly problematizing ways. In 1852, for example, an article in the *New York Times*, writes: "It is wonderful, this tide of immigration as it surges towards the Pacific (3 Dec 1852:3). This is a time period when population expansion is seen as necessary to the continuing success of the US national project, and so the metaphor of *tide* to describe the movement of migrants has an intended positive meaning. By 1869, however, this hydraulic movement has become more forceful. In an article titled, "The Flood-Tide of Immigration", for example, (*New York Times* 9 May 1869:4), the unnamed author notes, "From all parts of Germany...Great Britain, and particularly from Ireland, the news is that peasantry and mechanics are emigrating to America in numbers unprecedented" (ibid). Concluding that, "the tide of immigration is swelled", the author opines: "So long as those who come are good citizens, the more the better" (ibid). This discursive formation uses the hydraulic metaphor to create the conditions of possibility for immigration to be seen as unstoppable (not just a tide, but a flood-tide), and also elevates the citizen subjectivity as desirable.

The hydraulic metaphor becomes more forceful as immigration becomes increasingly problematized throughout the remainder of the nineteenth century. When Congress meets to discuss loopholes to Japanese exclusion following the Gentlemen's Agreement of 1908, for example, the *New York Times* reports the discussion under the headline, "ROUSED BY HAWAIIAN FLOOD" (23 July 1921:2). In the ensuing article the unnamed author elaborates that it is a *human* flood we are talking about, and notes that, "Hawaii [is] being flooded with Japanese" (ibid). This use of the flood metaphor to problematize the migration of people is illustrative of the manner in which metaphors can transfer ideas from one discourse to another. Floods of water are *known* dangers, and flood stories are among the oldest fear narratives in human storytelling, dating back to at least 2000BC when the Sumerian poem titled *The Epic of Gilgamesh* provides us with an ancient precursor to the Noah's Flood narrative. Just as when problematized sparrows are connected with problematized migrants, connecting the age-old fear of floods with the nascent fear of mass human mobility makes sense of the human migrant problematization.

The metaphor of the melting pot is employed in the US at the beginning of the twentieth century to illustrate the potential benefits of 'racial' mixing. The metaphor comes from a play of the same name written by Israel Zangwill in 1909. Explains one character: "America is God's Crucible, the great Melting-Pot where all the races of Europe are melting and re-forming!...the real American...will be the fusion of all races, perhaps the coming superman" (1909/2007, Act 1). But after a series of increasingly restrictive and racist immigration policies are passed in the early 1920s—policies that work to restrict southern and eastern European migration to the US—the metaphor begins to turn. Now, the migrant is indigestible in the American melting pot. We see this in the comments of popular author

Kenneth Roberts in *The Saturday Evening Post*: "a law that will ... give America a chance to digest the millions of unassimilated, unwelcome and unwanted aliens that rest so heavily in her" (in O'Brien 2003:37). This metaphor reinforces the ideology that there is a fundamental and irreconcilable difference between people, and that because of this, "unwanted aliens" (ibid) cannot dissolve or assimilate into US culture. In this metaphoric view of the world, immigration does not function like a melting pot where incomers lend some of their values and cultural variants to the mix. In this version of homogenous national culture, migrants are produced as spoiling the stew. As Ali Behdad (2005) notes on the flimsiness of the idea of the melting pot: "Cultural and ethnic differences were tolerated only to the extent that they could be melted into a single national form" (2005:12). The migrant who spoils the stew, therefore, makes visceral how aliens represent a threat to a supposedly homogenous US culture. As Ghussan Hage (2000) points out, such ideas are indicative of what he terms 'Measurement and Numbering Pathology' (1990:123). Notes Hage: "Such worries about mixing and mixtures are a constant feature of...media reporting about immigration and multiculturalism" (1990:125).

Discourse analysis allows us to filter through metaphoric formations and ask what everyday commonsense beliefs they are indicative of or even produce. As Wodak and Meyer note, this is because metaphors conceal, "the more hidden and latent type of everyday beliefs" (2009:8). When an official White House press release (2018), for example, refers to migrant children as UACs—standing for Unaccompanied Alien Children—it communicates a value system in which such children are framed as unwanted, problematic, and also potentially dangerous. And if these subjects are defined in discourse as fearful, the political and material effects are that people will fear them and even discriminate or attack them. Such ideas lend political support to hegemonic conceptions of the US as a nation-state being ruled for a specific people and add weight to calls for a prophylactic border wall in order to keep migrants out. I return to this concept in chapter six in which I show how such discursive formations are characteristic of a moral panic. For now, I posit that such metaphors contribute to the hegemony of migrants being perceived as symptomatic of a crisis.

MULTIMEDIA IN DISCOURSE

Where much discourse analysis focuses on the written or spoken word as the unit of analysis (see Habermas 1979, Wallerstein & Balibar 1991, Doty 1993, or Wodak 2001), a discourse is never just words. As many cultural studies scholars have noted (see Foucault 1965, Hall 1988, Mirzoeff 1999, Shirato and Webb 2004, Behdad 2005, or Shapiro 1985 and 2012, for example) discourse includes an array of sign activity such as images, design, layout, color, and sound. Such elements have tangible effects on how a text is received (including a visual 'text' such as a film or television news item), how a subject is framed, and how an idea becomes 'commonsense knowledge'. It could be argued that when image, text, and sound are combined it has a far more visceral effect than either images or texts by themselves. Writing about the interrelated nature of media in the discourse on madness, for instance, Foucault notes that, "painting and text constantly refer to one another—commentary here and illustration there" (1988:17). Focusing on how different media transmit ideological notions, Stuart Hall (1988) sees television as the medium *par excellence* for transmitting knowledge and sees it as, "the dominant medium of social discourse and representation in our society" (1988:71). Hall elaborates:

> Much of television's power to signify lay in its visual and documentary character—its inscription of itself as merely a 'window on the world', showing things as they really are. Its propositions and explanations were underpinned by this grounding of its discourse in 'the real'—in the evidence of one's eyes. Its discourse therefore appeared peculiarly a naturalistic discourse of fact, statement and description.

Television, in other words, is seen as a particularly vibrant medium for creating 'commonsense knowledge'. By logical extension, other visual media that purport to 'show things as they really are'—media such as film and photography—likewise have this potential.

The following example from *Fox News* illustrates this point. In a 2013 television news report, guest-anchor Chris Wallace describes what he terms, "more proof of the economic impact of the immigration debate" (Wallace 2013). The report focuses on an estimation by LA County officials about the number of children of undocumented parents who receive aid. Accompanying Wallace's report are several images that do not relate to what Wallace is talking about, but which inform our knowledge about migrants in very particular ways.

Image 6: Fox News Special Report with Chris Wallace, 2013

A man is seen climbing over a barbed wire fence with dollar bills hovering over this head—a visceral image of both financially motivated criminality and of a failing border fence. This image contributes to the discourse of the migrant as an illegal. It also points to the trope that 'they' come here to get 'our' money thus shoring up the message that the 'economic impact of immigration' is a negative one. This image highlights the notion that the southern border is an insufficient structure to maintain security (this report appeared some two years before Trump ran for office on a pledge to 'build the wall'). The headline to this corner image with its blood-red background states, "CHILDREN OF THE CORN" and later changes to "ALIEN NATION" while the image remains the same. Neither the seemingly strange headlines nor the image are referred to explicitly. Instead, the viewer may remember that *Children of the Corn* (1977) is the name of a popular horror story by Stephen King that is adapted for film. Further, corn could popularly be assumed to be the staple diet of 'Latino' immigrants in Los Angeles. Likewise, *Alien Nation* is the name of an anti-immigration treatise written in 1996 by Peter Brimelow that is often promoted on Fox News. Put these symbols together and the picture of 'criminal alien immigrants' threatening the cultural and economic well-being of the US nation-state is made commonsense.

Further analysis is warranted at this point in order to explain how such discursive articulations become knowledge and how this leads to political and material effects. In other words, to explain how commonsense ideas, "become part of the lives of ordinary people, or even how they become institutionalized and made part of the structure of institutions" (Hacking 2011:278). This news report on one of the US's most watched television stations answers that question. First, because Wallace does not refer to the image nor to the headlines, the audience is left to make their own connections, engaging their consent in what is a racializing (by which I mean race-constructing), nationalizing, and criminalizing process. In this manner, the audience *becomes a part of* how negative associations are made, building on and reinforcing damaging social constructions. Multiple ideas about migrants are drawn upon and perpetuated in this report: that they are aliens, criminals, worthy of fear, not to be trusted, and that their food choices make them Other. This collective symbolism links together all the strands of discourse (Jäger 2001:33).

Second, the ideas in Wallace's report create the reality

they purport to name. When Wallace states he has, "more proof of the economic impact of the immigration debate" (Wallace 2013), he is not just hypothesizing that some migrants are a burden on the economy; he is stating he has *more proof* that generations of migrants *from south of the border* are bad economically for the US. For viewers of this show, as well as those who hear about it, this framing points to the southern border as a site of incursion into the US nation-state, and also reinforces a 'problem about numbers' framing of the discourse on immigration. This definition of the situation is not created by Wallace, but it is mobilized by him. A combination of his 'proof' and the visceral images in his report make this framing 'relevant' in the realm of rational, critical debate, and support the hegemony of the discourse of Latino immigration to the US as a problem. It is a discursive iteration that echoes discursively with prior historical iterations and adds its own details to the discourse. Foucault's historical analysis of the discourse on sexuality reveals that it is the multiplication of discourses that creates, "a determination on the part of the agencies of power to hear it spoken about, and to cause it to speak through explicit articulation and endlessly accumulated detail" (1978:18). The details spoken about and shown in Wallace's report lend support to the knowledge that the US needs a more secure border to stop unauthorized migration. And Trump's call for a border wall indeed draws upon this discursive commonsense.

What is essential for discourse analysis is to examine how such collective symbolisms function to support structures of power. Wallace's report strengthens the notion of the US as under attack from aliens because of the US's weak borders, reinforces the idea that the US economy is threatened by immigration, and hints that aliens pose an insidious threat to US culture. Now the idea that the US has a single, homogenous culture is characteristic of a national-style of identity, and is, itself, one of the hallmarks of the nation-state form of power. Such identities denote, "a fundamental and consequential sameness among members of a group or category...expected to manifest itself in solidarity, in shared dispositions or consciousness, or in collective action" (Brubaker and Cooper 2000:7). Only in a nation-state where it is imagined there is a single, homogenous culture defined, in part, against the people living south of the US border, would "children of the corn" (Wallace 2013) be a threat.

A key principle in discourse analysis is that social phenomena neither present in their entirety nor are they ever concluded. Threats to a nationalized 'US culture' exist because there is no concrete definition of what US culture is. Like an old building in permanent need of support, the ideological concept of US culture is always under construction. "Meaning can never be ultimately fixed and this opens up the way for constant social struggles about definitions of society and identity, with resulting social effects" (Jørgensen and Phillips 2002:24). When it comes to idea of the nation and 'national identity', however, because the struggles operate in a dialectic, pushing and pulling into ever more distant binaries, we have a sort of congealing of definitions. The effect is to force ideas about nation and national identity into an increasingly stark 'us and them' framework. Through this process, the 'American' becomes one homogenous national identity that co-constitutes against the identities of other nationals. And likewise, the homogenous identity of the 'citizen' co-constitutes against the homogenous identity of the 'alien'. Such identities lend support to contemporary strategies to strengthen the US border, since, within this ideological reasoning of distinct and discrete identities, the only way to maintain the wholeness of an identity is to prevent mixing or dilution. In the following chapters I return to this theme when I explore the figurative subjects of the nation and the utility to the nation-state of such symbolic constructions. Here I just want to emphasize that a discourse gains its meaning and power by relating to other discursive ideas, and by positioning itself in contrast to other discursive ideas.

△△△

Discourse has been shown as an effective vehicle for forging commonsense knowledge about people, places, and people's positionality in the nation, as well as for ensuring the continued dominance of the status quo. In the US's immigration discourse, migrants are framed as problematic alien Others who threaten the socio-economic and cultural welfare of the nation. The best solution—in this ideological mindset—is to eject such illegals and strengthen 'our' southern border to prevent future incursions In this manner, the legitimacy of the nation-state and its practices of immigration restriction and exclusion are strengthened.

A discourse emerges out of specific socio-historical and political contexts and leads to specific strategic outcomes. A discourse can be thought of as ideological when the utility to dominant groups—as well as the social relations out of which such a discourse emerges—are concealed. A discourse achieves the status of a hegemony when the economic basis out of which such a discourse emerges becomes far removed, and when what is represented becomes accepted as commonsense.

Discourses rely on prior, parallel, and even seemingly unrelated discourses to achieve meaning. Discourses operate dialectically, echoing discursively across time so that dominant ideas are reinforced, often in a process of mutual constitution so that ideas such as the alien Other represent as dichotomously opposed to the national citizen. Discourses promote subjectivities in imaginative and transformative ways, leading towards a hegemony of fixity that lends support to contemporary strategies to strengthen the US border.

2/RELATIONS IN THE NATION

Ideas of belonging and exclusion that code desired and undesired national subjects are intrinsic to the concept of the nation. The citizen is central such understandings, because it is the citizen who is seen as heir to national resources, the citizen who legally and politically 'belongs' to the imagined community of the nation, and the citizen who is afforded certain rights and privileges (and must exercise certain responsibilities) on account of their status. By contrast—in fact co-constituting itself through this contrast—the alien is both the legal subject name and figurative identity that demarcates the symbolic Other. Constructed through regimes of practice, represented in discourse, and shored up through legal statutes, the alien is produced as the internal enemy of the nation who must become a 'naturalized citizen' in order to neutralize their 'unnatural' and always-already threatening 'nature'. The legal and figurative identities that are demarcated by the labels *citizen* and *alien* are seen as essential both for political practice and for constituting the imagined community of the nation[12].

In this chapter I undertake a review of some of the core theoretical concepts of subject-making and the nation. Rather than figurative subjects like the national or the migrant having some intrinsic or fixed meaning, I argue that they are social constructions that emerge out of relations of power and that work as technologies of domination. Since ideas of national belonging in the US are from the very outset bound to ideas of race, in this chapter I provide a theoretical overview of ideas of race in relation to ideas about the nation. I examine the relationship between immigration practices and immigrant stereotypes in discursive representations of early immigrants. I explore how the discourse on racism shifts after the delegitimization of ideas of race at the end of the Second World War amid a new discourse of civil rights and 'post-racism' in the 1950s. And I show how articulating notions of race and nation produce the degraded alien migrant subjectivity as well as co-constitute the citizen as a subjectivity of value.

SUBJECT-MAKING

Three basic concepts of subject-making can be outlined here: that figurative subjects do not create themselves but are rather determined in form by both social and economic processes (Foucault 1982, Mamdani 2012, Becker 2963); that figurative subjects are co-constituted as 'normal' against the figure of some Other (Said 1979, Stoler 1995, Anderson 2013); and that the process of subject-making (also referred to as subjectification) is both homogenizing (Said 1979, Behdad 2005, Mamdani 2012), and divisive (Foucault 1965, 1982, Linebaugh and Rediker 2000).

The process by which power creates figurative subjects is a central concern of Foucault, one that we see evolve over the course of his work from *Madness and Civilization* (1965), to *The Order of Things* (1970), *The Archeology of Knowledge* (1972), *The History of Sexuality* (1978), and again in *The Subject and Power* (1982). For Foucault, power is seen as diffuse, "exercised from innumerable points, in the interplay of nonegalitarian and mobile relations" (1978:94). What is key for Foucault is to locate such subject-making practices historically in order to uncover what he terms their "strategical integration" (1978:102). In other words, what we need to ask is out of what particular sets of social relationships does such subject-making occur? And when we are looking at the political and material effects of a discourse—what Foucault terms "power effects" (1982:780), what we need to focus on is why a discourse is deployed—or even necessary—at a particular historical conjuncture.

Disrupting 'Normal'

A key theoretical concept related to subject-making and power is that of 'normalcy'. That the 'normal' is invoked against some kind of marker for 'abnormality' is central to the process of figurative subject construction. In *Madness and Civilization* (1965), Foucault postulates that in eighteenth century Europe, 'madness' becomes the object of scientific analysis and investigation. The brain of a 'madman' is weighed in comparison to that of a 'normal' man; these observations serve to constitute madness as an object together with its subject—the madman. In *Remarks on Marx* (1991), Foucault refers to such historical processes as, "the birth of a particular normalizing society" (1991:66). Madness is not just fashioned as a form of knowledge that speaks truth because it appears as knowledge ("madness fascinates because it is knowledge" (1965/1988:21)). Madness becomes a key part of a normalizing society that enables the spectacle of the 'mad', the disciplining of the mad, and —most importantly—the confinement of the mad. In short, the discourse on madness shores up the figure of the mad person and enables their removal from the society of the normal.

In translating the historical trajectory of such "formulas of exclusion" (1965/1988:9), Foucault notes that they are not unique to the mad but rather lean on prior understandings of people in 'need' of confinement. For example, the manner in which the mad are constructed as abnormal and thereby socially excluded mirrors how lepers have previously been excluded. Links are also found between the treatment of the mad of a particular society, and the treatment of the 'idle'. The Tudor Poor Laws of sixteenth century England, for example, confine an increasing population of out-of-work poor people into institutions where they are obliged to work[13]. Such confinements—of the mad, of lepers, and of the idle—might seem at first glance unrelated. But in his discourse analytic method, Foucault sees the connection, noting that, "in a hundred and fifty years, confinement had become the abusive amalgam of heterogeneous elements" (1965/1988:45).

What Foucault reveals here is that discourses with diverse subjects can share ideas to produce similar political and material effects. In other words, what he finds is discursive crossover. And so, the discourses that produce the abnormal —whether rooted in 'differences' of class, morality, sanity, or wellness—also produce the same 'solutions' of confinement and exclusion. In this example we can see how discursive crossover produces subjects as well as solutions. There is no 'origin' of the abnormal subject as much as there is anxiety over the abnormal Other that transmutes at specific historical moments to focus on different kinds of Other for particular political ends. This transformation is not a rupture but rather what Foucault might call, "a torsion within the same anxiety" (1965/1988:16).

Foucault's focus on the diffusion of power and on processes of normalization are useful in explaining how consensus is achieved and how 'things' become 'known' as commonsense. As Foucault shows in regard to both madness and sexuality (1965, 1978), and as Laura Ann Stoler shows in regard to sexuality and race (1995), the 'will to knowledge' is a priority of medical, legal, and educational professionals. Positivist determinations for what constitutes corruption or perversion are constructed by such professionals in difference to expectations about what constitutes the 'norm'. The person with sexual perversions, or the person with criminal tendencies, are willed into existence by such professionals as 'abnormal' in contrast to their ideas about the normal person who is presumed as the rightful member of a civil society. As Foucault notes in *Discipline and Punish* (1975), "The power of the Norm appears through the disciplines...For the marks that once indicated status, privilege and affiliation were increasingly replaced—or at least supplemented—by a whole range of degrees of normality" (1975:184). And as the discourse shifts once the ideas of noble birth and hereditary power become discredited, for example, the concept of normality becomes the emergent ordering force, producing new ideas about the normal person and the co-constituted 'deviant other' that are taken as commonsense. These commonsense ideas concerning normality and deviance emerge through both practice and discourse and are seen as having a structuring effect on social relations.

People's subjectivities as well as their subject standing in the nation-state are often defined by the degree to which they are considered Other. For Nathalie Cisneros (2003), the quintessential Other today is the alien, an imaginative subject-figure who is constructed by an articulation of the discourses on race, nation, gender, and poverty. Such discourses relate to each other, inform each other, and so reinforce ideas of normalcy versus deviance. The idea that the citizen is the default or normal inhabitant of the nation, for example, is reinforced by the always-already threatening (and in Cisneros's view, sexually deviant) presence of the alien Other. And while the alien as 'threat' is made viscerally present through physical structures such as the US border, or through the material practices of Immigration and Customs Enforcement (ICE), it is through discourse that Cisneros sees the figurative subject of the alien coming to life. In addition, it is through the oppositional discourse of the alien as the deviant Other that the hegemony of the citizen as belonging is constructed and perpetuated.

When a particular idea is constituted in opposition to another idea we can say that it is co-constituted. The dialectical nature of co-constitution pushes ideas into ever more extreme versions of themselves until they become false binaries. Ideas about figurative subjects, for example, consolidate into homogenous versions of themselves and push further apart from each other until we have clear ideas about who 'we' are in direct contrast to who 'they' are. In this manner, the figurative subject identity becomes, "a master status that tends to overpower, in most crucial situations, any other characteristics which may run counter to it" (Hughes 1945:353). The alien label can thereby be conceived as a totalizing identity, a stereotypical signifier that has profound political and material consequences.

Figurative identities are co-constituted in a dialectic, that is, ideas about aliens and citizens swing from one extreme to another until such identities become absolutely dichotomous. Notes Theodore Adorno: "the dialectic advances by way of extremes, driving thoughts with the utmost consequentiality to the point where they turn back on themselves, instead of qualifying them" (2005:86). As with all false binaries, what emerges are stereotypical versions of the original idea, with the deviant alien stranger at one end of the spectrum and the citizen of the imagined national community at the opposing end. Because these identities are dichotomous, however, it is a spectrum devoid of a center. Furthermore, these identities are never complete; due to the socially constructed nature of identities —as well as the porous boundaries of identity definitions—they must continually be constructed and reconstructed. This process of construction and reconstruction of the figurative identities of the nation can be seen as a key part of what Billig terms the flagging of the national (1995:93); such identity flagging occurs through everyday practices and discourses.

The practice of co-constituting figurative identities originates in colonial discourse and has devastating and far-reaching effects. In his classic work *Orientalism* (1979), Edward Said argues that academic and literary texts on the 'Orient' have the effect of creating, "what is believed to be radical difference" (1979/2004:45), between the supposedly homogenous people of the Orient and those of the 'Occident'. Said shows that the discourse of Orientalism travels readily from imperial colony to imperial metropole, from port to the furthest hinterland, reaching far geographically and far into the consciousness of both colonizer and colonized. The Orient is constituted in dichotomous opposition to the Occident, or the imperial center of power. The people of the Orient are likewise co-constituted in contrast to people of the Occident with absolute disregard for the heterogeneity of peoples within these broad geographies. The textual depictions of people and places are seen as acts of creative scholarship, but such discourses also provide the foundation for a massive takeover of power. When Napoleon, for example, considers incorporating Egypt into the French Empire, it is because it is a place that he has considered, "tactically, strategically, historically, and—not to be underestimated—textually, that is, as something one read about and knew" (1979/2004:80). Imperial discourse on Egypt holds sway in Napoleon's imagination; the idea of it belonging to France is easily incorporated into his imperial geographic imaginary. But before positioning the French military in the region, Napoleon sends an advance front of Orientalist scholars selected from his own *Institute d'Égypte,* scholars who ingratiate themselves with Egypt's inhabitants. In this case, discourse is seen as informing the imagination and fostering consent for imperial invasion.

Central to discourses that co-constitute figurative subjects are highly reductionist stereotypes. Negative stereotypes are described by Stanley Cohen (1972) as folk devils, or, "visible reminders of what we should not be" (1972/2002:2). In the discourse on immigration these folk devils are the deviant alien Others, and because information about them tends to be framed in stereotypical ways, the effect is homogenizing. Alejandro Portes and Rubén G. Rumbaut (2006:122) point to this trend in *Immigrant America: A Portrait,* noting:

> The characterization and denunciation of immigrants as either a radical threat or an inferior stock that undermined the welfare of American workers was based on a stereotypical image of newcomers. Then as now, all immigrants were portrayed as having similar traits. The reality was quite different.

The media-consuming public accept such stereotypical and homogenous representations since, as Cohen notes, "our direct experience...in a highly segregated urban society is often nil" (1972/2002:11). The material outcomes of such stereotypifications can be devastating. Notes Étienne Balibar: "Collectivities of immigrant workers have for many years suffered discrimination and xenophobic violence in which racist stereotyping has played an essential role" (1991:20).

The immigrant stereotype emerges through regimes of practice and is illustrated in the media in a process that affirms these representations. It is then reaffirmed through interpretations of direct lived experience that activate the stereotype. In the late 1800s, for example, the Chinese laborer is represented in stereotypical form as a sojourner male; he who earns money in the US and then returns (with his money) to his family in China. But this stereotype is not just willed into being by imaginative journalists and given a sense of 'truth' by readers seeing lone Chinese males. Rather, this stereotype emerges out of the existing immigration controls that limit the ability of the Chinese laborer to either stay in the US or bring his family with him. Notes McKeown: "Mechanisms to control Asian mobility gave concrete reinforcement to the images and ideologies of difference that had inspired those controls in the first place" (2008:44). In other words, for McKeown there is an articulation between representation, ideology, and material practice that structures difference and gives it a sense of 'truth'. But this is not a truth devoid of power; this is a truth *willed into being* by power. The job of the genealogist is not only to describe and analyze such 'truths', but also to lay them bare to the historically specific conditions that animate their production and reproduction.

Defining Labels

While the label *alien* has been an official state category for un-naturalized people in the US since 1790, it is not a noun commonly used in everyday speech to refer to a person (foreigner might be a less archaic moniker). Rather, the term alien is used by certain politicians, journalists, and others in order to reinforce the idea that a person is *symbolically Other* to the nation. The addition of the word 'illegal' to the alien label emerges after the US Border Patrol is created in 1924, and the illegal alien subjectivity is shored up during the Bracero Program of the 1940s and 50s when unauthorized Mexican migrants are increasingly targeting by state and federal agents[14]. And while some media outlets refuse to refer to people as illegal aliens, many others still do. I argue that such labels rouse a host of negative associations that contribute to the discriminatory and often damaging treatment of those so labeled.

Since labels such as illegal alien refer to migrants in terms of deviance and criminality, it is instructive at this point to look to the criminological literature on labeling. In 1938, Frank Tannenbaum conceives of a model of crime in which there are two opposing "definitions of the situation" (1938:17). In Tannenbaum's theory, specific acts come to be defined as evil which are then extended, "to a definition of the individual as evil, so that all his acts come to be looked upon with suspicion" (ibid). Hall et al (1978/2002:19) offer further insights into how labeling works:

> Labels are important, especially when applied to dramatic public events. They not only place and identify those events; they assign events to a context. Thereafter the use of the label is likely to mobilise this whole referential context, with all its associated meanings and connotations.

In practice, however, the labels illegal and alien articulate with racisms and nationalisms so that *anyone* perceived to be in the same category as an illegal alien is liable to be stopped by state and federal law enforcement agents. This practice emerges during the Bracero Program in the 1940s and 50s, when, as outlined in the previous chapter, the Attorney General's office estimates that for each "Mexican alien" who is apprehended in the border region, three more slip away undetected (as reprinted in the Congressional Record of 1954:8129). From this point on in the discourse we have the intrinsic connection between Mexican-ness and alien-ness, and between Mexican-ness and illegality.

The connection between Mexican and illegal is shored up as a practice that is commonly referred to as, "rounding up aliens" (Miles 1995) intensifies. This occurs throughout the eighties and early 1990s in response to changes in immigration policy and enforcement practice that in turn affect how migrants are perceived and represented. An article from *The American Spectator* (Custred 2000) illustrates the press rhetoric that accompanies these changes, as well as the kind of everyday language Border Patrol agents use to make sense of their experiences during this time period:

> Throughout the 1980s and early 90s the 14-mile stretch of border in San Diego was hostile, violent, and out of control. Border patrol agents use terms like 'chaos' and 'anarchy' to describe it, saying that they faced riot conditions every night...almost daily thousands of Mexicans would gather on the U.S. side, then dash forward en masse in what were known as banzai runs.

The sense of fear and hostility that this article communicates is reflective of how the Mexican subjectivity has been represented but is also reflective of how Mexican-ness is being understood in lived experience. Just as with the stereotype of the lone male Chinese laborer in the late 1800s, here too the stereotype that emerges is a degraded caricature of a human whose subjectivity is reflective of—and related to—immigration policies and procedures.

In response to these 'riot conditions' and to the appearance of Mexicans 'dashing' about near the border, a series of caution signs are erected along the I-5 freeway near San Diego that shore up the 'illegal Mexican' stereotype:

Image 7: John Hood for CALTRANS/State of California, circa 1980s

Just as with the trope of the immigrant *anchor baby*, here in this illustration the child is depicted as an afterthought. The adults are the ones with the motives: the figure in the lead is disconnected, his head down, caring neither for traffic nor for those who follow him. The child in the image appears flying, un-tethered except through the woman's rough grasp. For southern Californian drivers this image serves as both CAUTION and cautionary tale. Watch out for these people, it says; they care little for their own lives, and even less for the lives of their children. I return to this topic in chapter six when I discuss changes in discursive representations of migrants that result from changes in immigration enforcement practices during this time period. Suffice to say here that an increase in border fencing in highly populated areas like San Diego results in migrants increasingly crossing the border either in 'banzai runs' or in more remote areas and at night to avoid detection. The more sinister or frightening appearance of these arrivals, coupled with an in-crease in unauthorized crossings as authorized routes become increasingly restricted, leads people to *experience* migration as an 'invasion' in the borderlands. In the article above, for example, Custred (2000) reports: "Besides the surging numbers Mrs. Robles noticed something else...whole families illegally crossing and streaming north. "That's when I realized it was an invasion," she said". The use of the military term *invasion* here is supported by the idea that migrants engage in so-called banzai runs. This is a term used by allied troops in the Second World War to refer to the terrifying rush attacks that Japanese troops engaged in (Sloan 2017). Using it here to refer to the movements of families with children is indicative of just how fearful people have become of the migrant subjectivity during this time period.

And then in the summer of 1997, buoyed by fear of the migrant subjectivity that is supported by the label 'illegal', police and Border Patrol agents in Chandler, Arizona, round up and detain *anyone* they suspect of 'being illegal'. Several hundred people racialized as 'Hispanic' are stopped and asked to prove they are 'legal'. Sixteen of them subsequently file a civil rights violation lawsuit in federal court (Fletcher 1997). This practice of 'rounding up aliens' could not have happened without the prior construction of the illegal alien as a demonstrably dangerous figurative subject. And neither could it have happened without there being a commonsense association between 'Hispanics' and illegality. Rounding up can be seen as an innovative deployment of state power with the overt function of exercising control over migrants and the border. Discursive crossover alerts us to the material outcomes that this kind of animalizing metaphoric framing can elicit, in this case suggesting that particular racialized subjectivities should be herded and fenced in like lowly and subservient animals. A further material outcome of this practice is to reify the understanding that US citizens are 'white', and any non-'white' person represents a potential threat to the nation.

In 2010 the Arizona state legislature attempts to codify this practice into law by adopting State Bill 1070 (US State of Arizona 2010). The bill requires police to determine the immigration status of any person arrested or detained where, "reasonable suspicion exists that the person is an alien and is unlawfully present" (US State of Arizona 2010, Article 8). Thereafter, in Arizona and other states in the US, every act or behavior of the assumed Hispanic is coated with a film of suspicion; every assumed Hispanic is always-already illegal.

Howard Becker's classic work *The Outsiders: Studies in the Sociology of Deviance* (1963) furthers Tannenbaum's theory of labeling by arguing that it is social groups who label certain acts or behaviors as deviant, rather than there being some intrinsic quality of the act or behavior that is deviant in itself. In other words, the alien does not create themselves; they are constructed by the society that emphasizes staying in the 'homeland' as 'natural', and the alien as un-natural (and not fit to be *naturalized* into national citizenship). The alien is thereby a social creation, "created by society...by applying those rules to particular people and labeling them as outsiders" (1963:6). The rules that create the deviant act are also a reflection of socially constructed norms. In the case of the immigration discourse, the agreed-upon rule is that allegiance ties a person to their 'birth nation'; aliens defy that rule when they leave their 'home nation'. The assumption in this logic is pointed out by Bob Sutcliffe (2001). It is, "that everyone in the world has a 'place', usually the country in which they were born, and that it is natural and desirable that everyone should stay there and not move to some other place" (2001:68). Migration (or, rather, as Sutcliffe emphasizes, migrations), is seen as the active disavowal of this rule; the figure of the migrant thus becomes the embodiment of deviance.

Use of the label *illegal* has declined in some institutions, but negative ideas about illegal immigrants—as well as policies aimed at deporting illegals or blocking their passage—have intensified since Trump rose to power. In 2013, the Associated Press decides it will no longer sanction the use of the terms *illegal immigrant* or *illegal* to describe people, and accordingly changes the terminology in their Stylebook that is used by newspapers and schools around the US. The move is described by a spokesperson for the AP as, "part of a broader shift away from labeling people and towards labeling behavior" (Weiner 2013). Such a shift is welcome news, but it still supports the hegemony of migrant *behavior* causing the immigration crisis. This understanding conceals that it is the restrictionist and exclusionary nature of the immigration system that produces such unauthorized migrants in the first place.

Labels are often used to refer to a biopolitical grouping of people assumed to share physical and cultural attributes. Their codification through state devices such as the census exerts a particular kind of symbolic power that has material and political effects. The label *alien*, for example, when used in everyday language, may refer to something strange or out of place. But when a person is codified as an alien through state classificatory systems such as the passport office or the census, this labeling heralds specific legal rights and responsibilities[15]. The power behind the entity that does the labeling, in other words, significantly affects the weight that the label bears. "The state is thus a powerful 'identifier', not because it can create 'identities' in the strong sense", as Rogers Brubaker and Frederick Cooper note (2000:16), "but because it has the material and symbolic resources to impose the categories, classificatory schemes, and modes of social counting and accounting with which bureaucrats, judges, teachers, and doctors must work and to which non-state actors must refer" (ibid).

Censuses are subjectifying technologies of the state that assign people to specific labeled categories in the interests of managing and controlling a population. Foucault argues that it is knowledge about the population through data and statistics that enables a government to manage the imbrication of people and things (by *things*, he means, "wealth, resources, means of subsistence, the territory with its specific qualities, climate, irrigation, fertility, etc." (1978/1990:93). This process he conceives of as governmentality, a practice core to the metropole of the Empire, the manifest purpose of which is, "the welfare of the population, the improvement of its condition, the increase of its wealth, longevity, health" (1978/1990:100). Prior to the mid-eighteenth century, Foucault argues, the government acts like a patrician over a family, demanding obedience, the end goal being the submission to the patrician's will. From the middle of the eighteenth century onwards, however, the use of technologies of identification and classification such as the census move us beyond this metaphor of government as family. The use of statistics brings into focus the population—its increase through births, its decline through famine, its ascendency through productive labor practices, the accumulation of wealth in certain segments but not others. These phenomena, Foucault posits, "are irreducible to those of the family" (1978/1990:99). The availability of such statistics both historically and today enables government to promote the population as its reason for governing. Not 'do as I say' (the patriarchal family model), but 'we the people' (the logic of governmentality). Notes the US Census Bureau: "The statistics of the Nation are an important and even indispensable tool in the proper portrayal of the status of the United States in various subject fields at various periods in time" (US Census Bureau 1949:V). In other words, techniques of governmentality produce both the nation and its people.

The people of the US are imagined as a 'national people', in part, because of this social counting. Technologies of governmentality such as the census, or the practice of counting people as 'immigrants', are key for both delineating a people and for exerting control over them. But this counting of people is never impartial. Until 1850, for example, reports of immigrant arrivals are only made at Atlantic and Gulf ports (US Census Bureau 1949). Those entering via Pacific ports, or from Canada, Mexico, Hawaii, Puerto Rico, and Alaska are simply not counted. In a compendium of statistics covering the period 1789 to 1945, the US Census Bureau (1949) notes that, "there existed, practically speaking, no inspection along the frontiers prior to October 1893... Until January 1, 1903, only steerage or third-class passengers were counted as immigrants, and cabin passengers or aliens who traveled first or second class were omitted" (1949:19). Land borders are practically non-existent then, and the class of an ocean-going passenger has more to do whether a passenger is counted as an immigrant than which particular nation they are a subject or citizen of.

Two further subject categories in the US illustrate the political nature of counting practices: African-origin slaves, and Indians. Enslaved people are routinely transported across the Atlantic from the west coast of Africa, but even after the US prohibits the importation of slaves in 1808, they are not considered 'immigrant', since their movement into state territories is neither regulated nor restricted as immigration. And while people designated 'Indian' are not counted in the US Census at all from its inception in 1790 until the year 1860 when they start to be counted, they are likewise never imagined as 'immigrant'[16]. And then when they are counted in 1860, this number excludes those in 'Indian Territory' and on reservations, who are not enumerated at censuses until 1890 (US Census Bureau 1949:27). Under the 14th Amendment that grants citizenship to persons born in the US, 'Indians' are still not interpreted as being US subjects and are not given their citizenship until 1924 when the Indian Citizenship Act specifically includes them.

After the end of World War II, however, there is a profound shift in both discourse and practice as the idea of national identity—as well as the practice of counting 'nationals' who enter the country—becomes entrenched. McKeown (2008) notes that, "one of the most widely recognized markers of the shift to national control over identity was the transformation of the passport into an internationally standardized certificate of citizenship" (2008:102). Like the census, the passport is a technology of governmentality that ascribes a totalizing identity to a person, binding that person to their national identity through the promise of protection that such a document of citizenship provides.

The drawing of boundaries works both for national boundaries and for those constructed through social process as 'identity'. The state uses technologies of governmentality to produce a homogenous people and its necessary Others, and to impose itself upon 'the people' and the Others; such subjectifications are seen as politically and materially important for imagining the nation. What is essential to each of these constructions is the understanding that they reap closure. Note Stuart Hall and Paul Du Gay: "The unity, the internal homogeneity, which the term identity treats as foundational is not a natural, but a constructed form of closure, every identity naming as its necessary, even if silenced and unspoken other, that which it 'lacks'" (1996:5). In other words, identity constructions shore up subjectivity boundaries, but they still do so around a central core of 'difference'.

IMAGINING THE NATION

The discourse on the nation and its desired inhabitants is necessarily passionate because from the very outset the nation is constructed as something to be passionate about. In Benedict Anderson's ground-breaking work *Imagined Communities* (1983), Anderson examines nationalism (and, given that term's multivariate meanings, nation-ness) as a specific type of cultural artifact that commands, "profound emotional legitimacy" (1983/2006:4). Tracing nationalism to its precursor cultural forms found in religious and dynastic systems, Anderson posits that the nation is three things: a limited space, that is ruled by a sovereign entity, and that imagines itself as a community (1983/2006:7).

Part of the way the imagined community is drawn together, Anderson argues, is through the mass media, the newspaper in particular. Other cultural artifacts like novels and works of visual art—as well as practices like pilgrimage—likewise have the ability to construct the nation. Notes Anderson of these diverse artifacts: "once created, they became 'modular', capable of being transplanted, with varying degrees of self-consciousness, to a great variety of social terrains, to merge and be merged with a correspondingly wide variety of political and ideological constellations" (1983:4). In the US, they are the newspaper messages that refer endlessly to the US, its desired and undesired subjects, its desired future, as well as to its carefully scripted history[17]. They are the street festivals of the 1880s in which the Chinese laborer is caricatured as the enemy to US progress. They are the nation itself, a place drawn together through the endless dissemination of such artifacts, a carefully crafted and essentially limited sovereign entity that commands what Anderson calls, "profound emotional legitimacy" (1983:4).

Anderson notes that over the course of the eighteenth century in the US the printing industry grows in both materials published and readership, resulting in a kind of "virtual revolution" (1983/2006:61). Though the impetus for growth of the print media industry is capital accumulation, the mass media inadvertently becomes a technology of nation-building that enables the reader, "to visualize in a general way the existence of thousands and thousands like themselves through print-language" (1983/2006:77). An outcome of this revolution is that bourgeois newspaper readers see themselves as part of a collective of like-minded readers: an imagined national community[18]. With the invention in the US in 1843 of Richard Hoe's steam-powered rotary press, prints finally became affordable, and printed materials such as books, pamphlets, and newspapers become widely disseminated. Newspaper enterprises start cropping up in remote outposts. Notes a Nevada editor in 1867: "American pioneers carry with them the press and the type, and wherever they pitch their tent...there too must the newspaper appear" (in Wheeler 1976:51). The number of newspapers and magazines in circulation in the US grows exponentially, and so does readership. By 1870 there are more than two and a half million newspapers being printed every day in the US, and by the turn of the century that number has blossomed to 15 million (Volti 2017:243). Concurrent with the growth of newspaper readership is an increase in competition among what are increasingly seen as rival publications. Illustrations start to accompany many publications, and stereotypical characterizations of Others find purchase in a broader audience than ever before.

This rapidly expanding media shapes ideas about national character just as the most profound issues of government are being wrestled with: whether slavery will be outlawed in its entirety, and whether the federal government has the right to set policy for all the states. The Civil War of 1861-1865 confirms both questions. The demands of war also prompt a number of decisions by Congress that create a far more integrated union of states than had existed before. In order to pay for the war, for example, in 1863 the National Bank Act is passed, and the first national currency system is created. With large numbers of working-age men fighting in the war, a national department is created in 1862 to support the continuing needs of agriculture. In order to facilitate the movement of supplies and troops necessary for the war effort, the 1862 Pacific Railway Act is passed to create the nation's first transcontinental rail line. The first wartime draft is created in 1863 with the Confederate Conscription Act. Then, in 1864, Lincoln signs into law the Act to Encourage Immigration that provides financial support to would-be immigrants on the agreement they pay back any associated expenses out of the wages of their first year of employment. Despite very clear wording of section 3 of the 1864 Act that forbids compulsory enrollment in military service, many of these early immigrants find themselves joining the civil war. As reported in the *New York Times*: "The Irish follow the invitations of their kindred to a land of high wages and are overpowered on their arrival by the allurements of the recruiting sergeant" (3 May 1894, p.5).

All of these bureaucracies serve as centralizing structures that support the idea of the US as an imagined national community. And each bureaucracy has its own technologies of governmentality that enumerates people, classifies them, and thereby renders them as useful political subjects of the national project. Such subjects find their way from official statistics to mass media reports; the growing number mass media mean a veritable explosion of discourses on the nation and its subjects, and a growing imagined community of readers who will be constituted through their media consumption practices.

Once established as an imagined national community, however, the ideological work of the nation does not rest. Billig (1995) argues that established nations reproduce themselves daily through ideological habits and ongoing daily reminders that he calls, "banal nationalism" (1995:6). Rejecting the notion that nationalism is an extreme and irrational ideology, Billig instead sees nationalism as an "endemic condition" (ibid) that inserts itself into the daily lives of people in such a way that they might *not* take particular notice. Notes Billig (1995:93):

> 'we' are constantly reminded that 'we' live in nations: 'our' identity is continually being flagged. Yet, this flagging cannot merely be a matter of the flag hanging outside the public building, or the national emblem...'national identity' is a short-hand for a whole series of familiar assumptions about nationhood, the world and 'our' place in that world...These assumptions have to be flagged discursively.

While symbols like the Stars and Stripes and practices like singing the national anthem help to affirm what Billig refers to as, " 'Our' common sense about nationhood" (1995:16), it is through the commonsense discourse of nationalism that Billig finds national identity becoming a form of life.

Giving a nation label to a person, species, or 'thing' feeds into the logic wherein the world is seen to be naturally divided into nation-states on account of assumed fundamental differences. A core idea within this nationalist logic is that of autochthony: that species, including humans, have a particular 'origin' to which they are 'native'. The word autochthon has a root in the Greek, meaning: "a person indigenous to a particular country or region and traditionally supposed to have been born out of the earth" (*OED* 2012, autochthon, noun. 1). Autochthony continues to signify a person or species belonging to a place, or rightfully of a place: something 'indigenous', or native.

The alien in both its legal and figurative forms is positioned as antithetical to the national and is presented in discourse as the quintessential social outsider. They are something akin to Simmel's stranger (1950), a person who is simultaneously an outsider, but whose outsider-ness is made visceral through their presence. The illegal alien, however, is a criminalized subject-figure that is produced through practices of immigration and then affirmed in practices and discourses that render them Other. Notes Saskia Sassen: "Border enforcement is a mechanism facilitating the extraction of cheap labor by assigning criminal status to a segment of the working class —illegal immigrants" (1988:36-7). Cast as the internal enemy, their insider-ness is organized through processes that simultaneously exclude and include them.

When the two identities of alien and citizen collide— and especially when one is seen as invading the other—it serves to illuminate what Jean Comaroff and John Comaroff call, "the tortured politics of belonging" (2001:233). Such politics are ideological, Comaroff and Comaroff argue, because they relate to an evolving set of ideas regarding sovereignty, citizenship, community, borders, and the integrity of such borders at a time when neoliberal global capitalism threatens to destabilize the global order (2001:237). In this new world order—one that purports loudly to be postcolonial and post-racial—the anxiety of belonging is ever present. Anxieties over state sovereignty manifest through what Comaroff and Comaroff refer to as a, "mass-mediated chain of consciousness" (2001:236) in which 'origins'—particularly national ones—become fetishized. So, when the integrity of borders is questioned—when the border is represented discursively as 'leaky' or 'porous', and when the migrant is able to enter the US with seeming impunity—there emerges the possibility that the nation-state itself is at risk.

This sense that western democracies have been breached by humans leads to a mindset that Doty calls "anti-immigrant-ism" (2003). Accompanying this is the idea that migration is a social problem, and both of these Doty sees as manifestations of anxieties over statist disorder. The anxiety is one that shatters notions of order and belonging, "where one feels a degree of security in the ground beneath one's feet, where one knows who one is and most certainly who one is not" (2003:6).

Focusing on the nation-state as an object of desire, Roxanne Doty (2003) notes that that there is no essential thing as 'the state', only a network of desires that are disseminated throughout the social realm and that manifest in what she terms practices of statecraft (2003:12). Such practices are seen as an articulation of the cultural and material and range from the work of a passport office clerk to the speeches of powerful figures and the practices of vigilantes in the borderlands. Such material and discursive practices are bent on coding the 'the state' and its inhabitants and are seen as an expression of desire: "desire for order, desire to overcome ambivalence and undecidability" (ibid). Such practices are seen as being essentially violent, however. And that violence is never so visible, Doty argues, than when it targets migrants coded as external to the state. Notes Doty: "they are excluded from that system, constituted as the outside, the other, the ones whose belonging is eternally called into question" (2003:14).

Resonant with this idea of desire, Slavoj Zizek (1993) sees the nation as structured by enjoyment. Equating nationalism with what he terms, "modern racism" (1993:203), Zizek posits that our hatred of the Other is really a hatred of their excessive enjoyment. "In short, what really bothers us about the Other is the peculiar way he [sic] organizes his enjoyment...the smell of 'their' food, 'their' noisy songs and dances, 'their' strange manners, 'their' attitude to work" (ibid). For Zizek, this explains the paradox of nationalism wherein 'our nation' is both out of bounds for the Other while also being threatened by them.

Discourses that construct the national and its desired and undesired inhabitants represent what Comaroff and Comaroff call, "ontologies of being, belonging, and difference" (2001:254). They are origins stories that speak to self, to place, and to one's the contrast with the Other. For Ali Behdad (2005) the construction of such Others helps to define the nation itself. Writes Behdad: "the figure of the alien provides a signifier of otherness through which the nation defines itself as an imagined community" (2005:168). And in the following section I show how such origins stories—in the national history of the US—are from the very outset structured by ideas of race.

IMAGINING RACE

While the US enshrines in its 1776 Declaration of Independence that "all men are created equal" (US Congress 1776), African-origin slaves are not included in this conceptualization, in part because their racialization as 'Negro' marks them as *Other than men*[19]. Previously, under British Imperial rule, slaves are not generally understood as subjects of the Empire (Brown 1999:276). Instead, slaves are understood as 'property', and this ideology continues into US rule[20]. This understanding is evident in a US Census Bureau document from 1805 that describes, in a section titled, "An Estimate of all the Real and Personal *Property* in the US" (US Census Bureau 1949:1, italics added for emphasis), that one million Negro slaves are counted as property valued at 200 million dollars. In a similar manner, in Timothy Pitkin's *A Statistical View of the Commerce of the United States* of 1835, the value of slaves as 'commerce' is estimated at approximately 300 million dollars (also found in US Census Bureau 1949:1). Importantly for the idea of race in the US, slavery (in contrast to servitude) is considered a permanent condition. Notes Robert J. Steinfeld (1991): "these conditions were passed by blood to a slave's...offspring [as a] permanent heritable taint" (1991:101). The conceptual difference means that Negro slavery is a totalizing status that links one generation to another through ideas of inheritance or 'bloodline'. Such ideas are pivotal to ideas of race.

Racialization refers to the practice of subjectifying uncategorized people and practices into race categories, categories such as 'Negro'. In the words of Michael Omi and Howard Winant (1986), racialization is used, "to signify the extension of racial meaning to a previously racially unclassified relationship, social practice or group. Racialization is an ideological process, an historically specific one" (1986:64). Such race categories carry the weight of something that is 'known'. It is seen as commonsense, for example, to refer to someone with a set of phenotypical traits as 'black'. Within this reasoning, along with the race label, are a set of assumed psychological and cultural traits that are central to the person, that is, supposedly part of their inherited condition, or what is sometimes called their 'nature', and thus assumed as fixed and unchangeable as their skin color. Racialization involves both the practice of subjectifying humans into racialized categories and a set of beliefs about human difference.

Subjectifying here is used in its double sense to mean both 'making a subject out of', and also 'bearing down upon'. There is no doubt that racialization is an often negative force that can be exercised upon a person or a biopolitical group of people. But what makes the concept of racialization complicated is the notion of identity. If Barack Obama refers to himself as 'black' as he does in *Dreams from My Father* (1995), or checks only the black box in the 2010 census (a census that for the first time allows for multiple boxes to be checked), is it an erasure of his mother who is widely racialized as 'white'?

Identity, for sure, is both a personal practice and a political concern. But what we need here is an explanation that links subjectivity, normativity, and some kind of internal dimension through which people willingly adopt such subject-categories as a part of themselves. In a later (and unfinished) volume of

Foucault's series on sexuality called *The Use of Pleasure* (1987:5), Foucault begins to address this concern, focusing on:

> the practices by which individuals were led to focus attention on themselves, to decipher, recognize and acknowledge themselves as subjects of desire, bringing into play between themselves and themselves a certain relationship that allows them to discover, in desire, the truth of their being.

The normative conception here is that there is an essential 'truth' to a person's being, something like an identity. Foucault of course would never use the term identity—heralding as it does something like an immutable and fixed 'nature'. What would be of interest to him are the *processes* through which a person ascribes to an identity—processes that have the effect of being self-regulating—as well as the relationship between such self-regulations and power. As Hall and Du Gay note, such processes are, "produced in specific historical and institutional sites within specific discursive formations and practices, by specific enunciative strategies" (1996:4). In other words, both the idea of race, and the identification of oneself as being of a particular race, are produced through material and discursive practices.

The problem remains, however, that if we attend to these racializing formations, we risk elevating such ideas to commonsense. Brubaker and Cooper (2000:6) articulate this difficulty:

> The problem is that nation, race, and 'identity' are used analytically a good deal of the time more or less as they are used in practice, in an implicitly or explicitly reifying manner, in a manner that implies or asserts that 'nations', 'races', and 'identities' 'exist' and that people 'have' a 'nationality', a race, an 'identity'.

The problem, they assert, is similar to the one of methodological nationalism that we encountered in the introduction, where analytical use of a term brings its being into concrete existence. The logic involved in identifying, labeling, or counting a person as one thing (whether it be a race or a nation) reifies the belief that there *are different types* of people. If we make commonsense of race, or use nation as a category of analysis, it solidifies our understanding of the globe as divided into discrete races and national units. But if we reject such notions because we do not want to reify something that contributes to injustice, then how then do we counteract racisms and nationalisms and other such subjectifications? The answer is to focus on the historically specific sets of social relationships out of which such ideas emerge. If we analyze the discursive formations that produce such notions—as well as show why and to whom such formations are politically and materially useful—we can begin to deconstruct hegemonic ideas of race and nation that are predicated on human difference.

Managing Difference

Ideas of human difference—whether structured by ideas of race or nation—make commonsense of the logic of separation. Discourses that support this logic are called anti-miscegenation discourses and depend on ideas of purity and contamination, as well as assumptions of hierarchy. This logic is behind the 'one drop rule' embedded in the "Racial Integrity Act" enacted by the Virginia General Assembly in 1924. The act's stated aim is: "correcting a condition...[to prevent] near white people, who are known to possess an intermixture of colored blood, in some cases to a slight extent...[from] declar[ing] themselves as white" (Virginia Health Bulletin, Vol XVI:2). The law asserts that these persons, "are not white in reality...their children are likely to revert to the distinctly negro type even when all apparent evidence of mixture has disappeared" (ibid). Accordingly, just one 'drop' of 'colored blood' makes a person 'colored'. The Act results in the official reclassification of thousands of Virginians, and the removal of some reclassified children from 'white' schools. It dichotomizes people into two essential races: white and colored. And it reinforces the notion that the 'white race' is hierarchically superior, and therefore something whose 'integrity' needs to be kept by avoiding 'mixing'.

Given the cruel application of the law such as the removal of children from their schools, why would people refer to themselves as colored? Here it is useful to remind ourselves of the dual nature of power that both Gramsci and Foucault concern themselves with. For Gramsci (1971/1999:145) there is the direct exercise of juridical power (that this Racial Integrity Act asserts), and the indirect exercise of power (through which ideas of colored and white spread throughout the popular imaginary). The juridical power, as Doty explains, creates subjects: "Subjects, by virtue of being subjected to the juridical function, are themselves constructed, defined as particular kinds of subjects, given particular identities" (1996:242). The indirect exercise of power is the means by which ideologies of the ruling class and state percolate throughout the culture at large—through repeated use by teachers, for example—and are accepted by the masses as commonsense. They are even accepted as if such ideas were not those of the ruling class and state. In Foucault's understanding of power as expressed in his *Society Must be Defended* lectures from 1976 there is again this dual process: both the juridical power that is exercised through the law, and then a cultural power through which, in this case, people are racialized as colored and imagine themselves as colored. In imagining themselves as colored, however, there is a repression at play, a repression of self. For Foucault, this repression is how power is exercised on the self, as, "the continuation of war by other means" (1976/2003:15). Legal power operates as a complement to productive power until the idea of colored and white as two 'different' types of people that should be kept apart becomes hegemonic (as Gramsci articulates it) or 'normal' (as Foucault does).

A key result is to divide colored people from white people, to divide such subjectified people within themselves, and furthermore to normalize these divisions. As such they are what Foucault calls, "dividing practices" (1982:777). Nandita

Sharma (2006) refers to such practices as, "exclusionary inclusion" (2006:29) and argues that, "[t]he social organization of difference…always works to create forms of separation" (ibid). Such practices are born of particular sets of socio-economic relationships and are not only useful for government rule; they also create powerful subjectivities that create 'knowledges' about life that have a disciplinary and regulating power over people's everyday lives.

A genealogical detour is instructive at this point because it shows that the historical classification of people into different groups is one of the ways colonial powers practice their statecraft. Mahmood Mamdani (2012) argues in *Define and Rule* that governmentality—or what he refers to as "indirect rule colonialism" (2012:3)—is enacted in the colonies along two modes of differentiation: racial and tribal. Notes Mamdani: "Both were based on legally sanctioned difference, and both were in turn taken as proof of that difference" (2012:3). In other words, such subjectifications are about, "the understanding and management of difference" (2012:43). After the crisis of empire (in India in 1857, and in Jamaica in 1865), Sir Henry Maine— legal member of council in colonial India—finds that the failure to analyze and understand the people of the colonies— particularly those of the remote interior—is a central cause of the crisis. The 'Indians' are not used to sovereign rule, Maine finds, but rather are familiar with authority through blood kinship, "the sole possible ground of community in political functions" (quoted in Mamdani 2012:17). The British Empire's response to the 'Sepoy Mutiny' (or Indian Rebellion) of 1857 is the doctrine of noninterference, that, as Mamdani notes, "turned into a charter for all around interference" (2012:26) because it specifies exactly who is to be 'protected'. This involves defining peoples into varying subjectivities based on sometimes arbitrary determinations about language, religion, location, and caste. And then in the last half of the nineteenth century, the categories of 'native' and 'settler' are imagined, with 'natives' separated into various subcategories through technologies such as the census, "a technical complement to a political agenda" (2012:30). In this manner, as Mamdani notes, "the British actively defined and shaped community identities" (2012:29).

The practice spreads from colony to colony, from India to Africa. Describing the use of 'native' by colonizing authorities in nineteenth-century Africa, Mamdani argues that such terms are deployed to segment people into differing 'tribes', such that, "cultural difference was reinforced, exaggerated, and built up" (2012:48). The technology of the census is once again deployed to enumerate people from supposedly different 'tribes'; once so enumerated, competition and discrimination ensues. Those classified as a member of a particular 'race' are treated as separate from those of 'other races', with European civil law applied to them as homogenous (but separate) groups of peoples marching on a progressive, but separate, trajectory towards 'civilization'. Those cast as of a 'native tribe' are treated under a different legal system, one that entrenches their practices as both 'unique' and 'customary' and fixes them both geographically and in some kind of antiquated past.

The idea of different groups of 'natives' continues to be highly dangerous. In 1994 an estimated 800,000 people are murdered over the course of three months as one 'native' group with little political power—the Hutus—attacks another 'native' group—the Tutsis—who are perceived, among other things, as having an unfair political advantage. The roots of the tragedy lie in German and Belgian colonial rule during which Hutu is constructed as a 'native' identity, and Tutsi as a 'settler' one. The two identities are co-constituted; the 'native' defined in contrast to the 'settler', but in such a manner that that the 'original' inhabitant—the autochthonous 'native'—is seen as the rightful heir to the nation. When Hutus attack, therefore, it is because they see themselves as clearing 'their' land of an 'outsider' presence.

Both 'race' and 'tribe' designations are seen by Mamdani

as subjectification practices that create subjects with, "a single, exclusive and total identity" (2012:74). In other words, defining various peoples as 'this tribe' or 'that race' is not just a practice of imagining and assigning group identities, it is also *productive* of 'tribe' and 'race' as authentic and different categories of people. "Tribalism is reified ethnicity," notes Mamdani (2012:7). "It is culture pinned to a homeland, culture in fixity, politicized, so that it does not move" (ibid). Such subjectification practices are technologies of political rule that have specific political and material effects: they create imagined peoples, reinforce the imagined geographies to which such people are seen as belonging, and reify ideas about people staying fixed in those geographies.

Counting Subjects

The idea of fixity that is central to such subjectivities reveals a curious paradox; if 'race' is seen as a fixed attribute (you are born a certain race and you stay that way), then race classifications would also stay fixed over time. But that is not what we find in US government documents. In notes on how to classify taxable 'Indians' in the 1870 census, for example, it is written in the Compendium: "Where persons reported as 'half-breeds' are found residing with whites, adopting their habits of life and methods of industry, such persons are to be treated as belonging to the white population" (US Census Bureau 1870:19). This note on classification in an official government document demonstrates the porous boundaries of ideas of race. It also demonstrates how ideas of race are bound to biopolitical classificatory systems that are enacted by and for those in power. And then in the 1930 census—a census taken at the beginning of the Great Depression—people who are born in Mexico, or whose parents have been born in Mexico, are recorded as being of 'Mexican race'. But prior to the 1930 census, and from the 1940 census onwards, they are recorded as 'white' along with an additional designation, an 'ethnicity' (US Census Bureau nd, "1930"). The change has more to do with understandings about who is deserving of national jobs—and who is seen as belonging to the nation—than it has to do with the actual people being counted. As Juan Garcia notes, "For Mexicans the depression was disastrous. As jobs became scarce, they were among the first fired and were replaced by 'Whites' and 'American citizens'" (2004:223). And so the categorization of Mexicans as a 'race' in the 1930 census can be seen as a technology of government that supports those socio-economic decisions. Following this explicit racialization comes further nation-state exclusion in the form of the involuntary expulsion of as many as 500,000 people to Mexico, many of whom are packed onto trains hired specifically for that purpose (Daniels 2001:26).

As these examples show, the idea of race exerts a strongly material and experiential force. Exclusionary practices based on ideas of race are significant enough in labor markets that they form what Miles (1989) terms, "a structural constraint… maintaining a hierarchy…and setting ideological limits to the operation of the labour market" (1989/2003:133). Even after labor laws prohibit exclusionary practices based on race in the UK, Miles finds that exclusionary acts are, "widespread, although they became more covert" (ibid). And part of the way that race continues to structure the labor market is through the practice whereby real or imagined phenotypical characteristics are imbued with certain meanings; in other words, through racialization.

The idea that humans belong to distinct and separate races is finally discredited after the murder of millions of people of Jewish and other supposed races during World War II by Nazi Germany (and others). In 1950, geneticists and physical anthropologists gathered by the United Nations declares: "all men [sic] belong to the same species" (UNESCO 1950). In a revised version of the document that appears the following year, it is noted: "The use of the term race in speaking of such groups may be a serious error, but it is one which is habitually committed" (UNESCO 1951). And yet almost seventy years since that statement, the term 'race'—as well as 'ethnicity' (what Balibar (1991:49) rightly refers to as "*fictive* ethnicity")—are still used everywhere from everyday speech to government documents. It is still normative to think and speak of people in terms of divergent 'races' of human, or as belonging to different 'ethnic' groups. Accordingly, despite the UNESCO statements, the race discourse remains hegemonic. Furthermore, ideas of race assume the stance of commonsense, even if we are unsure exactly what specifies a person as belonging to one race or another. Race means different things at different historical times and is employed in differing forms and with differing functions. In this sense, race has what Ann Laura Stoler refers to as a "polyvalent mobility" (1995:69). This is because race is not a stable idea or a coherent signifier but rather a socially constructed ideology that conceals the social relationships that shape racialized hierarchies. In other words, it is because of the utility of the idea of race that it has stayed with us.

For us to understand why race has remained a hegemonic concept even after such a bold attempt at discourse correction by UNESCO, it is useful to consider Foucault's notion of biopower, which he first outlines in *The History of Sexuality* (1978). For Foucault, biopower is a political technology that serves both to discipline the individual and exert controlling force over the 'population' at large, which it has constructed. Foucault finds biopower to be a result of the discourse on sexuality that begins to proliferate from the eighteenth century onward. The endless ways of talking about sexuality—scientific studies on sexual health and pathology, rules about sexual morality and pedagogies on childhood sexual development, religious ordinances on matrimonial relations and contraceptive practices, and the whole "will to knowledge" (1978/1990:55) that supports the proliferation of scientific discourses—all exert a governing pressure on what is considered 'normal'. Significantly, biopower, "brought life and its mechanisms into the realm of explicit calculations and made knowledge-power an agent of transformation of human life" (1978/1990:143). Thus, biopower is the multi-faceted application of 'truths' about life that are deployed in order to discipline and regulate life.

It is through this notion of biopower that we can link the discourse on sexuality to the discourse on race; when the discourse on sexuality gathers momentum from the eighteenth century onwards, ideas of race enter the domain of the everyday. Both precocious childhood sexuality and perverse sexuality are framed, for example, as a threat to the race. And continuing this theme, in the second half of the nineteenth century, Foucault finds the discourse on sexuality is employed with a focus on, "the perfecting of the species" (1978/1990:148). Notes Foucault (1978/1990:149):

> Racism took shape at this point (racism in its modern, 'biologizing', statist form): it was then that a whole politics of settlement (peuplement), family, marriage, education, social hierarchization, and property, accompanied by a long series of permanent interventions at the level of the body, conduct, health, and everyday life, received their color and their justification from the mythical concern with protecting the purity of the blood and ensuring the triumph of the race.

In other words, race is deployed in the discourse on sexuality as an ordering apparatus, transforming social relations, and normalizing ideas of anti-miscegenation. In *Race and the Education of Desire* (1995), Ann Laura Stoler highlights the ways that Foucault links the concept of biopower to the discourse on race in *The History of Sexuality* and in Foucault's published and (then) unpublished lectures. Stoler notes that Foucault is not centrally interested in race; his focus in these texts is on the manner in which knowledge is deployed as a technology of and for power. However, Stoler finds race to be a significant subtext, one that is centered on beliefs about normality. Notes Stoler, "modern racism is the historical outcome of a normalizing society" (1995:35).

△△△

This chapter has provided a review of some of the core theoretical concepts regarding subject-making, race, and the nation. I have shown how such subject-making emerges out of historically specific sets of social relationships that are imbued with power, and that are useful to power. Key to such constructions are ideas of 'normalcy' and co-constituted ideas about the abnormal or deviant person who is seen as not belonging. Such ideas make sense of the logic of separation, or anti-miscegenation, which is predicated on concerns of purity and contamination.

The practice of constructing subject categories that define a person by race or nation is enabled through technologies of governmentality such as the census. Such technologies do not just imagine people; they are productive of people, and strategically so. The concept of biopower, for example, illustrates how knowledge about people becomes a tool for disciplining and regulating their everyday lives. Such processes divide people and normalize ideas about difference based on ideas of race and nation. In the following chapter, I elaborate on how these ideas intersect in discourse, and explain the outcome of such discursive articulations.

3/ARTICULATING RACE AND NATION

In the previous chapter I explored modes of subject-making that are key to the nation and its figurative Others. In this chapter, I show how ideas of race and nation articulate to produce the figurative subject of the migrant. Such articulations contain within them—and are supported by—a series of related and negative ideas about poverty, gender, sexuality, and criminality, that together create the polyvalent subject-figure who is the migrant.

This chapter traces a historical genealogy of the migrant subjectivity by looking at a range of symbolic Others who are found mostly *within* the geographic bounds of the US nation. Beginning with the political exclusion of the 'Indian native', I show how co-constituting stereotypes about natives and citizens work to produce ideas about US national character and belonging. Turning to the figure of the migrant, I show that the roots of the migrant subjectivity are found in the criminalization of the mobile poor. Such figurative subjects emerge in 16th century England after the radical shift to capitalist modes of production pushes people from their livelihoods. Moving on to the mid-nineteenth century, and to new radical upheavals that accompany successive waves of industrialization, I show how ideas about alcohol consumption and criminality are used to construct and demarcate Irish and German people as deviant immigrant Others.

I then explore sexualized and criminalized representations of the migrant in a diverse range of media from satirical cartoons to street festival signs and state testimony. I show how stereotypical representations of immigrants racialized as Chinese are supported by the 'yellow peril' journalism that is prevalent in the US from the mid-nineteenth century onwards. I show how these negative representations begin to proliferate in the last quarter of the nineteenth century, supporting the passage of the Page Act of 1875 and the Chinese Exclusion Act of 1882. Finally, I show how historical ideas about the migrant subjectivity echo discursively with contemporary ideas, supporting an understanding of immigration-as-crisis, as well as legitimizing a series of increasingly discriminatory and exclusionary practices.

POLYVALENT IDEAS

As I noted in previous chapters, several scholars have focused on the articulations between discourses concerning race and nation and have shown how such understandings relate to practices of immigration (see Balibar 1991, Miles 1993, Cisneros 2003, Doty 2003, and Sharma 2006, for example). Balibar offers a good summary, noting how such discourses represent, *"a historical system of complementary exclusions and dominations which are mutually interconnected"* (1991:49, italics in the original). Such discursive exclusions and dominations articulate with each other but also echo discursively across time, such that, "the memory of past exclusions is transferred into the exclusions of the present" (1991:9).

Racism explains the persistence of the nationalist discourse: because it contains within it racisms that cannot be uttered in what Balibar refers to as neo-racist—or even 'post-racist'—nation-states (1991:9). So, in historical moments where we cannot use ideas of race to dominate and exclude, a host of other ideas that center on 'national difference'—ideas about

language, class, food, religion, education, culture, and so on
—stand in for, and support, ideas of race. In this manner racism is not just another form of nationalism, it is constitutive
of it. Or as Balibar explains, "racism is not an 'expression' of
nationalism, but *a supplement of nationalism* or more precisely
a supplement internal to nationalism, always in excess of it, but
always indispensable to its constitution and yet always still
insufficient to achieve its project" (1991:54, italics in the original). This illustrates the polyvalent nature of nationalism, an
ideology that is both multi-faceted and multi-functional. And
if a discourse is what can be said within the realm of the possible, then I posit that nationalism functions in contemporary
discourse as the sayable form of racism that (barely) conceals
this internal and supplementary ideology.

The fact that nationalism barely conceals racism is evident in the strong negative reactions around the world to
Trump's use of the term 'nationalist' to describe himself in
2018. As Peter Baker explains in the *New York Times*: "When
used domestically, [nationalism] is a word often tainted with
the whiff of extremism, not least because a variant of it, white
nationalist, describes racist leaders and groups" (23 Oct 2018).
But Trump knows that describing himself as a nationalist will
appeal to his core base of 'America first' supporters. And so, at
a 22 October 2018 rally in Houston, after querying the accept-
ability of the word, he states: "You know what I am? I'm a nationalist, O.K.? I'm a nationalist. *Nationalist!* Use that word! Use
that word!" (ibid).

Nationalist ideas have always articulated with racist
ideas, and a look at the etymology of the two words *nation*
and *race* is instructive since it shows these conflations from
the outset. The term nation emerges in the English language in
about 1330 and precedes the term race by about only 200 years.
According to the *Oxford English Dictionary* (2003), the word *nation* has its roots in the Anglo-Norman word *naciun* that is itself related to the classical Latin word *nātiō*, meaning, "birth,

race, nation, class of person" (*OED* 2003, nation, n.1). The word *race* relates to the Middle French word *race* meaning a, "group of people connected by common descent" (*OED* 2008, race, n.6). Such meanings help to construct the idea of 'a people' with a singular nature who are bound to 'a nation' in which they 'belong'.

An early conflation of race and nation appears in translation of the work of Giraldus Cambrensis (1187), a distinguished scholar who is appointed to court by Henry II. In 1187, Cambrensis travels extensively throughout Ireland and writes about his findings for the court. When he returns to Oxford, Cambrensis undertakes captivating readings of his work (Scott and Martin 1978:267), and it is likely that the ideas he puts forth about the Irish have a wide reach, adding to their legitimation and commonsense use. In the English translation of Cambrensis's work that dates to the nineteenth century, he summarizes the people of Ireland as: "a most filthy race, a race sunk in vice, a race more ignorant than all other nations" (1187/1894:134-5). Whatever words are used in the original Latin version of Cambrensis' work, by the time of this 1894 translation, race, nation, and something like personality or 'nature' are conflated, with the ideas articulating such that, "the fierce and barbarous Irish nation" (1187/1894:171) are seen as a homogenous people with a singular nature bounded by geography[21].

Reinforcing the idea of a geographically-bounded people with a homogenous (and negatively evaluated) culture, Cambrensis writes that, "the whole habits of the people are contrary to agricultural pursuits," (ibid) such that the fields remain, "barren for want of husbandmen" (1187/1894:124). Cambrensis here links the idea of the Irish as a barbaric race to the assumption that they are too lazy to maximize the profit of their lands. He continues: "thus secluded from civilized nations, they learn nothing, and practice nothing but the barbarism in which they are born and bred, and which sticks to them like a second nature" (1187/1894:126). This passage confirms racist ideas about 'a people' having an essentially negative 'nature' that ties them to their fixed geographies. Illuminating this supposed link between 'a people' and 'their land', Cambrensis describes the countryside of the Irish in anthropomorphic terms as, "rude and barbarous" (1187/1894:319), "demanding labour which is not forthcoming" (1187/1894:124). Because the Irish are seen as lazy and barbaric, Cambrensis' solution for Henry II is that he subjugate the people and take, "just title" (1187/1894:324) of their lands. In Cambrensis' history of Ireland we have an early example of the conflations of race, nature, nation, and geography. What is important to note here are the political and material outcomes of such articulations. In this case, colonial appropriation is seen as the 'solution'.

'Natives' in the US

If this story sounds familiar, it is. The removal of land from 'Indian natives' in the US is likewise based on widespread (and contradictory) ideologies that 'they' are a barbaric race of people who are simultaneously too lazy to cultivate the land. These two ideas—that of the 'lazy Irish race' and that of the 'lazy Indian race'—echo discursively with each other and inform each other. The Indian native identity becomes shored up through discourse and practice as a symbolic subject-figure who embodies ideas of the racialized Other. And just like the solution put forward for the Irish, so too for the Indian, the solution is one of land appropriation.

Needless to say, before the arrival of Europeans in the late 1400s, varying groups of Indians lived extensively throughout the Americas. As to how many is a matter of conjecture; scholars such as Charles C. Mann put the population estimate, "closer to the number estimated by 'high counters'" (2006:xx), that is, 100 million people for both the North and South American continents[22]. And new archeological discoveries—such as those uncovered at the Gault Site in Texas (Daley 2018)—continue to push back the date when people are believed to have first settled on the North American continent. Within a hundred years of the arrival of Europeans, however, as many as 90 percent of people from the varying 'Indian Nations' are dead, in large part from introduced diseases (Watts 1999). Some 30 to 40 percent of 'Indians' are estimated to have died from smallpox alone, according to Fenn (2001). However, as Mann notes in a discussion with Fenn, to focus on the number of people who died misses what is really important: "...that many people lived. The Americas were filled with an enthusiastically diverse assortment of peoples who had knocked about the continents for millennia" (Mann 2006:151).

The Indians that remain alive by the arrival of the Mayflower in 1620, however, are greatly impoverished through disease, armed conflict, and the diminution of their number; impressions about them reflect that loss. Just one year after arriving from England on the Mayflower, a New England preacher named Robert Cushman makes the earliest recorded sermon in North America. Notes Cushman: "The country is yet raw, the land untilled, the cities not builded, the cattle not settled; we are compassed about with a helpless and idle people, the natives of this country, which cannot in any comely or comfortable manner help themselves, much less us" (1621/1844:265). As with Cambrensis's impression of the Irish, here too we have an author linking an 'idle race' with unproductive land.

That Cushman's sermon is recorded and printed means it has a far greater reach than an oral sermon alone, indeed a global reach. It is noted in *The New England Historical and Genealogical Register* (1861:170) that the first edition of Cushman's sermon is printed in England and bought for about $60, a small fortune at the time. But printing technology improves over the years, with presses being constructed from more durable materials, meaning that more sheets can be printed in each run. By 1861, eleven editions of Cushman's sermon have been printed, editions that are printed in ever increasing numbers. How many people read or hear about his ideas is a matter of conjecture; what is far more important to note is that such things are *possible to say*. But the far reach of such ideas—and the fact that many people hear about them and talk about them—is important for understanding how such ideas as 'idle natives' become legitimated and enter into people's minds as commonsense.

Although Cushman's sermon of 1621 represents Indians in discriminatory ways, representations in early US history are not uniformly unfavorable. When Benjamin Franklin (1755) writes about "the natives" (1755/1918:4), for example, he notes they are, "hunters...having large Tracts" (ibid) and further states, "we have so fair an opportunity, by excluding all blacks and tawneys, of increasing the lovely white and red" (1755/1918:10). Although not unfavorable, this labeling of people by phenotype—in this case by their supposed skin coloring—is illustrative of racializing ideologies that mark people as essentially 'different' based on differential skin color. In the 1830s and 1840s, Indians are represented as, "important people, despite their not being Christians" (in Shapiro 1997b:31), so although once again they are not presented in a particularly negative light, they are still seen as different on account of their religious practices. Then in Frances Trollope's *Domestic Manners of the Americans* (1839), the Indian (as a homogenous, stereotyped 'people') is admired as a, "most interesting race" (1839:174), albeit one that is "fast perishing" (ibid).

As the US gears up for civil war, however, a shift occurs in the discourse on the Indian. Increasingly, Indians are seen as a threat to America's national future, and increasingly, Indians are represented as negatively racialized and stereotypical figures. In an article in the *New York Times* titled, "Interesting from Kansas" (12 Aug 1857:2), for example, it is reported:

> These Kawa Indians...are the meanest, most good-for-nothing, most lying, drunken, treacherous, cowardly, lazy tribe in the whole of Kansas. They are perfectly incorrigible, and, but for the rapidity with which they die off by disease, and drink themselves to death, would be a serious impediment to the future progress and prosperity of this portion of the Territory.

As with the discourse of the 'lazy Irish nature', this piece of reporting perpetuates and reinforces beliefs about Indians as lazy and does so in their entirety as a 'tribe'. Similar to the discourse on the Irish, the laziness of the tribal Indian is seen as part of their hereditary condition: "Work is something [the 'Indian'] has never done; his idleness and improvidence are his birth-right" (*New York Times*, 27 Oct 1886:9). And as with the Irish, the solution to the 'lazy Indian problem' and to the people who are seen as an impediment to US 'progress'—is to take away their lands.

A second representation that is commonplace during this time period is that of the Indian as a 'barbarian'. This stereotype is seemingly contradictory to the idea of the lazy Indian, but the idea of the 'barbarian Indian' does indeed form a perfect binary contrast to that of the 'civilized settler'. Reified through technologies such as the census, and shored up through discourse, the two identities co-constitute with specific political and material effects. In this case, the barbarian Indian stereotype is used as a rationale for sequestering the Indian on reservations, and many reports from such reservations are ripe with examples of their supposed barbaric nature. For example, in a letter from the Upper San Joaquin Indian Reservation of 31 August 1852, it is noted how the Indians are, "terribly excited" at the death of a member of their tribe known as "Major Savage" (in the *New York Times* 14 October 1852:3). "They threw themselves upon his body, uttering the most terrific cries, bathing their hands and faces in his blood, and even stooping and drinking it" (ibid). When not bound to the reservation, the Indian is seen as both barbaric and an impediment to economic 'progress'. In a report in *The Alta California* from the gold mining regions of northern California, for example, it is noted, "[T]he savages invariably murder every isolated individual. This state of things has a most disastrous effect upon the interests of that section of the State...It has stopped the working of many of the most productive mining tracts" (in the *New York Times* 20 October 1851:1).

A material reason for representing the Indian as barbaric

is a desire for their lands as both gold is discovered, and the population of European-origin 'settlers' grows from just over 17 million in 1840 to almost 40 million by 1870 (US Census Bureau 2017). The Homestead Act signed by President Lincoln in 1862 supports this land-grab, providing European-origin settlers with 160 acres of surveyed public land to which they can earn ownership. Notes Secretary of the Interior Columbus Delano in 1872: "our civilization ought to take the place of their barbarous habits. We, therefore, claim the right to control the soil which they occupy" (as reprinted in the *New York Times*, 2 Dec 1872:2). By the end of the nineteenth century, the idea of the Indian as barbaric and an impediment to progress and civilization has become hegemonic. Now, the Indian features in the landscape only as, "a rampant and intractable enemy to civilization" (*New York Times*, 27 Oct 1886:9).

Such discursive formations are of utility to the US as it begins to nationalize its state sovereignty, not only because they create a 'racialized tribal other' who stands in contrast to the 'ideal American'; but also because they allow for territorial expansion under the guise of progress. Such ideas are contained within the ideology of Manifest Destiny, a term first used in in 1845 by writer and politician John O'Sullivan to silence international opposition to the US's annexation of Texas. Writing in *The United States Magazine and Democratic Review*, O'Sullivan notes that it is the US's, "manifest destiny to overspread the continent allotted by Providence for the free development of our yearly multiplying millions" (1845:6). Prosperity, development, progress; all are seen as the 'just' providence of the growing and 'progressive' US nation. Writes O'Sullivan: "She is no longer to us a mere geographical space–a certain combination of coast, plain, mountain, valley, forest and stream. She is no longer to us a mere country on the map. She comes within the dear and sacred designation of Our Country" (1845:5).

This notion of 'our country' is of central importance to the nationalist discourse, because it comes with a fundamental assumption of who 'we' are. The civilization discourse used in reference to the Indian plays a key part in creating this sense of 'us' because it provides a racialized Other against whom it is possible to co-constitute the ideal national subject. So it is not just 'us' and 'them'—the 'civilized us' and the 'barbarian them'—rather it is the much more possessive notion of 'ours' and 'theirs'. It is an idea that will echo discursively throughout US history, reappearing in 1882, for example, to support ideas that Chinese workers threaten 'our jobs' as well as the future prosperity of 'our' nation.

CRIMINALIZING MOBILITY

I have used the term discursive echo in this chapter to refer to ideas that resonate historically, with prior problematizations and solutions lending support to contemporary ones. A key subject-figure that appears historically time and again in the discourse on immigration is the figure of the mobile working poor. Such a figure articulates at specific historical times with both nationalized figures—as in the 'huddled masses' of Europe that Emma Lazarus depicts in poetry form in 1883—as well as racialized figures—as in the 'migrant caravan' that is said to be approaching the contemporary southern US border. Notes Doty: "The figure of the pauper in the first half of the nineteenth century bears a significant resemblance to the figure of the illegal immigrant in the United States today" (2003:40). Two things are significant about these two subject-figures: first, that they are both are imagined in the collective; and second, that both subjectivities are imbricated with ideas of criminality.

A historical genealogy is instructive here to show how changes in social and economic structures related to capitalist accumulation produce the criminalized figure of the mobile working poor from the very outset. In sixteenth century England, according to Ellen Meiksins Wood (2002), a shift in agrarian social relations leads to the massive displacement of workers and the criminalization of the mobile working poor.

Prior to the shift, it is customary for people to graze their animals and collect firewood and other means of sustenance on both common and private lands. These customary rights afforded people the ability to feed, clothe, and support themselves—thus providing the tools for their own reproduction. Between the sixteenth and eighteenth centuries, however, a succession of rights to public and private lands is eliminated. Land ownership becomes ever more concentrated in the hands of private landlords and new conceptions of property emerge in which land is only to be used for capitalist production and the accumulation of profit. Since success is based on output—produce to market, for example—the focus of this new agricultural paradigm becomes productivity. "The result was a highly productive agrarian sector, in which landlords and tenants alike became preoccupied with what they called 'improvement', the enhancement of the land's productivity for profit" (Wood 2002:xx). This newly productive agriculture ensures that a large population can be sustained who are not in agricultural production, but it also means far fewer laborers are needed in agriculture. These propertyless people have no option other than to sell their labor power in order to survive. Many move to the cities in search of work; many others became part of an underclass of, "dispossessed 'masterless men' who wandered the countryside and threatened social order" (2002:108-9).

Some assume that capitalism has always existed in some form or other, that progress is linear and heads steadily towards civilization, and that competition is a 'natural' behavior for humans, who have, "a propensity in human nature...[to] truck, barter, and exchange one thing for another" (Adam Smith 1776:29). But as Wood shows in *The Origin of Capitalism* (2002), there is nothing natural about capitalism. Capitalism isn't just an outgrowth of industrialization, or an increase in global trade. It is never a 'transition', since, as Federici points out, that term, "suggests a gradual, linear historical development, whereas the period it names was among the bloodiest and most discontinuous in world history" (2004:62). Capitalism is brought about by a radical transformation in social property relations that results in, "the disintegration or subordination of non-capitalist forms of subsistence" (Sassen 1988:33).

Perhaps because of the rapidity of change, as well as the widespread nature of change, this mass movement of people throughout 16th and 17th-century Europe causes great consternation. New laws are enacted in an attempt to control the movement of the out-of-work poor, such as the 1597 Act for the Repression of Vagrancy (in Anderson 2013:21). Notes Silvia Federici: "Everywhere—if we give credit to the complaints of the contemporary authorities—vagabonds were swarming, changing cities, crossing borders…a vast humanity involved in a diaspora of its own" (2004:82). But as Bridget Anderson explains, their 'crime' is not just one of poverty, but also one of mobility: "The vagabonds and beggars were not simply people without jobs who were able to sell their labour in a competitive labour market, but they were people without positions…their mobility was a sign that they, quite literally, were not keeping to their place" (2013:17). Penalties for vagabondage include whipping, branding, imprisonment, and forced employment. The European mercantilist class rounds up such laborers, casts them as 'vagabonds', and ships them as criminals to varying colonies under conditions of unfree labor (Federici 2004:87). In England, thousands of people cast as vagabonds are shipped to America to carry out their penalty as workers (Linebaugh and Rediker 2013:20). From this historical period onwards, we have an inextricable connection between the out-of-work and the out-of-place, between (low) socio-economic 'class' and mobility. This connection echoes discursively through history, reinforcing and legitimizing hegemonic ideas about the mobile working poor as the criminalized Other.

Mobility in the Age of Industry

Just as with the advent of capitalism in the sixteenth century, socio-economic and political strife that accompanies industrialization in the nineteenth century displaces millions of people in Europe and around the world. In Ireland, for example, a combination of English colonial rule along with prolonged devastation to the potato crop after the introduction of industrial fertilizers (Coogan 2012) pushes some 1,186,928 Irish people to migrate to the US between 1847 and 1854 (US Census Bureau 1949:34). Political and social upheaval that accompanies rapid industrialization in mid-nineteenth century Germany likewise results in large numbers of people emigrating to the US: over 200,000 in a single year in 1854, and over 250,000 in the year 1882 (see figure 1).

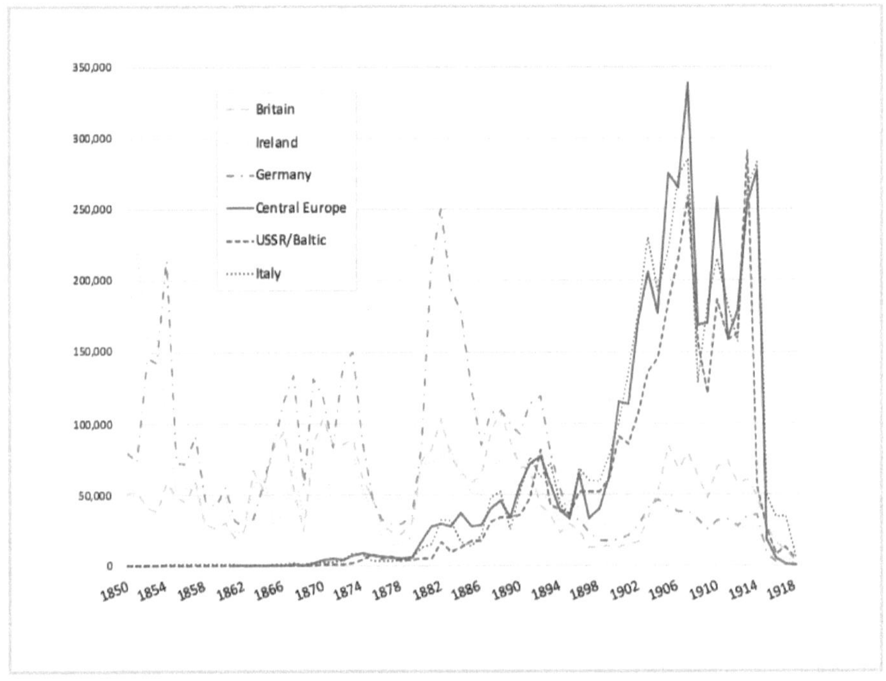

Figure 1: European Immigration to the US 1850 – 1918, US Census Bureau, 1949:33-34

Employment agencies spring up across Europe during this time period, promising work in the booming iron and steel industries in the US (Kraut 1982). Communication technologies are invented such as the telegraph, and printed newspaper become cheaper and more abundant; rail networks and steam-ships are invented, meaning that people can travel to places they hear and read about with increasing speed, ease, and safety. Many of the people who emigrate during this time period arrive at sea ports along the east coast. A result of this is that by 1860, as many as 47.2 percent of the population of New York is enumerated as having been born in a country other than the US (US Census 1999). And in a single year between 1887 and 1888, an estimated one million more people leave Europe for nations such as the US, Argentina, Brazil, Canada, and Australia (Kraut 1982:9). By 1890, over nine million people, or 14.8% of the total US population, are designated as "foreign born" in the US census (see figure 2).

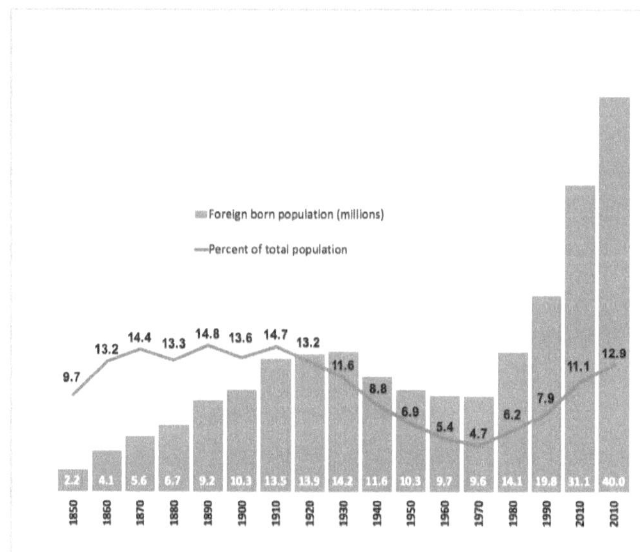

Figure 2: Foreign born population & foreign born population as % of total US population, US Census Bureau, 2011

For the US, this means not only a rapid shift in the ratio of the foreign-born population to the total population, it also means rapid economic growth for the nation. Notes Ali Beh-dad: "industrialization displaced peasants, transforming them into the proletariat of urban cities. This sociohistorical transformation, which forced the already uprooted peasants to come to the United States, was central to the nation's population growth and economic development" (2005:99). So, while the national economy grows rapidly during this time, there is a concurrent growth in the US in number of mobile working poor.

Those who migrate from Europe during this time period, for example, are primarily poorly educated and unskilled workers from rural origins (Model 1990). Or at the numeric pinnacle of US immigration from 1900 through 1910, up to 90 per cent of workers from Italy, Hungary, Italy, and Mexico are designated as manual workers, as are 65 per cent of Jewish immigrants, and 75 percent of immigrants from China and Japan (Morawska 1990:193). Such workers follow the lead of friends and relatives before them (people who often arrange and pay for their passage), settle in neighborhoods where they have ties, and move into jobs for which they are deemed suitable. They do not move randomly into industrial positions. "A combination of employers' stereotypes and workers' pre-emigration skills and preferences resulted in the channeling of particular nationalities into particular endeavors" (Model 1990:133). This channeling means that groups of mobile working poor from similar geographic and cultural regions settle in particular workplaces and neighborhoods within the space of a few years.

Because of the concentration of such groups of people in certain areas—in the Chinatowns and little Italies that still exist today, for example—what results is an increase in fear, suspicion, and hostility directed against both the racialized and nationalized figure of the migrant, as well as antipathy towards the system of immigration that has allowed so many mobile working poor to enter. These can be seen as an articulation of ideas about race and nation, ideas that are related to—and dependent on—a variety of ideas about poverty, education level, gender, sexuality, culture, and deviance.

The Criminal Migrant

A rapid population increase in the US in the last quarter of the nineteenth century, coupled with a steep downturn in the US economy, leads to a large increase in the number of people seeking poor relief and being convicted of crimes. Specific crimes and types of behavior deemed 'immoral' became associated with specific nationalized and racialized groups. From this point onwards there is a persistent focus in the discourse that works to promote the immigrant subjectivity as a criminal one. Under the title "Nationality of Crime" in a *New York Times* article of 1874, for example, are statistics of police arrests and commitments to New York City prisons from 1860 to 1872. The article notes that of persons committed to prison: "Foreigners and their children represent nearly 95 in every 100 prisoners" (ibid). Illustrating the articulation between racism and nationalism, the article is constructed for the perusal of, "those who take an interest in the development of races and nationalities" (*New York Times* 21 March 1874:9).

Irish and German immigrants bear the brunt of the animosity—particularly in the northern states—during this time period. People born in Ireland are seen as being particularly enamored of what are seen as the twin crimes of drunkenness and violence. Notes the *New York Times* in 1874: "the Irishman was never at peace unless he was in a fight" (21 March 1874:9). The article goes on to state that two thirds of the women in city prisons are found to be Irish, with prostitution named as their chief vice. In total, over three-quarters of all people listed as paupers and criminals are listed as having been born in Ireland. The Irish are not only portrayed as being prone to poverty and criminality, they are also portrayed as *preferring* to live in this state, "never so satisfied as when in the hands of the Police or in prison" (ibid). Focusing on the 'vice' of drunkenness, in particular, the article notes that, "The inflammable 'potheen' maintained its proud supremacy, showing more than twice as many victims as it should, while stupid 'lager' lags considerably behind its ratio" (ibid). These are not just any alcoholic beverages, however. Potheen is a distillate of the potato customary to the Irish, while lager is the name given to German beer. The beverages are picked upon as demonstrative of the kind of criminal disorder that is intrinsic to the migrant subjectivity. Such ideas, in other words, construct an association between migrants, vice, and crime.

The idea that migrants are alcohol abusers has a long and storied history in the US, dating back to the Temperance movement that begins in the early 1800s. According to Gusfield (1963), declining social status of the old elite combined with large-scale immigration from places like Ireland and Germany leads to social tensions during this time period. As the old elite attempts to uphold social control, they fixate on the newest immigrants, who Gusfield finds as representing, "the bottom of the class and status structure in American society" (1963:51). Whiskey and beer are seen as, "customary and often a staple part of the diet" (*ibid*) for such people, and so the Temperance movement turns alcohol abuse into a symbolic marker of degeneracy and criminality. Groups that have concerns about alcohol abuse raise the salience of their social 'problem' by joining it in discourse with the 'problem' of immigration[23]. Notes Gusfield: "While different wings of the movement represented assimilative and coercive attitudes toward immigration, the alien was seen as an opponent of Temperance and of middle-class life styles" (1963:155). In other words, while immigration as a whole is problematic for some members of the Temperance movement, it is the figurative subject of the migrant who is produced as being contrary to American values.

Thereafter, alcohol consumption—and its supposed moral counterpart, abstinence—becomes a symbolic means of differentiating the American-born citizen from the immigrant alien. Such symbolism is transmitted in the media, with Gusfield finding that, "fiction was probably the most effective media of mass persuasion" (1963:50). Pamphlets are distributed and gaudy fiction novels are written that graphically characterized the life of a drunk and contribute to the commonsense understanding that the alcohol abuse of the immigrant is symptomatic of a 'crisis'. Testament to the crisis-like nature of the Temperance movement is the exaggerated solution later proposed: prohibition. In large part due to the efforts of the Temperance movement, a nationwide ban on the production, import, transportation, and sale of alcoholic beverages is enacted from 1920 to 1933. To abstain from alcohol becomes what Gusfield refers to as a status collectivity (1963:187) in which American-born 'teetotalers' co-constitute themselves in opposition to immigrant drunks. In other words, it is not just the national individual who is co-constituted through this process: it is the collective subject-figure of the immigrant, as well as the entire system of immigration that allows them passage.

Utility in Anti-Immigrantism

In the mid-nineteenth century, the discourse of nationalism and anti-immigrantism finds a productive place in US politics for the first time. I contend that this forges the first significant transformation to the migrant subjectivity as both politicians and media enterprises realize the political and personal profits to be made from demonizing immigrants. Stirred by the appearance in Massachusetts of tens of thousands of people from Ireland after the famine summer of 1847, a secretive new party known as the Know Nothings fixates on three things: the 'problem' of Irish Roman Catholicism; the potential for immigrants to usurp the American-born 'native' as a wage-earner; and the concern that immigrants would become naturalized and get the vote (Haynes 1897:75). Once again, the practice of alcohol consumption is used to suggest that such immigrants are problematic. The following political cartoon from circa 1850 illustrates these problematizations:

Image 8: Unnamed cartoon by JHG. publication unknown, circa 1850

Seen running away with a ballot box are a club-wielding and unkempt man dressed in a barrel of Irish Whiskey, as well as a dopey-looking, pipe-smoking man dressed in a barrel of Lager Bier. Separating the two in the background is the image of the US flag, perhaps suggesting that such immigrants threaten to divide the US. To the left of the image, a scuffle breaks out by an election polling place, illustrating the kind of disorder that the Know Nothings aim to 'solve'.

The census returns of 1850 seem to verify the alarm of the Know Nothings, showing just how rapidly the population of people from Ireland has grown in states like Massachusetts. Writes the historian George H. Haynes, in language rife with hydraulic metaphor: "That in the midst of this time of doubts [in the 1850s] the tide of immigration should have suddenly risen to the flood was cause quite sufficient to fill timid souls with grave apprehension for the safety of American institutions" (1897:79). The Know Nothings fixate on this rise in the number of immigrants, constructs it as a crisis that threatens US patriotism and interests, and stokes public fears for political advantage. And as John David Bladek (1998:39) notes, this strategy is highly successful:

> By promising to overturn the old political structure, 'annihilate these two parties', and inaugurate an 'era of patriotism', the Know Nothings increased in stature almost daily. Their popularity was hard to ignore. By the fall of 1854, their nativist rhetoric dominated political discourse in much of the country.

In the November elections of 1854 the Know Nothings make a number of surprising wins, including the election of Governors in nine states, as well as new members and supporters in the House of Representatives and the Senate (Haynes 1897:67). While the success of the Know Nothing party is ultimately short-lived (in part because of their indecisive position over slavery), this strategy of stoking resentment against immigrants in order to win votes—especially among working class voters—proves productive. And it is this exact strategy that the Democrats employ leading up to the Page Act of 1875 in order to court votes. Except this time, there is a new figurative subject who is targeted for discrimination and exclusion. Notes the *New York Times*: "the Democrats bid for the support of the ignorant classes by proscribing the Chinese" (26 Dec 1874:4).

IMMIGRATION RESTRICTION

Before the Civil War erupts, many reports focus on the potential of Chinese immigrant labor to replace slave labor. A *Milwaukie Sentinel* article that is reprinted in the *New York Times* (27 Sept 1852), for example, waxes lyrical about Chinese labor, suggests that certain races are suited to certain climates, and advocates for Chinese labor as cheaper than slave labor:

> The Chinese—Asiatic in origin, inured to labor under a burning sun, and in morasses unfriendly to our race—could well be employed in the rice swamps and cotton plantations of Carolina—

> and in the sugar fields of Louisiana. He would be less costly than
> a slave to keep, more diligent and more reliable.

And then, just six weeks before the Civil War begins, in an article titled, "Coolies and Cotton" (26 Jan 1861:4), there are more optimistic reports in the *New York Times* about Chinese men as laborers. Calling such people "John Chinaman"—an early moniker pointing to the stereotypical nature of this immigrant subjectivity—the unnamed author speaks warmly of their abilities as: "Extremely industrious, docile and temperate" (ibid). The author further notes that, "the swarming millions of the Flowery Kingdom are capable, without diminution of supplying the world with labor" (ibid).

As large numbers of working-age men exit the workforce to fight in the Civil War, a growing number of Chinese immigrant laborers are employed to work on national projects such as the transcontinental railroad. Writing on the worker shortage faced by the Central Pacific Railroad Company, Kraus (1969) notes the project, "would have taken much longer were it not for the Chinese laborers who played such a significant role in building the railroad" (1969:42). Recruiting offices are set up in Canton Province, China to attract such workers, and the total population of Chinese in the US increases from just under 35,000 in 1860 to more than 63,000 by 1870 (US Census Bureau 1949:27) [24]. Though the Chinese are not the first choice for laborers, their racialization as Chinese—and the material practices that support such racializations—have the effect of producing them as the ideal replacement worker.

Articulating ideas about race and nation inform the discourse on the Chinese immigrant worker and inform labor practices that in turn legitimate such ideas. A letter written in 1865 by legal counsel for the railroads, for example, notes: "A large part of our force are Chinese, and they prove nearly equal to white men, in the amount of labor they perform, and are far more reliable. No danger of strikes among them" (as cited in Kraus 1969:43). The comparison of Chinese laborers with 'white men' in a hierarchical manner (nearly equal...more reliable) is commonplace in ideologies of race and nation. It is not important whether Chinese means *race*, or Chinese means *nation* in this context; the two supplement each other, articulate with each other, and in doing so produce commonsense understandings of hierarchical difference that are materially useful to labor relations. A report to Andrew Jackson written in October of 1865 likewise focuses on such hierarchies in regard to labor relations. The report notes both the expense and scarcity of war-time labor, as well as the merits of using cheap Chinese immigrant laborers: "as efficient as white laborers. More prudent and economical, they are contented with less wages" (as cited in Kraus 1969:45). In this case, such ideological thinking lends justification to an increase in Chinese wage labor exploitation.

By 1869, however, the Central Pacific railroad is finished. The Chinese immigrant laborer, racialized as industrious, reliable, cheaper, and less likely to strike, is now constructed as extraneous to the nation. And as he competes for employment with men who have returned from the Civil War, as well as with newer immigrants from places like Ireland and Germany, the Chinese worker is now increasingly represented as a threat. It must be emphasized once again that the number of Chinese immigrants counted as entering the US is miniscule compared to the number of European immigrants during this time period[25]. On average, just three Chinese immigrants a year are enumerated as entering the US prior to 1853. (US Census Bureau 1949:36). Compare this to the 361,576 immigrants who come from Europe in 1853, of which more than 162,000 come that year from Ireland alone (US Census Bureau 1949:34).

Anti-Chinese sentiment abounds, however, and is found in many media forms, including popular songs of the time. We can imagine such songs being sung in the mining camps and boom towns that spring up throughout California and other mining states during this historical period. Such media make negative ideas about Chinese laborers commonplace, adding to their legitimacy. The following extract is from a song called "John Chinaman", that is published in *The California Songster* in 1855. The song opens with the un-named author lamenting having welcomed the Chinese laborer and descends into fear-mongering over imagined negative values and culturalist beliefs. The song posits that 'John Chinaman' is deceptive, and thieving, with little regard for the conventions of the law. The song promotes stereotypes of Chinese people eating vermin as well as dogs (puppies, no less), and ends by fixating on the gold that is becoming increasingly hard to mine as the California Gold Rush of 1848-1855 draws to its end:

> *I imagined that the truth, John,*
> *You'd speak when under oath,*
> *But I find you'll lie and steal too—*
> *Yes, John, you're up to both.*
>
> *I thought of rats and puppies, John,*
> *You'd eaten your last fill;*
> *But on such slimy pot-pies, John,*
> *I'm told you dinner still.*
>
> *Oh, John, I've been deceived in you,*
> *And all your thieving clan,*
> *For our gold is all you're after, John,*
> *To get it as you can.*

In this popular song that produces and reproduces the stereotype of the Chinese immigrant laborer, he is demonized for his supposed greed, when in reality it may have been that a majority of Californians are swept up in a fervor over gold at the time. But there *has* been a rapid increase in the number of Chinese people entering the US during the gold rush—from 42 people in 1853, for example, to 13,100 Chinese people in 1854 (US Census Bureau 1949:36). This rapid population increase, along with an increasingly vocal and negative discourse on the Chinese, leads to further animosity and outright violence, particularly in mining areas. In 1862, the State of California passes the Anti-Coolie Act, whose stated purpose is: "to protect free white labor against competition with Chinese coolie labor, and to discourage the immigration of the Chinese into the state of California" (State of California 1862). So although the initial focus is on restricting coolie labor, the overall intent is restricting *all* Chinese immigration.

And in each city in which Chinese people amass in any numbers during the last quarter of the nineteenth century, press reports speak of them as a threat, with many of these iterations producing racializing stereotypes of disease and contamination. In 1876, for example, a committee of the Senate of the State of California investigates, "The Social, Moral, and Political Effect of Chinese Immigration" (State of California 1876). In the recourse of their investigation, seven California State Senators gather public testimony from a diverse array of Californians, from police officers and city employees, to physicians and customs officers. When asked how, "the Chinese compare with the white races in morals" (State of California 1876:40), the reply from Charles Wolcott Brooks (1876:41), the owner of a trading company in San Francisco, is:

> I have been very little in the Chinese quarters here, but I know it is filthy, indeed, and that they are very much overcrowded. They live in a filthy condition here, and in a filthy condition at home, in their own districts. The buildings here are crowded pretty much as they are at home. Buildings once occupied by Chinese are unfit for white occupation, but real estate dealers obtain from them double and treble the rent they receive from the whites.

So although Brooks has hardly seen where Chinese people live, he 'knows' they live in squalor, and further iterates that the Chinese contaminate such buildings, even after out-competing 'whites' in rent. Such stories accompany a new age of so-called 'yellow peril journalism', in which newspapers like Joseph Pulitzer's *New York World* or William Randolph Hearst's *San Fran-*

cisco Examiner print increasingly lurid and sensational stories in order to attract readers. Thanks to the completion of the US transcontinental railroad in 1869, such yellow peril stories are now shared readily from coast to coast, adding to the intense competition between media enterprises. In these stories, articulating ideas of race and nation produce and reproduce hegemonic ideas about the threat of the Chinese Other. Explains Gina Marchetti (1994:2):

> Rooted in mediaeval fears of Genghis Khan and Mongolian invasions of Europe, the yellow peril combines racist terror of alien cultures, sexual anxieties, and the belief that the West will be overpowered and enveloped by the irresistible, dark, occult forces of the East...As slavery ended and immigration to the United States increased in the latter half of the nineteenth century, the yellow peril became a flood of cheap labor threatening to diminish the earning power of white European immigrants, thereby deflecting criticism of the brutal exploitation of an expansionist capitalist economy onto the issue of race [sic].

Such stories, in other words, not only attract readers, they also distract readers from salient social issues, and do so by transferring blame onto ideas of race. Such an ideology, for example, distract the worker from considering it is capitalists who are exploiting their labor power. Or, as evidenced in the testimony from Brooks, that it is real estate dealers who are making the real gains by exploiting racist ideas of the Chinese to charge them higher rents. Why the 'white' workers of California do not form a stronger alliance with Chinese workers during this time period can be understood in such a context; because 'yellow peril' narratives foment lasting social divisions between differently racialized peoples. Summarizes McKeown, "In short, Chinese played into the hands of capitalist interests that wanted to dominate and degrade the living standards of the working man" (2008:123).

Chinese Restriction

The hegemony of negative ideas about the Chinese immigrant subjectivity during this time frame is illustrated in the Page Act of 1875. It represents a significant turning point in the discourse on the migrant. Not only is it the very first law in the US that restricts immigration, significantly, the restrictionist nature of the law is bound to articulating ideas of race and nation. Following the Civil War and the end of slave labor relations, the Page Act purports to prevent the entrance of unfree laborers—those illegally bound by unlimited terms of servitude. However, the Page Act restricts the immigration of only one racialized and nationalized collectivity: "any subject of China, Japan, or any Oriental country, without their free and voluntary consent" (US 1875, Ch. 141, Sec. 2).

Although the Page Act targets unfree subjects from China and Japan, as well as people from 'Oriental' countries, prior to the passing of the Act there is limited data collected about people arriving from the Orient[26]. This reminds us how technologies of governmentality are both selective and bound to those in power. As for Japan, very few Japanese people are recorded as *ever* having entered the US prior to the passing of the act. Full records of immigration from Japan are not even kept until 1869 (US Census Bureau 1949:21), and by the 1870 census only 55 people are recorded in the US as being Japanese (US Census Bureau 1949:27). Therefore, Chinese restriction can be seen as the most likely target of the Page Act.

While the Page Act purports to be about preventing slave labor relations in the post-Civil War era, the initial focus of the Act is on ideas of deviant migrant sexuality and criminality. Accordingly, the Page Act begins by directing US port officials to, "ascertain whether such immigrant has entered into a contract or agreement for a term of service within the United States, for lewd and immoral purposes" (US Congress 1875, section 1). And although it goes on in the following section to talk about "free and voluntary" immigration, this focus in the first section of the Act on lewdness and immorality highlights the fact that assumptions about Chinese immigrants as sexual deviants have become hegemonic. Likewise, the entire third section of the Act concerns prostitution. And then in the fifth section of the Act, the focus turns to prohibit: "aliens of the following classes...persons who are undergoing a sentence for conviction in their own country of felonious crimes other than political... and women 'imported for the purposes of prostitution'" (US 1875, Ch. 141, Sec. 5). This section further allows port officials to inspect a vessel, "if he shall have reason to believe that any such obnoxious persons are on board" (US Congress 1975, section 5). Surveillance, then, is produced as the 'solution' for Chinese immigrant deviance. Contained within the wording of this Act are a litany of offences that the immigrant could have committed—or had the potential to commit. The Act also highlights the increasingly specific number of ways immigrants are seen to negatively impact the US. These ideas represent an articulation of ideas about race and nation, sexuality, and criminality. And, like the intent of the Act, the material outcome of the Page Act is directed squarely at the Chinese.

Although a woman imported for the purposes of prostitution from any country could have been targeted, in practice it becomes *all* Chinese women who are targeted. After the Page Act is signed into law, the US consul in Hong Kong creates an application form that requires Chinese women to be investigated by the director of the Tung Wah Hospital (McKeown 2008:109). Like the inspections of vessels in US ports, such surveillance is seen as the 'solution' to the 'problem' of deviant sexuality that is said to accompany Chinese immigration. Notes Eithne Luibhéid (2002), "Chinese women coming to engage in prostitution were the first of the peripheral sexual figures to become delineated by the US immigration apparatus" (2002:xiv). One reason for the focus on Chinese prostitution is the unequal ratio of men to women in early Chinese migration. In 1850, for example, there are only seven women of Chinese origin living in San Francisco, compared to 4018 men (Takaki 1998). Prostitutes are transported to meet the sexual demands of men in the context of racist strictures against 'miscegenation'[27]. By the 1870 census, 61 percent of the 3536 women in California of Chinese origin have their occupation listed as prostitute (ibid)[28].

According to Peffer's account, *If They Don't Bring Their Women Here: Chinese Female Immigration Before Exclusion* (1999), as many as 90 percent of early arrivals from China in the US as a whole are unmarried men (1999:4). To service their needs are as many as 1,500 Chinese women whose occupation is enumerated as 'prostitute' by census-takers in the 1870 US census (US Census Bureau 1999:11). As I have noted, provisions under the Page Act enable port officials to detain women suspected of being prostitutes upon their arrival at US ports. Whether these women are prostitutes, concubines, or the brides or relatives of men already in the US, many are detained and returned to China.

While the number of women enumerated as 'prostitute' may have been overstated (Chen 2002:84), public perception at the time is that nearly *all* Chinese women are prostitutes. In the California State Testimony taken in 1876, for example, when questioned—in the words of one Senator Pierson—whether, "the great bulk of the Chinese women that come here are prostitutes", a Mr. F.F. Low, replies, "That is to be presumed. I assume that as the fact" (1876:8). Such iterations do not *present* fact, however, but rather *construct* ideas as such. Another witness, on being questioned by Senator Haymond as to the, "general repute" of women who arrive by steamer from China (1876:21), replies, "these women are, as a rule, prostitutes" (ibid). One police officer, employed at the barracoon where women are held for inspection after arriving at the port of San Francisco, notes, "The whole Chinese population may be regarded as being criminal" (1876:60). Of the prostitutes, Officer Rogers notes they are held, "As slaves—bought and sold" (1876:59), adding, "There is really no escape from the life" (ibid). On the eighth day of testimony a doctor Toland is sworn in and the nature of the threat of Chinese prostitutes is made plain. Reports Doctor Toland: "these Chinese houses of prostitution are open to small boys...

a great many have been diseased" (1876:103). Noting that his patients believe in racialized ideas of contamination, that, "diseases contracted from Chinawomen are harder to cure than those contracted elsewhere" (1876:104), Toland concludes by pointing out his patients are lured in by the cheap cost of services: "the prices are so low that they [the boys] can go wherever they please" (ibid). Two things are notable in these statements. First, that we are seeing the same economic argument that is being made of male Chinese workers at the time: that they are to blame for the cheapness of their services (rather than this being the logic of racism in capitalist labor markets at work). And second, while the sexuality of the Chinese prostitute is seen as deviant, the use of prostitutes by 'our boys' is recused of its deviancy. Such discourses have the effect of regulating certain forms of sexuality; key to these understandings are articulating ideas about the race and nationality of the subject.

Reports about Chinese prostitutes in California can thereby be seen as an evocation of a racialized, nationalized, and gendered Other. The evocation of such figurative subjects is not just about the Chinese, however. It is also about regulating the sexuality of the citizen, guarding the citizen from the threats posed by miscegenation of the races, and guarding the nation from the threat of certain biopolitical groups. Buoyed by such reports that focus on the propensity of Chinese prostitutes to spread diseases and offer services below market rate, port inspectors step up their work. The census from 1880 shows a massive decline of nearly 75 percent in the number of women whose occupation is enumerated as 'prostitute' from a decade earlier (Peffer 1999:6). In this reduction, the logic of restrictionism informing the Page Act of 1875 produces powerful political and material effects.

Chinese Exclusion

If the intent of the Page Act is to limit Chinese immigration, the number of people enumerated as Chinese wavers only slightly and then increases after the Act is passed.

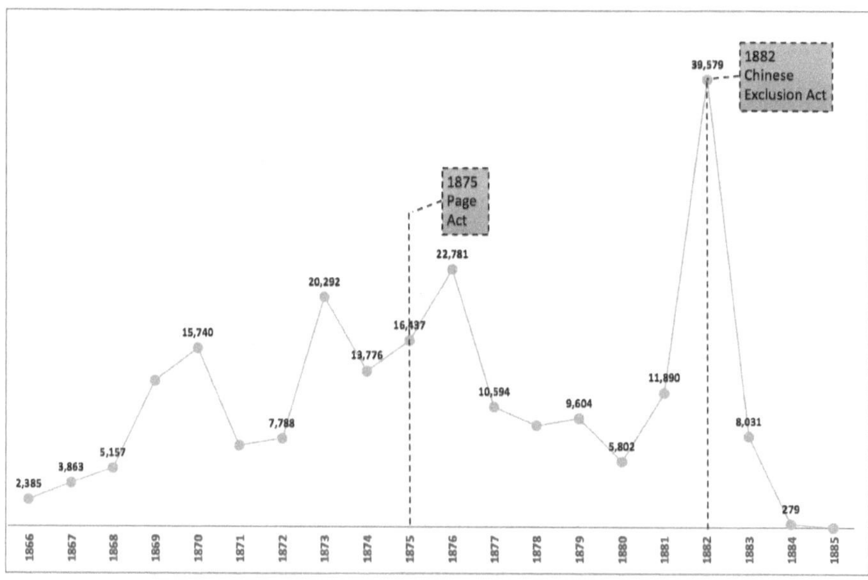

*Figure 3: Chinese Immigration to the US 1866-1885,
US Census Bureau, 1949:34-35*

It is important to emphasize that the number of people entering the US from China in 1882 represents only 5% of the total number of people who emigrated to the US that year (US Census Bureau 1949:34-5). But hysteria over Chinese immigration is rife, particularly in states such as California that have a large population of Chinese subjects. And while there are some complaints about the Page Act being, in the words of a *New York Times* article, "suspiciously like a new form of an old and violent protest against all Chinese…all the bitter prejudice against the race is aroused" (*26 Dec 1874:4*), these prejudices are about to be supplemented by a proliferation of visual media that, I contend, lead to increased discrimination and then outright exclusion.

As the media industry grows more competitive towards the end of the nineteenth century, illustrated publications multiply. One result is an increase in stereotypical and negative representations of those produced as Other. Cartoons and illustrations from this period formulate articulating ideas of race and nation that are soaked up by the reading and non-literate population. The following illustration from the cover of *Harper's Weekly* (1879) is a good example. As with other works of satire, this illustration is aimed at showing the folly of a particular way of thinking. Much more likely is that such representations promote the stereotypes they illustrate as commonsense. Titled "'Every Dog' (No Distinction Of Color) 'Has His Day'", this illustration focuses on a hierarchy of differentially racialized men, suggesting that each, in their time, will 'have his day'. Central to the illustration is a stereotypical Indian holding a peace pipe (and a barely concealed long rifle). He talks worriedly to a stereotypical Chinese man. Underneath the image the "Red Gentleman" says to the "Yellow Gentleman": "Pale face 'fraid you crowd him out, as he did me" (1879:1).

"EVERY DOG" (NO DISTINCTION OF COLOR) "HAS HIS DAY."

RED GENTLEMAN TO YELLOW GENTLEMAN. "Pale face 'fraid you crowd him out, as he did me."

Image 9: "Every Dog (No Distinction Of Color) Has His

Day." Thomas Nast for Harper's Weekly, 1879

This illustration is published ten years after the completion of the Central Pacific railroad and depicts the finished railroad at the top of the image, as a train laden with goods chases an Indian west. A Chinese man bangs a drum labeled "cheap labor" and is seen industriously chasing a train east. Implicit in this part of the illustration is the hegemonic understanding that workers from China are to be blamed for being 'cheap'. There is no culpability for the employers who pay them exceedingly low wages. In this manner, social inequalities structured by the labor market shift the responsibility from the employer to the worker. The race and nationality of the Chinese laborer is produced as a salient factor in denying American-born workers access to the labor market.

Stuck on the wall to the right of the two main characters are bill posters that talk about "The Chinese Problem" and list the "Laws Providing for Their Banishment" (1879:1). Denis Kearney—a contemporary labor leader from California who is known for his outspoken racist views—is described as "A Real American" and is quoted as saying: "The Chinese Must Go". Further down there are posters from, perhaps, less 'real' Americans: "Pat. Irish. Esq.", who states, "Foreigners Not Wanted"; and "Social Fritz", who states "Lager Bier Government We Must Have", reproducing the negative stereotype of Germans consuming alcohol. To the left of the main characters, sitting on a bale of cotton, is a newly emancipated—and starkly idle—man racialized as black. "My Day is Coming" is scrawled on the wall behind him, but quite what that day will bring or when (or if) that day will come is left unspoken. He is positioned on the far left of the illustration, his idleness seemingly his own doing, and nothing to do with the deadly hostility of the KKK who have the statement "DOWN ON THE NIGGER" posted on the wall at the top right of the illustration. The separation of these two—the KKK bill poster and the idle ex-slave—contributes to the understanding that race is a salient factor in determining a person's ability or willingness to work.

Finally, in the bottom right-hand corner there is a bill poster titled "Knownothingism of the PAST. Down with the Irish. Down with the Dutch". This reminder of the anti-immigration stance promoted by the Know Nothing political party of the mid 1850s is like a discursive echo, transferring memories of past exclusion into present exclusions (Miles 1991:9). The title of this illustration, however, seems to suggest that the future will be better for the people racialized in this image. Every race, every national person, will be treated as a 'dog', but at some point also, every 'dog' will have his day. And while this title could be taken optimistically, this *Harper's Weekly* illustration still reinforces ideas about difference based on articulating notions of race and nation. In its graphic use of homogenizing stereotypes it exerts a kind of political pressure that reifies people as having as essential and unchanging 'nature'. Such ideas are always employed as a totalizing identity, one that co-constitutes an imagined Other. And such ideas are invariable used to discriminate and exclude. Notes Robert Miles: "The ideas of race and nation are categories of simultaneous inclusion and exclusion. They identify socially constructed boundaries which separate the world's population into discrete groups which are commonly (although not exclusively) alleged to be naturally distinct" (1993:56). I argue that such ideas become visceral in the illustration form that becomes popular during this time frame, and further, that such illustrations push the discourse on the migrant closer and closer to crisis.

The following image that is published the succeeding year is from a widely popular illustrated publication called Puck. An early pioneer of political humor, Puck is published from 1871 to 1918 and employs cigar box illustrators such as Joseph Keppler to create full-page illustrations of key political characters and issues. Such vivid characterizations are not just for entertainment, however; they can be seen as having important political functions. Notes Alex Dueben (2014), "At Puck's height, the cartoons were among the country's most important political pronouncements of the week" (10 Sept 2014). The Keppler cartoon on the following page is typical of the fare that Puck disseminates and is illustrative of the stereotypical characterizations that such satirical cartoons thrive on.

This center-fold illustration features nine separate image sets that illustrate the past, present, and potential future of the US as it undergoes the "Chinese Invasion" of its title (*Puck* 1880 vol. 7, no. 158, pp. 24-25). The central figure of the illustration is Lady Liberty, kneeling on a book of law while doling out "Liberty and Justice" and life preserver rings labeled "Humanity", "Protection of Industry", and "Treaty Obligations". In the ocean all around her is evidence of the "Chinese Invasion"—desperate, skeletal men clawing at the rock of Manhattan Island, or the rat-like swarm of men fleeing the sinking vessel "CALIFORNIA".

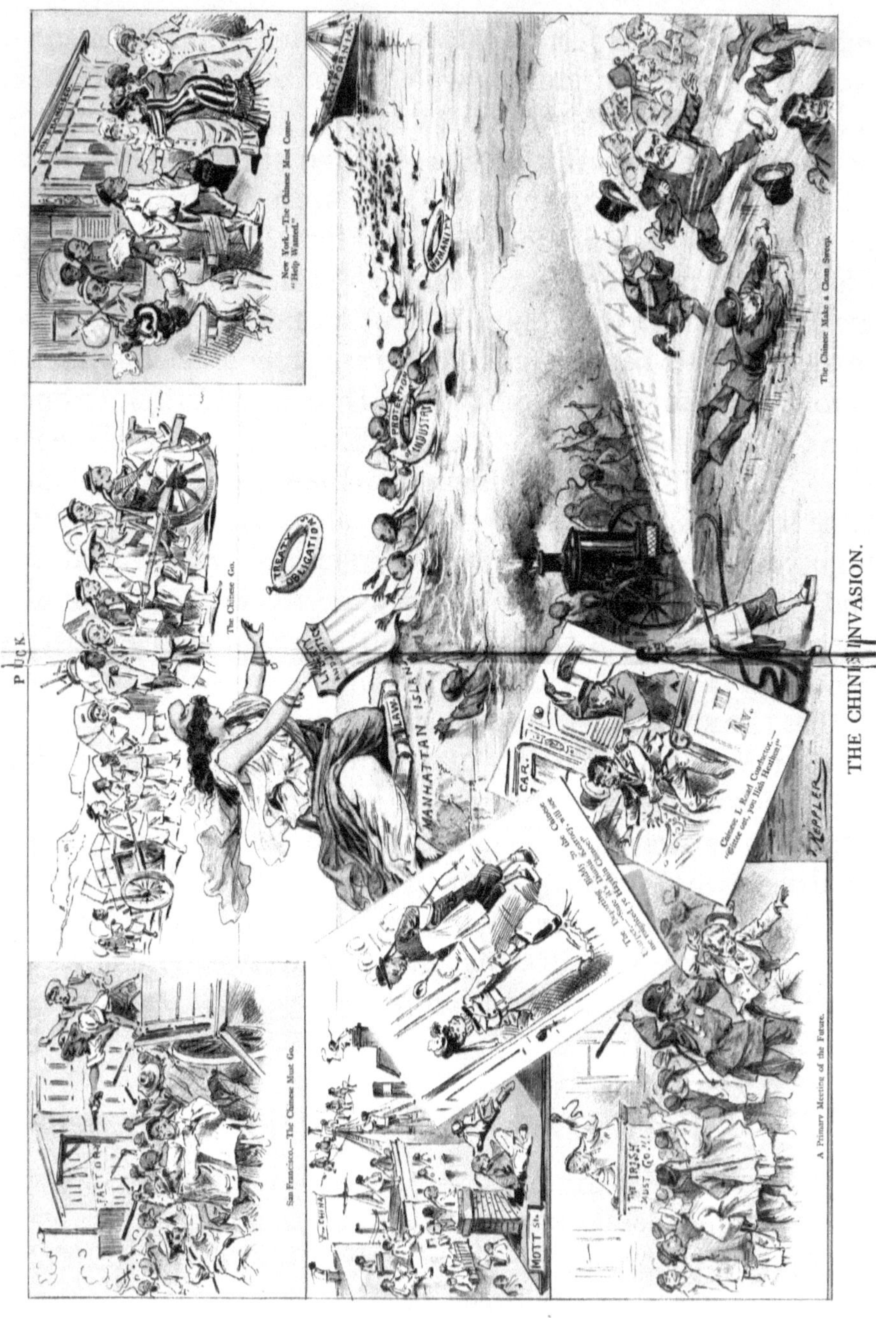

Image 10: "The Chinese Invasion." Joseph Ferdinand Keppler for Puck, 1880

Just under Lady Liberty are two pig-tailed Chinese rail-road workers: one is a conductor who pushes out an ape-like Irish man while yelling "Gittee out, you Ilish Heathen!" (ibid); the other operates a powerful hose labeled the "Chinese Wave" that washes away stereotypical caricatures of Irish and German workers in his "Clean Sweep" (ibid). In the top left of the image, outside the factories of San Francisco, pistol-waving workers skirmish with Chinese laborers. In the top right of the image, the well-kept ladies of New York greet older, more prosperous Chinese workers off the San Francisco train with open arms. And in the bottom left at, "A Primary Meeting of the Future" (ibid), a pig-tailed Chinese man takes the lectern labeled "The Irish Must Go!!!" (ibid) as a pig-tailed police officer raises his baton to an ape-like Irish worker. This illustration produces and reproduces a number of stereotypes: of the brutish, ape-like Irish man whose position in the police force and as a political candidate is being usurped by the "Chinese Invasion"; and of the Chinese immigrant, either industrious and eminently employable, or the rat-like detritus of California's failing immigration experiment. All the immigrant characters in this illustration appear to be swarming, degraded to their lowest animal forms, floating in on the tide, or washing away previous unwanted immigrants, and only the women in this illustration are giving out anything other than a beating. These are the starring characters in what is increasingly being produced as a *crisis* over Chinese immigration.

IMMIGRATION EXCLUSION

Popular support for anti-Chinese immigrant sentiment is stoked by the media as well as by politicians in the years leading up to the Chinese Exclusion Act of 1882. This anti-Chinese rhetoric is both reinforced by the edicts of politicians but is also manufactured in popular anti-Chinese demonstrations that have a decidedly holiday spirit. For example, on Saturday

4th March 1882—just two months before passage of the Chinese Exclusion Act—a festival is held in San Francisco. According to the *New York Times*, festivities include the hiring of a popular actor to read a series of resolutions that address, "the grave dangers that would arise from unrestricted Chinese immigration" (as reported in the *New York Times*, 5 March 1882:2). Dispatches of support are read from the governor of Nevada and the California State Senator. To court large audiences as well as to appeal to the workers of the city, the governor of California makes the day a state holiday. Meanwhile, according to the *New York Times,* a procession of workers pulls a wagon of children down Montgomery Street bearing the motto: "Shall Our Boys and Girls, or Chinamen, have California?" (ibid). The use of children in the demonstration and as the focus of the placard is a tactic designed to stir visceral feelings of protectionism. The motto also vividly illustrates how animosity against the Other shores up ideas about the national to whom 'Our Boys and Girls' are seen as belonging.

This notion of 'Our People' is key to both racist and nationalist rhetoric, as well as to notions of national belonging. We see it in O'Sullivan's iteration of "Our Country" (1845:5) in his article on manifest destiny in 1845. And we see it illustrated in print a day before the march in San Francisco. In the following illustration from *The San Francisco Illustrated Wasp,* a range of perceived traits of the Chinese worker are presented. What is key is that he is graphically presented as overwhelming "Our Boys" (Keller 1882) with his industrious labor. The publication is the most highly read weekly on the West Coast at the time (West 2004:86), and it is likely that the authors of the Montgomery Street wagon motto have seen the illustration.

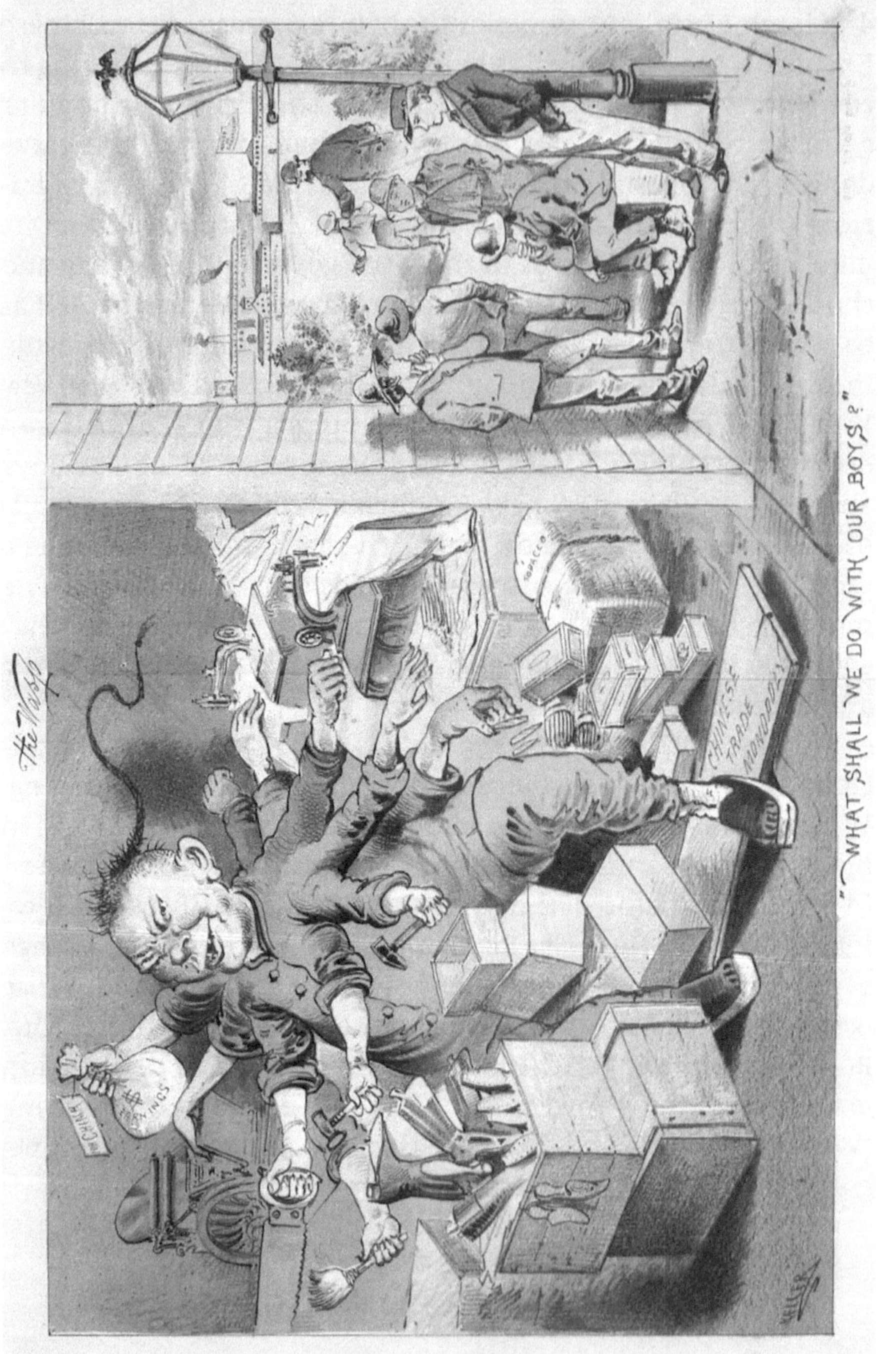

Image 11: "What Shall We Do With Our Boys?" George Frederick

Keller for the San Francisco Illustrated Wasp, 1882

In this illustration, the Chinese immigrant laborer is portrayed doing the work for which they are stereotypically known at the time: tobacco, laundry, sewing clothes, and construction, but note that the laborer works voraciously, his tentacle-like arms reaching into everything all at once. He is animalistic, unstoppable, barely settled in place, working hard at his "Chinese Trade Monopoly" while his dollars are tagged "For China", the place of his assumed allegiance, in an act that purportedly deprives the local community of the benefits of his earnings. The Chinese laborer occupies fully two thirds of the page, leaving "Our Boys"—a collection of working-age men racialized as white—standing around apparently locked out of the factories in the distance. Idle, clean-cut, pale, young, they loiter apprehensively, bathed in the light of day under the American-eagle-topped lamppost. Meanwhile the scowling and unkempt Chinese immigrant labors away in the darkness. This cartoon reinforces the ideas that the system of immigration promotes a monopoly of Chinese trade, and that Chinese labor poses a threat to 'our boys' of the nation.

Both these Kepler and Keller illustrations focus on Chinese immigrant labor competition and construct it in visceral terms as a crisis. The stereotypes deployed in such popular media produce and reproduce the Chinese immigrant subjectivity as a threat to labor competition, and as a threat to the future of 'our' nation, thereby producing consent for immigration restriction and exclusion. The stereotypical and derogatory manner in which the Chinese immigrant is produced and reproduced in the mass media, by powerful leaders, and in everyday speech is seen as influential in creating immigration-as-crisis. This Keller cartoon is published just two months before President Arthur signs the 1882 Chinese Exclusion Act into law. The Act severely restricts immigration from China, as well as allows for the deportation of Chinese people already in the US.

There are two significant power effects of this exclusionary legislation. First, to un-nerve previously demonized immigrant groups, and second, to raise the conditions of possibility for *all* immigration to be seen as a threat. In the following cartoon from *Harper's Weekly*, a stereotypical German and an Irish man are shown lazily smoking their pipes and (yet again) drinking their customary drinks as they ponder the situation. A worried 'Fritz' asks an ape-like 'Pat': "If the Yankee Congress can keep the *yellow* man out, what is to hinder them from calling us *green* and keeping us out too?". The cartoon supports the hegemony of German and Irish immigrants as problematic. It also points to a growing anxiety over the racisms and nationalisms that are increasingly being used as a reason to deny entry to the US and to citizenship, and to deny participation in its labor force. So rather than it promoting the idea that 'every dog will have his day' as the Nast cartoon of 1879 iterated, now—as the title of this carton suggests—it is 'who will be excluded next'.

WHICH COLOR IS TO BE TABOOED NEXT?

Fritz (*to Pat*). "If the Yankee Congress can keep the *yellow* man out, what is to hinder them from calling us *green* and keeping us out too?"

Image 12: "Which Color is to be Tabooed Next?"
Thomas Nast for Harper's Weekly, 1882

△△△

I have shown in this chapter how negative ideas about the race and nation of the migrant subject-figure—combined with internal and supplementary ideas about poverty, gender, sexuality, and criminality—produce vivid stereotypes that foster consent for practices of immigration restriction and exclusion. Through analyzing a range of historically specific media, I have shown how ideas of race and nation articulate with one another, strengthening essentialist ideas about 'a people' who 'belong' and those who should be excluded. Under this logic, wholeness must be maintained. And so ideas and laws prohibiting the mixing of races articulate with ideas and laws prohibiting the mixing of peoples. Such ideas lead to the first restriction-oriented immigration law, the Page Act of 1875, and then to the Chinese Exclusion Act of 1882. These laws target people from China and elsewhere as part of a strategy to limit and then stop immigration from negatively racialized populations deemed 'undesirable'. Co-constituted in this process are ideas about America as a 'desirable' national and positively racialized space.

Figurative subjects help structure the nation because they support ideas about who the nation is for, as well as specify who is seen as a threat, and the nature of that threat. From the onset of capitalism in sixteenth century Europe, through successive technological revolutions, there is massive political and social unrest that pushes the worker to become mobile. When such migrant workers are seen as being in unfair competition with US workers, we see an increase in hostility both from citizen workers and from the politicians whose votes they court. The utility found in demonizing immigrants by both the Know Nothing party and the emerging mass media of the

1850s prompts future demonizing of the migrant subjectivity. The discursive formations that produce such subject-figures are shown as concealing underlying political and economic realities.

4/ATTENDANT ALIENS

As the previous chapter illustrated, migrants are represented in historical discourses as out-of-place Others who by their very existence threaten the safety and economic stability of the US nation-state. These discursive formations rely on ideas of race and nation that articulate to structure a 'we the people' and a co-constituted migrant Other. A political and material effect of these formations is the hegemonic understanding that immigration is a crisis that can be resolved through restrictionist and exclusionist state 'solutions'. Such ideas echo discursively through time such that previous solutions make 'sense' of contemporary ones. This historical resonance lends credence to the calls of those, like Trump, who would strengthen the US border using prophylactic barriers like a wall. These measures are seen as necessary in order to counteract what Trump calls, "aliens...who have violated our borders" (8 Jan 2019). And these measures are commonsense if we understand the alien migrant[29] as a threat. But how is the migrant understood as a threat? What are the discursive mechanisms at play that rouse this sense of threat in our commonsense understanding of those produced as migrants? And what are the socio-economic and cultural consequences when the migrant subject-figure is produced as demonstrably dangerous to the nation and 'its people'.

This chapter examines the construction of the migrant subjectivity as a threat through what I term discursive crossover. This occurs when entirely different discourses become connected to transfer ideas, problematizations, and 'solutions' from one arena to another. I employ this original theoretical concept to analyze a range of media, from newspaper articles of the 1850s, to contemporary movies, presidential tweets, White House press releases, and protest art. Through my analysis I answer a number of key questions: How does discursive crossover between the disparate alien discourses impact the human migrant subjectivity? What are the significant developments in the human migrant subjectivity as a result of these crossovers? How does discursive crossover result in some bodies being privileged in their ability to cross borders, while other humans and non-human species are produced as a threat and targeted for surveillance, detention, and even eradication? And how does discursive crossover produce the power effect that the US nation-state is 'home' for some, while other human and non-humans produced as alien must simply 'go home'?

Theoretical Roots and Diversions

The idea that one discourse can be deliberately connected to another in order to define social problems derives from a number of related concepts. Frist, there is Kristeva's (1986) understanding of intertextuality—as well as Bakhtin's from which it draws—that both assume an *a priori* relationship between texts. In other words, inter-related texts share meaning because they share the same subject or object of discourse. Discursive crossover adds new nuance to Kristeva's formation of intertextuality because it announces the process whereby *unrelated* texts have the potentiality to share meanings.

A second theory that discursive crossover draws from is that of metaphorical linkage as constructed by Gary Alan Fine and Lazaros Christoforides (1991). Metaphorical linkage explores how nascent social problems gain status when a well-recognized problem is linked to an emerging public concern through use of the same metaphorical framing. Connecting one thing to another through metaphor, the authors argue, helps people make 'sense' of things, promotes an unestablished topic so that it can, "survive the competition of public discourse" (1991:376), and also provides dramatic images to illustrate concerns. Now, while metaphorical linkage examines how dissimilar topics are framed in nearly identical ways—the example the authors initially give is how the metaphor of 'addiction' is used to lend status to emerging problematizations about food or sex—discursive crossover goes further to highlight not only the productive ways that radically different discourses interact, but also the wide-reaching political and material effects that result when discursive crossover is deployed.

When an official in President Ford's cabinet talks about a, "silent invasion of illegal aliens" (Chapman 1975), for example, he is using the metaphor of invasion to suggest that unauthorized migration is demonstrably similar to what the dictionary describes as, "The action of invading a country or territory as an enemy; an entrance or incursion with armed force; a hostile inroad" (*OED* 1989 invasion, noun, 1.a.). But the term alien invasion evokes one more specter: the duplicitous space alien who threatens to plunder national resources using advanced intelligence and superior weapons technology. Discursive crossover prompts us to attend to the political and material outcomes of Chapman's metaphorical framing: to frame migrants as a duplicitous threat (not just an invasion but a silent one); and to promote his idea of an appropriate response (only the military can deal with an invasion). Accordingly, the metaphor of invasion and the phrase invasion of illegal aliens doesn't just make 'sense' of the movements of migrants, and doesn't just frame the debate about unauthorized migration in a recognizable way (as a crime, for example). The discursive crossover deployed here modifies our understanding of the migrant subjectivity by reminding us that aliens represent duplicitous hostility. And such a framing, I contend, legitimates an armed response.

One other theoretical concept is employed in this chapter in order to explain how meanings can transfer from one discourse to another: the Deleuzian attendant. In analyzing the triptych paintings of Francis Bacon, Gilles Deleuze (1981) employs a concept he calls the attendant character in order to explain how a figure in one canvas can modify the understanding of figures in other canvases across the triptych. In this chapter I extend the concept of the Deleuzian attendant to highlight the imaginative ways that *meanings* in one discourse modify the meanings in another through this process of discursive crossover.

I employ these theoretical concepts not only to add my own contribution to our sociological understanding of the world, but also to raise the conditions of possibility where our understanding of human and other species mobility and connectivity can be reimagined in a more positive way. Because my concept of discursive crossover focuses on the relationship between disparate texts and broader socio-cultural and political structures and materialities, it represents a productive addition to the method of discourse analysis.

DISCURSIVE CROSSOVER

In the previous chapter I leaned on the term discursive articulation to illustrate how the discourse on race acts as internal and supplementary to the discourse on the nation. Discursive crossover goes one step further to point to the productive links between discourses that are tangentially or even radically different. Crossover between discourses—between ideas about alien migrants, alien species, and space aliens, for example— occurs routinely in the discourse on immigration and prompts both meanings and solutions to transfer from one domain to another.

Discursive crossover between the three alien discourses supports the hegemony of a world divided into nation-states because it promotes and upholds ideas of 'difference' that logically require prophylactic borders and other anti-miscegenation measures. In the so-called alien species discourse, for example, these concepts of alterity are tied to ideas about the 'natural', the 'native', and overly competitive entities who threaten to 'take over' or 'invade'. And in the space aliens discourse these ideas of alterity are commonly magnified into a threat such that duplicitous and deadly 'invading aliens' destroy 'national resources' and threaten to probe and breed with earthlings. I contend that when invoked in the immigration discourse using discursive crossover, such alien ideas negatively modify the alien migrant subjectivity, legitimating political and material structures that repress and exclude on account of 'difference'. In other words, while discursive crossover is evoked through a language of ideas, I contend that this crossover effect also carries through into material practice. And so, while metaphorical linkage is centrally interested in how problems are constructed when concepts transfer from one domain to another, discursive crossover goes one step further to show that material solutions also transfer.

This chapter argues that the migrant subjectivity is significantly transformed when the alien species discourse and the space alien discourse interact with it through discursive crossover. This occurs at distinct historical moments and produces distinct political and material effects. So when we see late nineteenth century stereotypes of Chinese immigrants fleeing rat-like in the cartoon from the previous chapter titled "Chinese Invasion" (Keppler 1880), for example, it evokes a problematized species discourse. Nobody wants rats, and discursive crossover makes is plain that nobody should want Chinese immigrants either. But the power effect of these evocations is not just to transfer problematizations from one discourse to another: solutions also transfer. This means an increase in violence against Chinese immigrants during this time frame, but it also means political solutions. And so following the widespread stereotyping and demonization of the Chinese immigrant subject-figure comes the Chinese Exclusion Act of 1882.

Discursive crossover also occurs between the alien migrant discourse and the space alien discourse. Discursive crossover between these two very different kinds of alien may seem like an entertaining pun, but I contend that crossover with the space alien discourse leaves an indelible and dangerous mark on the human migrant subjectivity thereby promoting militaristic solutions. This is because discursive crossover functions to connect ideas inextricably, so that ideas about the space alien as a dangerous and duplicitous subject-figure are productive of negative ideas about the human migrant subjectivity, particularly when such people are labeled alien. The first discourse speaks to the second discourse and has a modifying and perverse influence upon it. The power effect of discursive crossover is to elevate the fearful nature of the migrant subjectivity, and thereby legitimate policies and practices that deal with humans and other entities deemed out-of-place.

For example, in the hit sci-fi film *Men in Black* (1997), we see a government agent inspecting a line of "nervous immigrants" (1997:4) for a space alien dressed in what the script describes as, "a 'Mexican' disguise" (1997:7). This is a pun: looking for space aliens in a line of 'Mexican aliens'. However, the lining up of the immigrants, the surveillance and interrogation at the border; these are the ongoing actual practices of federal agents who 'round up' Mexicans (and others) targeted as *alien* in contemporary border states. The discursive crossover evoked in this scene in *Men in Black* not only makes 'sense' of this discriminatory and racializing practice by government agents, it also makes it a light-hearted matter.

In reality, of course, the fear of being 'rounded up' leads many millions of people to live shadow lives as they modify their daily routines to avoid suspicion, arrest, detainment, and deportation. Reagan hints at this when he signs the Immigration Reform and Control Act of 1986, "to improve the lives of a class of individuals who now must hide in the shadows, without access to many of the benefits of a free and open society" (Reagan 1986). But discursive crossover in this scene also makes fun of 'rounding up'[30]. This allows the audience to laugh at this aggressive state practice and laugh at the 'nervous immigrants', rather than thinking critically about the moral implications for the US of this ongoing state practice. Discursive crossover in this scene also reifies the essential out-of-placeness of the alien migrant, reaffirms their alien-ness as an indicator of duplicitous threat, and thereby aids the hegemonic understanding that immigration is a social problem.

Invasive Discourses

A central outcome of discursive crossover, I argue, is to produce the migrant as a degraded and fearful subjectivity. One of the ways this is achieved is through the deployment of human-animal crossovers that not only dehumanize the migrant and reify their essential 'difference', but also irreversibly modify the migrant subjectivity to a lowly animal form who paradoxically, also poses a threat of invasion to the nation[31]. A genealogy is useful here because in historicizing the emergence and proliferation of human-animal crossovers we can trace its development as a novel political technology.

Discursive crossover between humans and animals is first used in the last quarter of the nineteenth century in order to promote the migrant subjectivity as a threat. In an article about migration by the Union Pacific Railroad in 1875, for example, the author refers to a, "swarm of emigrants...unprecedented in the history of railroading" (15 April 1875:9). The evocation of migrants as a swarm reminds us of deadly stinging wasps, perhaps, or some other kind of invasive animal pestilence. Through discursive crossover the verb *swarm* modifies the essential nature of the migrant, transforming their movement from human migration into animal invasion. And it is this transformation, I argue, that lends legitimacy to material practices of restriction and exclusion. This article, for example, appears just six weeks after the Page Act is signed, the very first restrictive immigration law in the US.

And then in the late 1800s, an ornithological dispute known as the Great English Sparrow War is tied discursively to the 'problem' of immigration and this has a number of political and material functions. Chiefly, it makes commonsense of the threat of species invasion and over-abundance, ties this to the threat of human invasion and over-abundance, and in doing so reifies ideas of national difference and the necessity of fixity. Talking freely about one threat—the English sparrow—allows fears about 'foreign species' over-population to transfer to fears about 'foreign human' over-population.

Gary Alan Fine and Lazaros Christoforides (1991) explore these problem constructions in their study, "Dirty Birds, Filthy Immigrants, and the English Sparrow War". Noting what they term, "the power of metaphor to shape the perception of so-cial problems" (1991:377), Fine and Christoforides argue that examining metaphors—in particular examining metaphors en-gaged in what they call "metaphorical linkage" (ibid)—is a pro-ductive way of looking at how social problems are constructed. "Ultimately," Fine and Christoforides caution, "this suggests that the constructionist view of social problems should not only examine the creation of issues in isolation, but as part of a nexus of images, symbols, beliefs, and metaphors: a master problem" (1991:389).

This 'problem' begins after the English sparrow is intro-duced in the early 1850s as a tool to combat the dropworm. Once sparrow numbers reach a critical mass, however, the dis-course becomes one of pestilence and invasion. And then from the 1880s onwards, Fine and Christoforides note, English spar-rows—now recognized popularly as "little beasts" (1991:380) —are metaphorically linked to what is increasingly seen as the "blight" of immigration (1991:379). English sparrows are anthropomorphized, and human migrants are animalized as moving in 'swarms' and 'herds' (1991:382). The authors con-tend that framing both social problems in nearly identical ways allows anti-foreign feeling against the English sparrow to transfer to anti-foreign feeling against immigrants. Note Fine and Christoforides: "Our claim is not that the proponents of attacks on sparrows cynically manipulated nativist rhetoric in order to inflame passions, but rather this set of nativist beliefs made sense in explaining the dangers of a foreign interloper to the community of American birds" (2001:377). In other words, metaphorical linkage makes 'sense' of a nascent threat by drawing on existing 'knowledge' that 'foreign-ness' and outsider overpopulation poses a threat to the nation. In this manner, immigration increases in saliency and validity as a recognized social problem.

Crossover between out-of-place animals and out-of-place humans is a discursive formation tied to specific socio-historical conditions that produces the migrant subjectivity as a hostile symbolic figure who can be restricted, excluded, and even attacked at will. A good example lies in an article in *The American Naturalist* by Joseph Grinnell (1919). It is written just two months after the end of the First World War that causes the mass displacement of people worldwide. The article —titled in part "An Experiment in Nature"—illustrates how discursive crossover between animals and humans constructs negative ideas about species mobility and species overabundance. Articulating ideas of race with those of nation, the author anthropomorphizes the 'English' sparrows as living in a "thriving colony" (1919:469), with, "their main headquarters" (ibid) in some trees near a ranch house. They are birds that, "crossed [a climate] barrier" (1919:468), and who should be, "strictly isolated and kept from genetic contamination by new influxes" (1919:472). Failure to do so, Grinnell posits, will result in a, "differentiation of the mass" (ibid). In other words, miscegenation—or genetic mixing—between differentially nationalized species risks a change in the supposedly homogenous national whole.

But these are not benign creatures; much as migrants are routinely seen as being invasive, these, too, are birds who, "self-impose" themselves on the US, "through their powers of invasion" (1919:472). And furthermore, they are seen as intentionally disrespectful of natural boundaries, a species who, "gradually advanced its frontiers and overleaped all the faunal boundaries which hem in the habitats of our native bird races" (ibid). In other words, the birds in this article are presented as belonging in their namesake country, but willfully and invasively crossing barriers[32]. This discursive crossover reifies ideas about national belonging as 'natural', and also lends legitimacy to the idea of barriers to fix everything in place. Grinnell writes wistfully about the order wrought by such fixity: "In the Old World, each race 'stays put'...each in its own faunal area" 1919:471). But because these birds are anthropomorphized as humans, they are given agency, and this agency is exercised in a manner that apparently evidences disrespect for national borders. And so, they are, "continually overstepping the bounds of the habitats of the races to which they belong" (1919:472). Such discursive crossover promotes as commonsense the idea that nationalized and racialized people should stay put or be isolated in order to prevent a disastrous change to the homogeneity of the nation.

My concept of discursive crossover goes further than that of metaphorical linkage to focus not just on problem construction as Fine and Christoforides do, but also to look at the broader political and material outcomes of such a process. A material outcome of the English Sparrow War, for example, is the understanding that the over-abundance of the out-of-place can be solved by extermination. The *San Francisco Bulletin* puts forward this solution for the birds in 1883, when it decries: "There is just one remedy, and that is to kill every one of them" (in the *New York Times,* 11 March 1883:4). This practice persists, as is noted on a contemporary hunting forum blog in which a user reminisces how it was customary in his Michigan youth for children to be employed at two cents a bird to shoot English sparrows and deliver them to the court house (timbergsp 2007).

But it is not just birds and other animals that this logic of extermination extends to. I argue that discursive crossover transfers this logic of extermination for the problematized and out-of-place *back* to humans. Stoler (2017) hints as much when she argues that, "the conceptual and concrete apparatuses to constrain and contain the movement of people conjoin with and borrow from those strategies deployed for the animal and botanical orders of the world" (2017:3). So while Fine and Christoforides argue that, "immigrants should have been grateful that they were not birds. Despite the violence targeted at them, they were never threatened with mass extermination in nineteenth century America" (1991:386), I argue that linking out-of-place animals with out-of-place humans results in a number of mass exterminations of humans during this time period, both migrant and racialized Other. In Clear Lake, California, in 1850, for example, as many as 250 Pomo Indians are killed by US troops led by one Captain Lyon who describes the location as, "a perfect slaughter pen" (in Field 1993: 54). It is no coincidence that he uses this animal term to describe the site of a human massacre, and neither is it an isolated incident. Notes Benjamin Madley (2017), such killings, "ignited an inferno of anti-Californian Indian violence that would last until 1873 and beyond" (2017:144). Madley goes on to quote the editor of the *Daily Alta California* as saying there, "will then be safety only in a war of *extermination*, waged with relentless fury far and near" (ibid). Anti-Chinese violence is also rife in this time period. As McKeown (2008:157) details, twenty-eight Chinese people are murdered in 1885 at the hands of a mob in Rock Springs, Wyoming, in an incident that is far from isolated. I contend that promoting these humans as unwanted through discursive crossover makes their extermination a 'logical solution'.

Discursive crossover that raises the specter of possibility for the migrant to be seen as a threat are deployed at key moments in the discourse. Such crossovers are not only used to make sense of the problem of migrants, they are also deployed to legitimate related solutions. This occurs at a number of discrete moments that shift the immigration discourse ever closer towards crisis. As mentioned previously, we see it in the last quarter of the nineteenth century as the Page Act and Chinese Exclusion Act are passed. And we see it again after the First World War and then throughout the 1920s. It is a decade in which Congress passes a series of increasingly restrictive quota acts that reduce immigration based on racist and nationalist concepts of hierarchical difference (Behdad 2005:20). And accompanying these successive acts are an assemblage of crossovers and other discursive formations that degrade the human migrant subjectivity to lowly and fearful animal forms.

Just after the first Emergency Quota Act is signed in 1921, for example, an un-named author in the *New York Times* makes 'sense' of the practice using a range of discursive formations. In an article titled the "New Age of Migration" (13 Nov 1921:2), after deploying hydraulic metaphors to produce migrants as a, "stream" and as, "surging masses", the author notes: "On a map of Europe the tracks of emigrants across the Continent and along the adjoining waterways would look as straggling and aimless as wandering cow paths on a pasture land" (ibid). The human-animal discursive crossover here not only reduces migrants to the lowly status of cows, but the use of hydraulic terminology and the verbs *straggling* and *wandering* also suggest that migrants are unable to control their movements. I contend that the discursive crossover that evokes migrants as straggling and meandering animals (who paradoxically also stream and surge) modifies the migrant subjectivity to one devoid of agency and intelligence. And it is these very same ideas about migrants that the 1917 Immigration Act seeks to address when it mandates a literacy test for immigrants.

Non-Vital Lifeforms

The use of animal terms and hydraulic metaphors to refer to human migrants continues today, with historical discourses echoing with contemporary ones, lending a sense that such 'problems' have a thorough grounding in the past. In northern France near Calais, for example, a migrant camp known widely as 'The Jungle' exists from 2015 to late 2016 when it is dismantled. Perhaps we can be charitable and posit that the name *The Jungle* is an evocation of Upton Sinclair's (1906) book of the same name—a book that empathizes with the plight of impoverished immigrants in early 1900s America. Or perhaps use of the term *jungle* is simply an essentializing way of saying that such migrants 'belong' in such an animal place (and, further, that such an animal place is out-of-place in metropolitan France). Certainly articles about The Jungle seem to animalize its inhabitants. In a *New York Times* article on the encampment, for example, Nossiter and Hicks note that, "Dazed and ragged, new migrants stumble" to the camp every day (26 Sept 2016). This description echoes discursively with the portrayal of migrants as *straggling and aimless* in the 1921 article quoted at the beginning of this section. Nossiter and Hicks continue, nothing that the jungle is, "a highly visible symbol of Europe's inability to cope with the migrant influx". The deployment of the term jungle and use of the hydraulic metaphor work to construct migrants as animals who are entirely devoid of human agency. The effect of such discursive crossovers, I argue, is to legitimize the confinement of migrants in inhumane conditions.

Unwanted mobile humans are not just described using any animal metaphor, however; as Bridget Anderson (2017) points out, the animals deployed in the contemporary discourse on migration are on the order of vermin, "forms of non-vital life, low down on the animal phyla" (ibid). Those cast as migrant—and Anderson makes it clear that the label *migrant* has become a derogatory one (2017:12)—are described or pictured using the metaphors of rats, cockroaches, and insects. Such animals are associated with invasions into urban life, and, particularly, with urban decay. All are competitors for human food, and all are imagined as invasive interlopers in the urban environment that humans have crafted from the 'natural' environment. Just as claims-makers decry pigeons as "rats with wings" (Jerolmack 2008) in order to render them out-of-place in the cityscape, so unwanted mobile humans are described as 'lower order' interlopers. The power effect of this discursive crossover is to reduce the moral compunction about excluding or even eliminating the out-of-place human migrant.

Lower-order human-animal crossovers are deployed by Trump, for example, as he describes what migrants might do to the US nation-state. Such animalizing crossovers, I argue, negatively impact the migrant subjectivity and lend justification to brutal state responses. And because of both the ubiquity and alarmist nature of these crossovers in the era of Trump, I contend that Trump's entrance onto the political scene as a candidate in 2015 marks a significant turning point in the discourse on immigration.

In a tweet from 2018, for example, Trump states: "[Democrats] want illegal immigrants, no matter how bad they may be, to *pour* into and *infest* our Country" (@realDonaldTrump 19 June 2018, emphasis added). I contend that use of the verbs *pour* and *infest*—especially when it is done routinely and by powerful figures so that such language is accepted unquestionably—permanently modifies the migrant subjectivity with significant economic, cultural, and social consequences. Trump makes this statement, for example, just as the Department of Homeland Security (DHS) begins to implement its 'zero-tolerance policy' at the southern US border, a policy that removes children from their parents, and inters them in separate facilities. Visiting one such facility, US Senator Chris Van Hollen tweets, "Just left Border Patrol Processing Center in McAllen—aka 'the dog kennel.' Witnessed loads of kids massed together in large pens of chain-linked fence separated from their moms and dads. @realDonaldTrump, change your shameful policy today!" (@ChrisVanHollen 17 June 2018). Due to the lack of an integrated data system, many such children—referred to by the government as UACs for Unaccompanied Alien Children—became untraceable by their parents, lawyers, or even agents internal to the DHS or HHS. Two such children even die in custody (Jordan 25 Dec 2018).

Although only children, UACs are the focus of particular suspicion in the contemporary discourse on immigration. And in a White House press release titled, "What You Need To Know About Loopholes Allowing Unaccompanied Alien Children To Stay In The Country" (4 April 2018), such 'alien' children are produced in both invasive and animal ways. First, they are seen as taking advantage of 'loopholes'. This is a very old military term dating to the sixteenth century, described in the *OED* as, "A narrow vertical opening, usually widening inwards, cut in a wall or other defense, to allow of the passage of missiles" (*OED* 1989, loophole, noun, 1.a.). In other words, loopholes are themselves border breaches, cut for the purposes of warring invasion. The problem with such loopholes, as the White House press release articulates, is that they, "continue to hamstring efforts to enforce our immigration laws and secure our border, ultimately resulting in catch and release" (White House 2018). The use of the transitive verb hamstring meaning to cut tendons and cripple is a visceral metaphor designed to evoke a sense that UACs—and the loopholes they take advantage of— cause disabling pain. Finally, the term 'catch and release' is used here unproblematically, as it is in much contemporary anti-immigration rhetoric. Catch and release, of course, is a fishing practice in which anglers return fish to the water alive after catching them, "in order to sustain stocks" (*OED* 2018, catch-and-release. adj. A). In other words, White House use of this term evokes 'alien' children as animals who invade and multiply, devious young people (always plural) who take advantage of, "Catch and release practices [that] have enabled the vast majority of UACs who enter the United States each year to avoid removal" (White House 2018). Deploying this range of militarist, animalistic, and viscerally painful metaphors is a clear example of discursive crossover that appears at the same time as Trump's zero-tolerance is enacted at the border. I argue that the principal effects of this crossover are not only to modify the migrant subjectivity but also to lend legitimacy to practices that separate, detain, and result in the dehumanizing treatment of such children.

Functional Discourses

A final function of discursive crossover, I argue, is that it allows for discussion in one sphere that cannot justifiably be discussed in another. We can talk freely about the need to eradicate alien plants in order to protect 'native' environments, for example, in a way that we cannot talk about so-called alien people[33]. As Jean Comaroff and John Comaroff (2001) argue in their article titled, "Naturing the Nation: Aliens, Apocalypse, and the Postcolonial State", while some plant and animal species act as signifiers of the state (2001:243), 'alien invaders' serve as powerful symbols that warn against mixing. In this manner, plant and animal invaders become alibis for the state to enact strict measures because they can be invoked in discourse to shore up understandings of national origins for people, and also to warn about the implicit dangers of crossing borders and mixing different types of being. Such discourses rely on ideas of national belonging, and nation-state invasion. This makes them useful allies in the political project of the nation, one whose borders must be both open and closed. In this manner, plant and animal species that make up the 'natural' world are useful for shaping new social and political distinctions because they can be employed both to solidify our understanding of national 'origins' and also serve as visceral threats of the dangers of border breaching and species miscegenation.

This same function of discursive crossover to permit the transference of topics also works in space alien movies in which an association is made between space aliens and human migrants. Analyzing the 1996 movie *The Arrival*, for example, Jodi Dean (1998) notes that the crossover between the two different discourses, "channels anxieties around security, otherness, and immigration into a story of extraterrestrial invasion.

The audience can express its squeamishness about aliens without experiencing guilt over racism or political incorrectness" (1998:155-156). In other words, discursive crossover between space aliens and human aliens functions to allow us to address our negative feelings about immigration calmly, and without fear of being seen as xenophobic[34]. This topic transference is a common tactic employed across the arts, for example, *War of the Worlds* (1898) can be seen as an allegory in which the space alien invasion of the story prompts us to question colonial practices of 'invasion' without specifically mentioning them. Fine and Christoforides (1991) also detect this function when historical problematizations are purposefully connected with contemporary ones: "Past problems permit us to examine the development and usage of a social concern without passion, if occasionally with a smug and ironic detachment" (1991:376).

But not all humans, animals, and plants are portrayed as invaders, just as not all human mobility is problematized. While some mobile humans are vaunted as 'world travelers', for example, animals such as the grey whale, wildebeest, or monarch butterfly are cherished in their mobility. The butterfly, in particular, is fetishized as a symbol of environmental wonder and fragility. Notes Bob Sutcliffe: "Monitoring the arrival of the monarchs from the south each spring has become something of a naturalists' and schoolchildren's cult in the USA" (2001:80). And while monarchs are watched with awe and delight as they migrate from their wintering sites in Mexico to the global north and back again, the situation could not be more different for the human migrants who make the same circular migratory journey. This difference is exemplified in Kingsolver's best-selling novel *Flight Behavior* (2012), in which characters venerate the monarchs that appear in their rural Tennessee village, yet treat the Mexican and Caribbean-origin human characters who have appeared in their village with outright hostility.

And just as some migrants are treated with hostility, so too are some animal and plant species. The mosquito, the quagga and zebra mussel, the algae that blooms turning Great Lakes into green swamps; all are sorely blamed for being willfully out-of-place, disrespectful of nation-state borders, a threat to national security, as well as a threat to the national economy. And as with the discourse on the unauthorized human migrants, in the discourse on alien species it is always the alien who has disrespected the laws of the land. "Mosquitoes don't go through customs", notes Obama at the height of the zika virus scare. "This is not something where we can build a wall to prevent it" (Mohney 2016)[35].

In both the discourse on the migrant, and the discourse on invasive plants and animals, the language, themes, and central ideas correlate with startling similarity; so do the tactics deployed to counteract the assumed threat. In contemporary Europe, for example, species considered 'aggressive' and 'non-native' are termed Invasive Alien Species (IAS) by the European Environment Agency. Reports on IAS are replete with terms that emphasize militarized intent, prolific breeding, and lack of respect for nation-state borders: "Report tracks threats from Europe's alien invasion" (Kinver 2013); "Range of plant invaders examined…amazing cases of invaders that expand seemingly without bounds or in unexpected ways" (Matsushima 2012). Such discourses anthropomorphize motives of plant and animal species such that, "Invasive ladybirds wage 'biological war' on natives" (McGrath 2013). The motives attributed to IAS are to terrorize, wage war, and cause purposeful financial loss to 'natives'. An article titled "Counting the cost of alien invasions" (Steiner 2010) warns of billion dollar losses to crops as a result of IAS, "massive population surges", and sinister "sleeper" species "who become embedded in a community to be activated some years later" (ibid). The concept of discursive crossover allows us to link the militarized war on terror to the war on IAS; plant and animal species are given anthropomorphic motives and are targeted using military force. Extermination is always the recommended answer. Methods for the extermination of IAS include Herbicide Ballistic Technology to ensure "invasive weed trees [are] targeted and eliminated" (hawaii.edu news 2016); or poisoned dead mice slung from a helicopter to "fight the voracious brown tree snake" (Borenstein 2017). The use of discursive crossover connects problems; it also makes sense of the same solutions.

Alienating Discourses

A clear case of discursive crossover is illuminated when unwanted human migrants—just like unwanted plant and animal species—are labeled *alien*. While the label has been an official state category for un-naturalized people in the US since 1790, its use today is contentious, which is why many media outlets refuse to use it. The concept of discursive crossover makes sense of why some media, politicians, and others *would* use the term however: to provoke the idea that such people are essentially Other, to invoke fear, and to foster consent for restrictionist and exclusionary responses.

In the case of the term 'illegal alien', such labeling works to assign criminality onto migrant workers, rendering them as cheap laborers, as well as producing them as socially and politically powerless (Sassen 1988:37). While committing an illegal act is not necessary for a person to be labeled illegal alien (or simply 'illegal'), the terminology is used broadly for both authorized and unauthorized migrants, as well as for asylum seekers who have not yet reached the southern border. As I referred to in previous chapters, although hundreds of thousands of Mexicans are expelled from the US during the Depression era (see Nevins 2002:54), the understanding of such people as *illegal aliens* does not emerge until the Bracero Program of the 1940s and 50s. Today, it is even used of people racialized as Hispanic who by their very appearance arouse suspicion (the practices in Arizona around the time State Bill 1070 is passed in 2010 confirm this). Notes Doty: "there is often a slippage between the categories of illegal immigrant and legal immigrant. Both get constructed as 'other' to those who naturally belong and become associated with a host of social dangers and disorders such as crime, drug trafficking, and terrorism" (2003:41). The label *Illegal alien* can therefore be seen as a broad, catch-all term used to signify the essential Otherness and criminality of the migrant, as well as to justify exclusionary responses. I return in some detail to the illegal alien subject-figure in the following chapter in which I explore the construction of immigration-as-crisis. First, however, I want to focus on use of the term *alien*.

The word *alien* has a long and storied history and an etymological detour is instructive at this point to illuminate how the label alien comes to be associated with threat. The word is ancient in origin, and according to the *Oxford English Dictionary* (2012) is partly a borrowing from the Anglo-Norman word *aliiene*, and partly a borrowing from the word *aliēnus* in Latin. The word emerges in medieval English circa 1350 as a verb to mean, "To make averse, hostile, or unsympathetic to someone or something; to alienate, estrange, put at a remove" (*OED* 2012, alien, verb. 1). In this sense there are profound meanings of threat and rejection that are made visceral by its active verb form.

The noun and adjective forms of alien are first seen some thirty years later in a medieval English bible known as *The Wycliffite Bible* (c1382). The meaning of alien in the Bible is infused with threat, first when it is used in Genesis to describe an outsider goddess among people (Genesis xxxv.2), and second when it is used to describe foreign sins that threaten a servant (Psalms xviii.13). Today there are three forms of the word— noun, adjective, and verb. The noun form of the word has multiple meanings: "A person who does not belong to a particular family, community, country, etc.; a foreigner, a stranger, an outsider" (*OED* 2012, alien, noun. B.1.a.); also, "strange, unfamiliar, different…hostile, repugnant" (*OED* 2012, alien, noun. 2). The adjective form is commonly used to describe someone or something that belongs to another person or place, thus emphasizing the sense that is of utility to nationalism that each person or thing has a place to which they belong. In other contexts, the word alien is used to highlight exclusion, meaning someone, "separated or excluded *from* a particular community, country, custom, etc." (*OED* 2012, alien, noun. 2a).

The conjoining of alien meaning foreign as well as a potential threat has been entrenched in US legal understanding since the Naturalization Act of 1790. Both the legal subject of the alien and the figurative subjectivity of the alien is further modified in 1798 when the Alien and Sedition laws are enacted. The laws are passed as hostilities between the US and France grow and are designed to identify internal threats to the US, giving the President the right to imprison and deport, "all such aliens as he shall judge dangerous to the peace and safety of the United States" (1798 5th Congress, S.I), either because of specific acts or in the case that the President has, "reasonable grounds to suspect [such aliens] are concerned in any treasonable or secret machinations against the government" (ibid). So this sense that the alien subject is either a threat or can reasonably be suspected of being a threat has been present in the US since the legal inception of the word, with the 1798 laws adding a further sense of duplicitousness and potential hostility to the alien subjectivity.

The word *alien* has a broad array of uses outside of the ones I have described so far in reference to people; in each use there is the sense that the alien is always-already a threat because of its essential out-of-placeness. Alien is used both as a noun and as an adjective to describe flora and fauna that are, in the words of the *OED* (2012, alien, adj. A.1.b), "brought from another country or district and subsequently naturalized; not native." So in Watson's *Cybele Britain* (1847) we have reference to a plant that is, "an imperfectly established alien" (in *OED* 2012, alien, noun. B.3). This botanical sense of the word also reinforces the idea useful to nationalism that there is a place hemmed in by national boundaries to which some people and plants are 'native', and then there are contrasting non-native alien species that seek to establish themselves. That the same word is used for both people and plants is not coincidental; and neither is the fact that these dual uses emerge in the mid-nineteenth century when goods and people are increasingly being shipped around the world. What it is important to analyze are the potential social and political materialities that are produced by such discursive crossovers. As Comaroff and Comaroff note, it is possible that the human alien and the non-human-alien are deployed, "as alibi, as a fertile allegory for rendering some people and objects strange, thereby to authenticate the limits of the ('natural') order of things; also to interpolate within it new social and political distinctions" (2001:257). In other words, ideas of *alien-ness* that are seen as intrinsic to both out-of-place species and out-of-place people by this time frame have important political functions. And discursive crossover promotes these ideas: the alien plant that has established itself imperfectly reminds us of the alien migrant who is imperfectly established—or, in an even more loaded term in the discourse on migration, not yet *assimilated*—in the national homeland.

The word alien is also used for ideas, traits, and—perhaps especially—vices, that are, in the words of the *OED*, "strange, unfamiliar, different" (2012, alien, adj. A.2). So in Shakespeare's *Henry IV* (1598) we have the King lamenting that his son's affections are, "almost an alien to the hearts of all the court and princes of my blood" (Pt 1. III.ii.34). The word is related to alienation in the anomic sense that it summons ideas of estrangement—and strangeness—of a person who is so far apart from fitting in, assimilating, or even understanding the norms and mores of a particular social situation that they are like a stranger. The sentiment is used in contemporary discourse to indicate a separation of cultures, and fears about migrants who refuse to relinquish their culture or assimilate to a supposedly homogenous American culture. So on the front page of the *New York Times* under the headline: "Far From Mexico, Making a Place Like Home" (Sack 2001), the author notes, "a huge wave of migration in the 1990s has created large pockets of Latino culture". The practice is not new, the author argues:

"For more than a century, immigrants to America…have settled close to one another, forming enclaves of familiarity in an alien culture" (ibid). This article reflects a nationalist discourse that posits hydraulic 'waves' of migration result in 'cultural enclaves' of people who either refuse to assimilate or cannot on account of the co-constituted strangeness of American and migrant culture. To describe such strangeness under the banner *alien* is to highlight two assumptions: 'their' essential difference and inability to assimilate.

ATTENDANT ALIENS

I have argued that discursive crossover functions to link seemingly disparate discourses to produce the migrant subjectivity as a threat, and also works to frame and legitimate aggressive solutions. A further concept I extend to explore these crossovers is that of the attendant character. The idea emerges in the work of Gilles Deleuze (1981) from looking at the triptych paintings of Francis Bacon—from his "Triptych, Three Studies for Figures at the Base of a Crucifixion" (1944), to the painting named "Triptych" that Bacon paints in 1983[36]. These triptychs are single works painted on three canvases in which there is a main event supplemented by figures who might appear at first glance to be incidental. Deleuze argues that such attendant characters seem to be, "a kind of spectator, a voyeur, a photograph, a passerby" (1981:13); but they are not just a witness to the main action. Rather the attendant functions, "as a constant or point of reference in relation to which a variation is assessed" (ibid). In other words, the attendant character (or characters) tells us something about the central character. The attendant is the side-show to which our eyes dart briefly before flitting back to the main theme. It is related to the main theme, but only as a point of reference, as something variable that clarifies through its difference.

In order to see how attendant characters work, consider the following diptych by artist Shepard Fairey (2017) in collaboration with Ernesto Yerena. Ironically titled, "Welcome Visitor", the illustration on two canvases juxtaposes two characters: a tourist-style poster-girl on one side, and an immigration officer on the other. Fairey notes that the diptych, "is an exploration of the contradictions between America's tourism industry and it's immigration policies; the uncomfortable collision of economic opportunism and xenophobia" (2017 obeygiant).

Image 13: "Welcome Visitor." Shephard Fairey, obeygiant, 2017

The central character is the flower- and scarf-wearing figure on the right side of the diptych, but it is not long before our eyes flit to the attendant character on the left: an officer wearing an ICE hat (signifying Immigration and Customs Enforcement). He shouts "PAPERS! Please OR DO NOT ENTER", underneath which is written "SPEAK AMERICAN!". Our eyes travel to snippets of newspaper, articles that report the internment in 1942 of "ALL PERSONS JAPANESE", and it is not long before we realize that Fairey is using what I term discursive echo to link two historical events: the internment of Japanese people during the Second World War, and the contemporary practices of immigration officers. Notes Fairey on the purposeful connection: "I hope that the level of relative comfort most people feel towards Japanese people presently puts in perspective the irrational and disproportionate fear of Muslims and Latinos that is going on now" (2017 obeygiant). So while the central character appears at first glance to be the poster-girl for travel, the attendant character of the ICE agent refers us to ongoing practices and laws that surveil and control human movement. The attendant character tells us something about the main character: that she is not just a flower-wearing poster-girl; she is also a figure who is blind to the world—the headscarf-wearing focus of immigration discrimination and exclusion.

Just as Deleuze extends his concept of the attendant to analyze both Bacon's paintings and the writings of Beckett, Michael J. Shapiro (2008) argues the Deleuzian attendant is, "robust enough to apply to other visual media such as film" (2008:52). I posit that the Deleuzian attendant can be extended even further to illustrate the process by which *meanings* cross over, not just between related images, but also between discourses that are only tangentially related. The Deleuzian attendant thereby prompts us to consider the discourse on the alien as a cultural product in three parts: the alien migrant is the symbolic figure who is central to the triptych, and our understanding of this figure is informed by the attendant presence of two other kinds of alien. The first is the alien species; plants and animals who are seen as invasive and willfully out-of-place. The second attendant is the other kind of alien who lurks menacingly in our cultural repertoire: the space alien.

I should note at this point that to write about space aliens is to raise a certain flag. In the introductory remarks at The New School conference on "The Invasive other" (2016), for example, space aliens are mentioned very briefly, and the comment is met with laughter and then never again revisited. Others note how studying space aliens as a science or studying those who *believe* in space aliens can be stigmatizing (Dean 1998:6). But belief is not a necessary condition for us to consider how space aliens relate to—and are productive of—ideas about other kinds of alien. Notes Debbora Battaglia: "A striking feature of the idea of the extraterrestrial is the extent to which conventionally distinct fields of knowledge cross-connect, collide, or pass through one another under its influence" (2005:2). Battaglia finds such crossovers useful for studying the subject-figure in the context of contact (2005:6), as well as for studying ideas about boundary negotiation (ibid). John Rieder (2008) analyzes science fiction narratives in the context of colonialism, arguing that other-worldly narratives decentralize the Earth in our universe, offer a reversal of the colonizer-colonized perspective, and are productive of ideologies of the Other that are useful for political and material rule. Jutta Weldes (2003) focuses on the legitimizing function of the space alien narrative, noting: "to the extent that it reproduces the content and structure of dominant foreign-policy discourses, it helps to produce consent to foreign policy and state action" (2003:7). In other words, discursive crossover between space alien discourses and political discourses aids in the production of consent for political and material actions.

Alien Invasion

Extraterrestrial narratives are centrally productive of the space alien as Other. As an attendant character in the discourse, and working through discursive crossover, I argue that the proliferation of the space alien in the 1950s—particularly in narratives of the alien invasion genre—leads to a significant negative transformation of the alien migrant subjectivity. This is because the extraterrestrial is not just any kind of Other; the most common trope of the invading space alien is that they are devious, invasive, and resource-hungry: in other words, a total threat to the nation and 'its people'.

The words *alien* meaning space alien and *alien* meaning human are homonyms—two words with the same spelling and pronunciation but with different meanings—but the *OED* nonetheless confirms the crossover effect of these two word forms. For example, at the end of the dictionary entry on the noun form of alien—"A person who does not belong...a foreigner, a stranger, an outsider" (2012, alien, noun. B.1.a)—the *OED* notes, "In later use sometimes *influenced* by sense B.5" (ibid, emphasis mine), that is, "An (intelligent) being from another planet; an extraterrestrial" (2012, alien, noun. B.5). In other words, when we use the word alien to describe an out-of-place human it invokes the attendant character of the space alien who says they 'come in peace', but then goes on to wreak havoc and destruction.

Use of the word 'intelligent' in this *Oxford English Dictionary* definition of space alien is somewhat paradoxical since while human intelligence is highly valued, space alien intelligence is commonly portrayed as a threat. Intelligence in humans marks them as 'extraordinary' and makes them eligible for migrant status. The US Citizenship and Immigration Service, for example, will grant O-1 visas, "for the individual who possesses extraordinary ability" (USCIS.gov).
In science fiction narratives, however, the intelligence of extraterrestrials is routinely seen as a threat, either because they use

that intelligence to develop advanced technology, or because they use it to deceive humans. In many contemporary science fiction narratives—Tim Burton's *Mars Attacks!* (1996) springs to mind—alien intelligence is used to outwit humans with the goal of using earth for their own consumption[37]. These aliens are not to be trusted; like the alien human conjured by the Alien and Sedition Acts of 1798, there is a discursive echo here that aliens are engaged in, "secret machinations" for their own nefarious ends (US Congress 1798).

Mars Attacks! (1996) is an alien invasion movie that poses a satirical counterpart to the alien invasion blockbuster *Independence Day* (1996) that is also released that year. Written in the concluding years of a century that sees two world wars and the invention and use of nuclear weapons, *Mars Attacks!* (1996) paints a picture of deceitful and sinister alien invaders. It is no accident, however, that the movie opens to an idyllic rural Kentucky scene. If we are not attuned to the racisms and kinds of othering that are central to the logic of nationalism, we might miss the discursive crossover that this scene invokes. A pink-faced farmer drives up to a neighbor and questions him over his assumed cultural practices: "Hey, howdy there, Mr. Lee", he says. "What is this? Filipino New Year's?... you're cooking up a feast. I can smell it all the way from the interstate" (1996:1).

Image 14: Screenshot of opening scene of Mars Attacks!
Director: Tim Burton, 1996

We are expecting a space alien invasion in the American heart-land, but here is an allusion to another kind of alien invasion: a 'racial', 'ethnic', or cultural one. Perhaps this is a satirical poke intended to expose everyday racism on earth, but it presents as little more than a scratch at the surface of racism. Indeed, because the scene appears as light humor it allows us to laugh at the racism rather than thinking critically about the moral implications of such practices. The representation of Mr. Lee as 'different', while satire, could even *add* to the hegemony of human difference. A few scenes later, the space aliens in *Mars Attacks!* use their intelligence to play into a US diplomatic wel-come, then annihilate the US military and government. After repeating the trope, "We come in peace" several times, the aliens gleefully obliterate the welcoming committee in a mur-derous and indiscriminate rampage. Diplomacy is a failure and perhaps the takeaway is not to trust anybody; that all aliens are potentially deadly interlopers. *Mars Attacks!* employs another trope that is common to the alien invasion genre: the idea that an attack by aliens brings together a divided humanity. Perhaps the opening scene is there to remind us how divided humans are because of our everyday racisms. And this then serves to contrast with the narrative that follows; how in the common enemy of the space alien, 'we' become united against a new 'other'[38].

The routine assumption in science fiction narratives—particularly those of the alien invasion genre—is that space aliens use their intelligence for war (rather than, say, to develop advanced healthcare or education systems). And this trope of the intelligent yet hostile space alien has a long and illustri-ous history. From the earliest science fiction narratives such as Lucian's *True History* (~160-190), to the highly influential *Gulliver's Travels* (1726) and H.G. Well's *War of the Worlds* (1898), to contemporary alien invasion movies such as *Mars Attacks!* (1996), there is this trope of alien intelligence and belligerence. For example, in Lucian's narrative that is written at the height of the Roman empire, the protagonist happens upon, "a great country" (160-190:14), which he then goes on to attack. However, the inhabitants of this foreign land join forces with warriors from other lands. A foot and air war ensue, with the victors building a double wall that detains the losing side in perpetual night until a treaty can be established (160-190:27-29)[39].

The attendant nature of True History acts as a point of reference for our contemporary political landscape. Inhabitants from different places band together for outright war; they are defeated and put in place by a wall so formidable that it cuts off the sun and detains them in darkness. If we consider the migrants from varying Latin American nations at our contemporary southern border, how they are portrayed as an 'invasion' of illegal aliens, and how the 'solution' is seen as a great wall, then this space alien narrative acts as an attendant point of reference that affirms the proposed augmented contemporary wall as a commonsense solution.

Swift's narrative *Gulliver's Travels* (1726) draws on Lucian's *True History* and features strange beings who are both intelligent and belligerent. Organized into warring empires, such beings are represented as, "mighty powers [who have] ...been engaged in a most obstinate war for six-and-thirty moons" (1726/2010:52). Working in the manner of discursive crossover, this tale is another allegory that prompts us to question the racializing ideas of European colonialism without specifically mentioning the colonial socio-economic system that is materially supported by construction of the racialized Other. Reflecting these themes, the powerful and intelligent King of Brobdingnag notes to Gulliver: "I cannot but conclude the Bulk of your Natives to be the most pernicious Race of little odious Vermin that Nature ever suffered to crawl upon the Surface of the Earth" (1726/2010:222). And so, humans are not just a homogenous race of animals, they are satirized as odious vermin, lower-order scavengers. The switch in perspective that this type of satire offers is not lost on readers; it is, according to Rieder (2008) a, "satirical reversal of hierarchies" (2008:4), one that demands the audience imagine themselves on the losing end of history.

Another kind of homeland invasion takes place in the South African alien thriller *District 9* (Blomkamp 2009), a movie inspired by the physical separation of the 'races' during the Apartheid era (1948 – 1994). When a large alien spaceship is abandoned in the sky directly above Johannesburg, its sickly alien inhabitants are exiled to a government camp called District 9, and separation between aliens and humans is mandated. The plot, however, is more about a human who becomes sickly after using the alien's technology: "Hunted and hounded through the bizarre back alleys of an alien shantytown, [one human] will discover what it means to be the ultimate outsider on your own planet" (Sony Pictures 2014). The marketing campaign for the movie plays on the idea of both the hunted alien and species separation. For a year before the movie comes out, banners, posters, and stickers are distributed in public spaces across large metropolitan areas with an 800 number for people to "Report Non-Humans". No indication is given that it is a marketing campaign for a movie.

Image 15: Poster for District 9 Marketing Campaign.
Shaire Productions for Sony Pictures, 2009

When people call the number, they are directed to a fictitious company called Multi-National United. Perhaps this hints at the global magnitude of alien problems, of how all nations need to come together to fight a new 'us and them'. Upon visiting the Multi-National United website, users are offered the choice of entering either the human or non-human side. The implication here is one of species alterity, that even on a website, the alien and the human must be kept separate and have different experiences because of their species difference.

If discursive crossover highlights the possibility of attendant scenes of meaning, in H.G. Well's *War of the Worlds* (1898) we have both attendant aliens who comprise the informative side characters in the alien migrant triptych. In this one discursive artifact, Wells combines themes of warring space aliens and invasive alien plants. Such attendant characters serve as a point of reference that illuminates the frailty of human dominance in the universe and highlights the necessity of species separation in order to avoid destruction. As such, *War of the Worlds* can be thought of as an anti-miscegenation discourse, a common trope in space alien narratives, and one that functions as a dire warning against species mixing.

War of the Worlds is written at the end of the nineteenth century, some twenty years after Germany's swift and decisive victories in Eastern France lead to the unification and militarization of the German Empire. England, at this point, is heavily invested in its imperial project. Slavery has ended throughout the British Empire beginning in 1833, but trade in gold and ivory from western Africa, as well as the discovery of diamonds and gold in southern Africa, means that wars are being fought on many fronts on the African continent in an attempt to maintain imperial dominance. The story begins with a telling quote from *The Anatomy of Melancholy*: "But who shall dwell in these worlds if they be inhabited?... Are we or they Lords of the World?" (1898/2004:4). This quote is particularly telling if we consider the context that Wells is writing in. As I have noted, the last decade of the Victorian era is defined by aggressive colonial practices by the British and other Empires around the world. *War of the Worlds* can thereby be seen as a political allegory that prompts a reversal of perspective on colonialism by situating England on the receiving end of a brutal colonizing attack. Notes Rieder: "The dominant strain of Well's critique of colonialist ideology...is indignation against colonial arrogance, an emotion rooted in the political and historical moment from which is arises, that of the climax of British world dominion" (2008:133). Thinking on a universal rather than a global plane decenters the earth in the universe and allows Wells to postulate what might happen to humans if lifeforms exist on other planets who have a similarly ruthless colonial mindset. Using space aliens as the antagonists also allows Wells to highlight the brutality of earthly colonialism without specifically mentioning it. Once again, discursive crossover allows for an exploration in one domain that which cannot be safely explored in another.

Following the trope that we have become familiar with, the antagonist space aliens in *War of the Worlds* are highly intelligent and technologically sophisticated, "practically mere brains, wearing different bodies according to their needs" (1898/2004:248). They are from the outset untrustworthy, fearful characters, with, "intellects vast and cool and unsympathetic [who] regarded this earth with envious eyes, and slowly and surely drew their plans against us" (1898/2004:6). In this modeling of the universe, the aliens are the uber-rational beings on the 'brain' end of Cartesian dualism, while the humans are mere bodies, incapable of such intellectual and technological sophistication. When the space aliens do arrive, they are organized; their weapons catastrophic. And yet they, too, are vulnerable to the alien environment. After a weed-like plant brought to Earth by the Martians, "intentionally or accidentally" (1898/2004:246) grows out of control, developing on earth, in the words of Wells, with, "gigantic and of unparalleled fecundity" (1898/2004:280), the space aliens are destroyed. This conclusion to the narrative emphasizes alien plant species as invasive and over-competitive and reifies the supposed dangers of species mixing. As a character in the narrative, these invasive alien weeds might at first seem incidental. But as attendant characters they point to fearful ideas of species difference, as well as to the necessity of fixity to avoid national disaster.

The last passages of *War of the Worlds* are ominous. Concludes Wells: "we cannot regard this planet as being fenced in and a secure abiding place for Man" (1898/2004:347). In other words, fences (or walls) will not save humanity from the alien: mobility of the alien—and contact with the alien—will always be a threat. If we view this narrative using the concept of discursive crossover, we see the attendant aliens (both plant and space) as fetishized subjects that symbolize an entire order under attack: the order of a universe divided into secure places for humanity.

Contemporary extraterrestrial alien narratives make

good use of the dual ideas of species difference and anti-miscegenation and the kinds of doomsday scenarios that emerge when mixing occurs. In *Transformers: Age of Extinction* (2014), for example, a character called Lockdown decries: "All this species mixing with species, it upsets the cosmic balance" (as quoted on IMDb.com). For the scientists in *Alien* (1979), the mission is to collect a sample of alien life, but the story is inverted when the horrifying space alien uses the human body as a resource for its own breeding. The message is viscerally clear: when aliens and humans mix there are violent and deadly results. And even in space alien narratives in which the alien is beneficent and it is the humans who are not to be trusted, there is still the implication that each species must stay in its rightful place. In *E.T. the Extraterrestrial* (1982), for example, the driving force of the narrative is that E.T. must still *Go Home*.

Discursive Crossover for Subversion

Discursive crossover functions in alien discourses to naturalize ideas of species difference, belonging, and fixity; it can also be used as a tactic to subvert or counter the dominant narrative. In order to rally support for migrants, for example, artist Favianna Rodriquez deploys the symbol of the monarch butterfly with each wing showing a human face. Under the butterfly is the phrase "Migration is Natural" (2012 favianna.tumbler). The image is made into a sticker as part of Rodriguez's campaign called *Migration is Beautiful*. Notes Rodriguez on her purposeful connection between butterfly migration and human migration: "The monarch butterfly has come to represent the beauty of migration... Like the monarch butterfly, human beings cross borders in search of safer habitats. Like the monarch butterfly, human beings cross borders in order to survive" (ibid). In this image, and in subsequent posters, Rodriguez deploys discursive crossover between migratory animals and migrant humans in order to counter negative ideas about human migration, and in order to promote positive social change. Within one month of the image's creation in 2012, the butterfly symbol begins to appear on buses, banners, murals, and in demonstrations all over the country (nd culturestrike.org). The symbol of the butterfly is used widely in the immigrant justice movement to highlight that antipathy to species mobility is idiosyncratic as well as prone to political manipulation.

Image 16: Sticker from Migration is Beautiful campaign.
Favianna Rodriguez, 2012

Discursive crossover is also invoked to counter the animalizations that are produced by both immigration practices and the discourse on human migration. During the time Arizona enacts State Bill 1070, for example, artists Shephard Fairy and Ernesto Yerena create the "We Are Human" poster series (2009 obeygiant). They distribute the images widely, both online as free print-outs, and as posters available for free in Fairey's Obey Headquarters in Los Angeles. The posters are subsequently used at protests in major cities across the US. I highlight the ubiquity of these protest images not to suggest that the more popular an image is, the more currency it carries. Instead, the broad uptake of the 'We Are Human' message points to the dominance of the dehumanized migrant message. In other words, reaffirming the humanity of migrants through use of the 'We Are Human' message is seen as a necessary tactic to counteract the hegemony of a discourse that produces migrants as less than human.

Image set 17: Posters from We Are Human campaign.
Shepard Fairey and Ernesto Yerena. obeygiant, 2009

One last example of people using discursive crossover to subvert the discourse that stigmatizes the alien migrant centers around the practice of calling a government hotline number to report unauthorized migrants who may have committed crimes. Such a hotline is created in 2017 after Trump signs executive order 13768 titled, "Enhancing Public Safety in the Interior of the United States". The hotline is run by US Immigration and Customs Enforcement (ICE), who states its goal is to, "support victims of crimes committed by criminal aliens" (ice.gov 2018). The Department of Homeland Security Secretary John Kelly (6 June 2017) clarifies why such a hotline is important:

Effective border security must be augmented by vigorous interior enforcement and the administration of our immigration laws in a manner that serves the national interest. As with any sovereign nation, we have a fundamental right and obligation to enforce our immigration laws in the interior of the United States —particularly against criminal aliens.

The implication in this statement is that "criminal aliens" challenge "the national interest" (ibid). Hence, calling a hotline against your neighbor who may be an unauthorized migrant (or who equally may just be someone against whom you have a grudge) is not only your right, it is your patriotic obligation.

The hotline is launched—almost certainly unintentionally—on the same day of the year that fans of the *Alien* films annually celebrate the franchise, and the hotline is subsequently flooded with hoax calls (bbc.com 27 Apr 2017). Many of these calls refer to space aliens in order to subvert the efficacy of the hotline and in order to counter the material practices of immigration that arrest, detain, deport, and exclude people judged to be 'criminal aliens'. The discursive crossover is intentional, and ironic messages on twitter stoke the subversion. Notes one user: "The # for Trump's hotline to report 'criminal aliens' is 855-48-VOICE. Please do not call this number to describe plots of X-Files episodes" (@dubsteppenwolf 26 April 2017). Or another twitter user, who writes: "Seriously, I will be calling 1-855-48-VOICE very soon and very often about ET, Alien, probably Predator too, about the crimes they committed" (@XLeoTheGreatX 26 April 2017). Such subversive messages can be seen as deploying discursive crossover in order to stoke a counter-discourse against ideas and practices that discriminate and exclude people judged to be 'alien'.

△△△

Discursive crossover is deployed in the immigration discourse from the 1870s onwards to produce the migrant subjectivity as a uniquely degraded and animal-like Other, a person who invades the nation and who out-competes the national, and a person with whom mixing would be disastrous. Supported by these constructions, aggressive state responses such as indefinite detention, militarized border control, and family separation are produced as commonsense.

For out-of-place animal and plants species, the discourse is one of invasion, over-abundance, and contamination. For extraterrestrial aliens, the discourse is one of invasion, deception, and anti-miscegenation. I have suggested that these discourses act like attendant characters to the central discourse on the human migrant. Such characters may present as unrelated, but I contend their presence should not be ignored. Through their crossover interactions these attendant aliens modify the migrant subjectivity, degrading and animalizing such humans and promoting them as deceptive invaders of the national space.

Discursive crossover is deployed in the discourse on immigration through a language of ideas, but the power effects are both political and material. Such crossovers occur when the migrant is described using animal metaphors (hordes of foreigners, swarms of migrants), when migrant flora and fauna are described in anthropomorphic terms (invading alien plants, illegal animals), and when the arrival of migrants is spoken of as an invasion. And just as the descriptions crossover, so do the 'solutions' proposed. This is because such crossover formations legitimate ideas of species difference and so the logic of species separation. The effect of discursive crossover, on other words, is to produce consent for practices and policies of immigration restriction and exclusion.

Discursive crossover heightens the sense of the unwanted human migrant as always-already a threat, but it does not just help define the migrant subjectivity in problematized ways; it also helps make commonsense of restrictive and exclusionary material solutions. In the following chapter I focus on contemporary discourses that promote the subject-figure of the migrant as symptomatic of immigration-as-crisis, and on the primary solution that Trump and others have proposed: the wall.

5/IMMIGRATION-AS-CRISIS

In this chapter, I explore the discourse of the 'illegal alien' and show how the language and symbolism used to produce such people contributes both to their denigration and to the construction of immigration-as-crisis. Leaning on the concept of moral panics as explored by Stanley Cohen (1972), I question whether today's understanding of the 'crisis' on the contemporary southern border is characteristic of a moral panic. This chapter defines moral panics and situates the immigration discourse in the moral panics literature in order to answer the call made by Cohen in 2002 that the theory, "be updated to fit the refractions of multi-mediated social worlds" (1972/2002:xxxviii).

Using a genealogical approach, I look to the figurative subject of the Mexican in the US from the early 1800s. In this discourse—through a series of articulating racisms and nationalisms—the Mexican is produced as a particular kind of Other to the US: the 'internal enemy' figure who must be excised through both discursive and material means. I then turn to three contemporary collective subject-figures who are frequently evoked by Trump in discursive formations that amplify their deviancy: criminalized Mexicans, the 'animal gang-members' of MS-13, and the 'caravan of migrants' that is said to amass at the contemporary southern border. Finally, I show how discursive echo between historical subject-figures and contemporary ones makes sense of immigration-as-crisis, as well as legitimating Trump's 'solution' to 'build the wall'.

PATTERN OF A PANIC

When we hear in horror headlines, "An Army of Illegal Aliens is About to Storm our Border" (Poff 2018), or read, "Homeland Security says surge in illegal border crossings is a 'crisis,' warrants military deployment" (Miroff 2018), or hear Trump declare a national emergency because, "[t]he southern border is a major entry point for criminals, gang members, and illicit narcotics" (Trump 2019b), there is little doubt that the US's immigration discourse is in crisis mode.

Such stories are characteristic of what Marshall McLuhan (1964) first terms a moral panic, in which "Western values, built on the written word [are] affected by the electric media" (1964/1994:82). But to what extent is the current discourse on immigration a moral panic? Does the multi-media nature of contemporary discourse amplify that sense of panic? And do the central characters in the discourse on immigration —the illegal aliens—represent folk devils (to use Cohen's 1972 term), a sort of stereotypical scapegoat to whom we can transfer both our fears and focus our solutions?

Although the term moral panic first emerges in the writing of McLuhan (1964), it is Stanley Cohen (1972) who crystallizes the term into its present meaning of an exaggerated reaction to newsworthy 'things' compared to less exaggerated reactions and also compared to other social problems that may be more problematic (1972/2002:vii). In other words, such stories can be seen as episodic fear narratives containing fearful central characters that together promote exaggerated reactions. The media operate as a channel for the general dispersion of such stories and help to produce such stories and characters as commonsense. As Goode and Nachman (1994) note, such media operate as, "a vehicle to elevate a latent fear or concern into wide-spread, mutual awareness" (1994:163).

Mass media stories such as the one titled, "An Army of Illegal Aliens is About to Storm our Border" (Poff 2018), for example, are exaggerated characterizations that do three things: create a stereotypical scapegoat (the 'illegal alien' who is said to be the source of the crisis); help to produce consent for exaggerated reactions (only a military solution can combat 'an army'); and attract far more attention than larger social problems such as income inequality, or the loss of 5.5 million manufacturing jobs in the US since 2000 (Hernandez 2018). Furthermore, in stating their 'army' is about to 'storm our border', such reporting organizes a visceral 'theirs vs ours' definition of the situation, one that pushes blame onto the 'illegal alien'. Bonnie Honig (2001) notes that an analysis of scapegoating forces us to attend to what she calls: "the *politics* of foreignness—the cultural symbolic organization of a social crisis into a resolution-producing confrontation between an 'us' and a 'them' (2001:34). In other words, the illegal alien scapegoat is not just the consummate figurative subject; rather the production of such subjects organizes immigration-as-crisis, and it is this understanding that lends legitimacy for political and material 'solutions'.

For Cohen, moral panics are painted in predictable discursive patterns that contain a number of seeming contradictions. The objects or subjects of the panic are both new and familiar (illegal aliens are about to storm our border; migrants have been journeying for centuries). The objects or subjects of the panic are dangerous in themselves but also flag-bearers for underlying social ills (an army of illegal aliens will work for cheap; millions of manufacturing jobs have been lost in recent times). The panic is predictable, but also requires claims-makers, "accredited experts [who] must explain the perils hidden behind the superficially harmless" (1972/2002:viii).

Claims-makers today can take the form of individuals or groups seeking political or social change as well as those who seek to frame public debate or provide collective definitions. While they can be public figures seeking to promote policies, or church leaders seeking to define deviant acts, they can also be news pundits making over-reactive and fear-filled claims to further their own fame and increase viewer ratings. When it comes to lurid claims in the discourse on immigration, there is both money and power to be gained. The story about illegals storming the border, for example, is written for the website of Fox News radio host Todd Starnes, a journalist who—in his own words—courts the attention of, "freedom-loving patriots who want to fight back" (Todd Starnes 2019). As Portes and Rumbaut (2006) point out, "playing on these fears has...proven lucrative for a host of nativist associations, agitators, and pundits" (2006:118). The claims-maker (or what Becker (1963) calls the moral entrepreneur) has the ability to shape the discourse, but also has the *incentive* to do so. There is something to be gained, for example, when Trump calls Canadian-born Ted Cruz an "anchor baby" during a campaign stop in 2016 (Diamond 2016). Such verbiage denigrates Cruz by suggesting he has less of a right to run for office because of his birthplace. It also reinforces the idea that so-called 'anchor babies'—the children of unauthorized migrants—are deserving of less rights than the children of citizens[40]. In using such lurid symbolic language to denigrate the nationalized Other, Trump drums up the support of nationalist sympathizers. One of the political and material effects of this evocation is to promote himself as the 'rightful' national candidate.

Cohen's initial use of the term *moral panic* is in reference to the Mods and Rockers, groups of youths that emerge in 1960s seaside Britain during a period of widespread social change. In the process of shaping societal reaction, the media characterize the Mods and Rockers in highly stereotypical ways, focusing on traits that present them as a public threat. Such stereotypifications are highly exaggerated, so while little actual violence occurs, for example, it is presented in the news media as if *all* the Mods and Rockers are engaged in deadly violence. Following is such an article from the *Daily Express* in 1964. It is printed the day after a Bank Holiday weekend, a time in which seaside towns like Margate attract holidaying families, as well as groups of youths venturing out for fun. Although only a handful of scuffles break out between the youths, the *Daily Express* defines the situation as if two differential and opposing groups —the Mods and Rockers—engage in a veritable orgy of crime. Notes the article: "The 1964 boys smeared the traditional post-card scene with blood and violence" (19 May 1964, in Cohen 1967). Such visceral characterizations create an 'us and them' definition of the situation: uber-violent youths who destroy Britain's 'traditional postcard scene'. But generalized beliefs about the supposed deviancy of the Mods and Rockers resonate with the *Daily Express's* readers. The definition of the situation as young people defying the norms of the 'traditional' makes 'sense' to newspaper readers, supporting widespread beliefs about juvenile delinquency in a time of rapid social change. The reaction of the public—or rather the exaggerated *over-reaction* —is in part why this episode is constitutive of a moral panic.

While Cohen is centrally interested in the process of deviance amplification, there is one more important step in this process: to produce consent for a series of escalating material state responses. Cohen (1967:126) explains as such:

> If you are dealing with a group that is vicious, destructive, caus-ing your community a financial loss, and symbolically repudi-ating your cherished values, then you are justified to respond punitively...By the logic of their own definitions, the agents of control have to escalate the measures they take and propose to take to deal with the problem.

In other words, *if* we have a crisis caused by deviant Others, then the outcome of such deviancy amplification is to pro-duce consent for dramatic punitive solutions. Fearful beliefs about the Mods and Rockers, for example, prompt hundreds of extra police officers to be deployed to seaside towns on busy weekends. This results in mass arrests of what the police label 'troublemakers' (although very few cases of malicious damage or violence are ever brought). A further result that Cohen men-tions is the idea of setting up road blocks to exclude such youths and, "to prevent any invasion" (1967:127). In other words, the panicked overreaction of both claims-makers and the public to the supposed deviancy of stereotypical folk devils lends legitimacy to a series of increasingly restrictionist and exclusionary responses.

Mediated Trials

A genealogical tangent is appropriate here to show how an early moral panic over a supposedly deviant subject-figure leads to deadly material outcomes. The folk devil in question is the essentially figurative subject of the witch, and in many ways both the witch 'crisis' and the deadly state responses to this crisis, are facilitated by the new and ready availability of textual media.

The panicked preoccupation with witches begins in fifteenth century Europe and spreads to the American colonies. Although Thomas Aquinas' *Summa Contra Gentiles* (c.1259–1265), has been around for a couple of hundred years prior to the invention of the printing press, the ideas it contains about witches have limited reach. After Gutenberg invents the press in circa 1450, however, there is suddenly an expansion of ideas about the witch, as well as an expanded reach of these ideas. Such ideas focus on the supposed immoral character of the witch, the many deviant behaviors of the witch, and tells readers—as well as those who are read to—how to identify and prosecute witches, as well as the best ways to kill them. In other words, *Summa Contra Gentiles* not only amplifies the supposedly deviant nature of the witch, it also lends legitimacy to extermination as a solution.

One further text helps to amplify the deviant nature of the witch and likewise provides for material solutions. The *Malleus Maleficarum* (or the Hammer of Witches), written by the inquisitors Kramer and Sprenger and published in 1486-1487, is perhaps the most influential text in the construction of the witch. The text is rife with passages from the Bible that support the idea of witches—particularly female witches—being the root of evil and, thus, in the Christian worldview, of all social ills. One of the outcomes of the publication and widespread dissemination of these ideas is to consolidate the figure of the witch into a single demonic—and demonized—character (Broedel 2004:3). In other words, while the construction of the witch is supported by claims-makers like Kramer and Sprenger—as well as by church leaders who have a vested interest in spreading such claims—the widespread dissemination of their claims turns an assortment of competing ideas about witches into a homogenous character that we recognize as a reductionist and stereotypical folk devil.

But the witch crisis is never just about supposedly deviant females; as Silvia Federici (2004) argues in *Caliban and the Witch,* the witch crisis has more to do with reorganizing social relations during the radical move to a capitalist market economy. Accompanying this transformation is a concerted effort to quell any kind of social protest, and central to this effort, Federici claims, is, "an attack… against all forms of collective sociality and sexuality" (ibid). In other words, Federici conceives of the witch crisis as a systematic re-ordering of gender and power relations that are necessary to facilitate the move to a capitalist world order. Notes Federici: "The sexual division of labor that emerged from it not only fixed women to reproductive work, but increased their dependence on men, enabling the state and employers to use the male wage as a means to control women's labor" (2004:75). The discourse that accompanies this new gendered division of labor produces the figure of the witch as a uniquely degraded scapegoat. Such scapegoating distracts from the root cause of the crisis: the radical shift in labor relations that are necessary for the 'success' of capitalism. So, the figure of the witch not only distracts from the economic basis of the crisis, such social practices also *produce* the subject of the witch. The stereotypical scapegoat, in other words, is produced as a deviant figure for political and material ends.

MEXICAN PERIL

Not all 'problem people' are characterized equally in the immigration discourse. Different problematized subjectivities take center stage at different historical periods according to the particular socio-economic and historical conditions that have animated their construction. A genealogical analysis attunes us to the shifts in such subjectivity problematizations, as well as to the technologies of power through which such subjectivities are administered. In the following section, I analyze the discourse that constructs one of the major scapegoats of the immigration system. It is a figure whose construction is aided by discursive crossover, and it is a figure who symbolizes an articulation of ideas about poverty, criminality, and mass mobility. Much like all scapegoats, it is a stereotypical and reductionist caricature, a figure who is represented as both cause and symptom of a failed immigration system. It is the Mexican, or rather *Mexicans* plural, since from their emergence in US media in the early 1800s, they are represented not as individuals with agency but as a collective who amass, surge, and otherwise threaten the nation and 'its people'.

While some theorists find animosity against migrants to be cyclical and linked to periods of economic turmoil in the US (see Bustamante 2002:7), a focus on discourse prompts us to see how the figure of the migrant is useful at particular historical moments for the varying constructions of the nation-state. Ali Behdad (2005), takes such an approach, seeing the prevarications between ideas of immigrant hospitality and hostility as having a productive function in national culture (2005:17). A genealogical backtrack is useful here to illuminate when the Mexican subject-figure is invoked for the first time in US discourse, and to show how this figurative subject helps co-constitute the national subject. This genealogical approach also shows how the discursive echo between historical representations of Mexicans in the US and contemporary representations helps to *produce* Mexicans (and others) as criminal migrants.

I should emphasize that when the collective figure of the Mexican appears in US media in the early 1800s, they are not represented as migrants. A system of immigration has not been created yet, and a system that restricts the immigration of people from Mexico does not emerge until well over a century later. And yet, from the start, the collective figure of the Mexican is represented in the US as a particular kind of Other. This othering takes the form of articulating racisms and nationalisms. In many senses, from the very outset, it is a colonizing discourse, one that concerns itself with creating and maintaining social boundaries through an evocation of 'internal enemies'. Ann Laura Stoler (1995:207) notes as much on the discourses of European colonizers:

> In this regard it is no accident that those discourses on nation and citizenship articulated so strongly with those on race. Both clarified the national, enforced class distinctions and affirmed the fiction of a North European centered homo europeaus at the same time. Both invoked an internal enemy. And both attempted to designate those interior frontiers that would guard bourgeois society's boundaries—and defend those it was feverishly making.

This internal enemy is a useful concept as we consider the collective subject-figure of the Mexican. Chiefly, this is because, from the very outset, Mexicans are constructed as an unwanted alien presence. Such ideas are seen as productive to the US, because through making the Mexican subject-figure as an internal alien enemy, there is a shoring up of ideas about what makes an American. In other words, nativist representations of migrants as alien enemies serve productive functions for national identity.

The collective figure of the Mexican first appears in media in the US in the 1830s as a negatively racialized caricature, summarized by one Texas plantation owner as: "ignorant, bigoted, and stupid and lazy, interested only in pleasure" (1836, in Kelley 2011:141). And then in the years surrounding the annexation of Texas in 1845, such negative representations abound. Travel writer Dr. Ferdinand Roemer of Germany, for example, describes the Mexicans he encounters in San Antonio in 1846 as, "a lazy, indolent race" (in Bremer 2004:42). Note that he is not just describing a specific person or group of people in San Antonio; he is using his observations to make pronouncements about an entire 'race' of Mexicans. Such racializing ideas about Mexicans are co-constituted against ideas of Anglo-Americans, people who are increasingly invoked as the 'rightful' inhabitants of Texas. This understanding is iterated in an article in the *Martinsburg Gazette* that is printed a few days after the annexation of Texas. The unnamed author (6 March 1845) writes:

> The spirit of Progressive Democracy now aims at universal empire, and the Anglo Saxon is proclaimed by them Emperor of the world. Where is this lust after territory now to cease?—the 'area of freedom' will soon begin to ask for more elbowroom, and then Canada, Mexico, Cuba and California must be ours.

This ideology posits Anglo-Americans as racially superior global overlords who have nothing but a 'lust' for 'freedom' (rather than a desire for land). This idea of being rightfully in Texas is supported by the ideology of manifest destiny that O'Sullivan conceives of in July of 1845 in order to support the annexation. But Mexican people already live in the area, of course, and so as part of a process of producing consent for annexation and expansion, Mexicans are invoked as internal enemies to US 'progress'.

But the discourse on Mexicans is not just about their supposed 'nature'; it is also about the negative impact of that nature on the lands that they work. Of the lands and people along the Rio Grande river, for example, Henry Smith Lane—future Senator and Governor of Indiana—writes in November of 1846 that they are, "very fertile but miserably cultivated; the people are lazy, ignorant and perfidious with no patriotism, no public spirit, no enterprise and it would be a great mercy for them to take their country" (in Guardino 2017:114). As with representations of the Irish and Indians that I discussed in chapter four, this ideology of a 'lazy people'—when conjoined with ideas about their unproductive lands—helps to produce consent for subsequent land appropriation.

After President Polk's proposition to purchase lands from Mexico is rejected, a war ensues. The Mexican-American War[41] is fought from 1846-1848, after which Mexico is forced to cede control of key territories, including areas that are now the present-day states of Texas, Arizona, New Mexico, California, as well as parts of Colorado, Utah, and Nevada. Now, more than ever, Americans see themselves as the 'rightful' owners and inhabitants of the lands. But the Treaty of Guadalupe that concludes the Mexican-American war does not stop the expansionist dreams of some members of Congress. Buoyed by the ideology of manifest destiny, many southern Democrats, for example, advocate for a continued expansion into the Mexican Republic (Tucker et al. 2013:514). Perhaps in order to support these expansionist ideologies, as well as to control the 'internal enemy' figure of the Mexican, the negative discourse about Mexicans continues.

Ideas about Mexicans in the US are continually co-constituted against ideas of the American during this time period. On the front page of the *New-York Daily Times* from 1851, for example, is a report titled "Mining Intelligence" from the *Stockton Journal* that states:

> Every American naturally desires to work on his own hook, to exemplify his independence, and when the chances are equal, ninety out of every hundred will prefer it. The capitalists are forced to pay heavier prices for hands, and in some cases can hardly get them for any sum. Mexicans...do the burthen of the work in the southern placers, and it is likely that they will continue to do it. Raised as serfs, they know no organization or restraint...Lazy and vicious, they work only when forced to do it, and then, to secure a living, naturally become dependent on the enterprise of others. Thus, the southern mines are peopled with a set of men equally as much slaves as the negroes on the plantations of Texas or Louisiana.

20 Oct 1851:1

This report in one of the most widely-read publications of the day (the precursor to the *New York Times*) is productive of the figure of the 'independent American'. Co-constituted against this is the collective figure of the Mexican, who (paradoxically) is seen here as both "lazy and vicious" (ibid)[42]. The American is constructed here as 'naturally' industrious and independent —so independent, in fact, that the capitalist is forced to pay more to secure his labor. Mexicans, in contrast, are represented as lower order laborers, disorganized, and uncontrollable. Furthermore, they are seen as being "raised as serfs" (ibid), rather than this being a form of unfree labor that is forced upon people, in part because they have been racialized as cheap. Furthermore, it is seen as due to their own 'nature' that Mexicans (always in the plural) become 'dependent' on the organization and enterprise of others.

This discursive co-constitution is widespread in the mid-nineteenth century. Writes John Russell Bartlett in 1854, for example: "Mexican indolence cannot stand by the side of the energy and industry of the Americans and Europeans" (1854:40). And this discourse extends from the Mexican individual to the Mexican nation itself, just as land disputes between the two governments—as well as 'incursions' by people from both nations—continue. In 1853, for example, the *New York Times* reports that the Mexican President, "has lost nearly all his former energy; [his government] is lazy and careless" (23 Sept 1853:2). (1854:40). And a report from Ringgold Barracks in Texas notes, "What a miserable country Mexico must be under such rule! She has elements of power within her, but never can they be developed under such turbulent rulers, and such a thievish, dirty, lazy population" (in the *New York Times* 13 April 1855:2).

In an attempt to end land disputes and incursions that stand in the way of completion of the southern intercontinental railroad, the Gadsden Treaty is signed in 1854. Although some members of the US government still believe expansion into Mexico will continue, the Gadsden Treaty solidifies the present-day political border between Mexico and the US. An actual border, however, does not materialize until seventy years later. Notes Douglas S. Massey (2009:7):

> Until this time, the Mexico–US border was little more than a line on a map and was mostly unmarked (Massey et al. 2002). In response to growing immigration from Mexico, however, in 1924 Congress created the US Border Patrol and for the first time, the border with Mexico became a tangible reality.
>
> The creation of the Border Patrol brought into existence a new category of Mexican in the United States—the illegal migrant.

In this understanding, it is creation of the US Border Patrol in 1924 that produces Mexicans in the US as 'illegals'. And as we turn to the contemporary discourse on illegals, we will see the discursive echoes with these historical discourses that animate and reify the Mexican illegal alien subjectivity.

CRIMINALIZING ALIENS

Surrounding the passage of many immigration laws is a discourse that amplifies the deviance and essential Otherness of the migrant figure. Such laws then reify those distinctions into official state categories such as: 'alien' (1790 Naturalization Law); 'coolie' (1862 Act to Prohibit the 'Coolie Trade'); 'pauper', 'vagrant', 'anarchist' (1917 Immigration Act); and 'illegal alien' (1986 Immigration Reform and Control Act), to name but a few. It is this last category of migrant that we turn to now, as I argue that the current push to 'build the wall' is, in part, a response to the deviance amplification of the 'illegal alien' migrant subjectivity.

Problematizations shift, and by the end of the twentieth century, it is the mass migration of the global poor, illegal aliens, and refugees that takes precedence in the immigration discourse (Doty 1996:172). Accordingly, when asked about the

US's most important problem in a Gallup telephone poll, "immigration" or "illegal aliens" has been the top answer for about 5 percent of Americans since 2001 (Newport 2018). Three times, however, that figure leaps to the 15 percent mark, with the latest figures showing that "immigration/illegal aliens" is seen as the second largest problem, right behind government dysfunction (ibid)[43]. The perception is divided along partisan lines; for those voting or leaning Republican, some 25% believe that immigration is the US's top problem, while for those voting or leaning Democrat, only 6% choose immigration. For a candidate styling themselves as a Republican, then, a focus on immigration-as-problem—and a scapegoating of 'illegals' as either a cause or symptom of that problem—makes good political sense.

In the contemporary mass media, we see such iterations time and time again. Republicans, in particular, evoke the migrant category of illegals in order to mobilize fear of the migrant, to appeal to traditionally Republican voters, and to lend legitimacy to future restrictions and exclusions. When Republican nominee Sharron Angle runs for a Senate seat in Nevada in 2010, for example, she employs a TV attack ad that speaks of: "Illegals sneaking across our border putting Americans' safety and jobs at risk" (Angle 2010). This discursive iteration places 'illegal migrant-workers' in competition with 'American national-workers', and also amplifies the deviance of illegals as an imminent threat to 'national security'.

Image 18: Screenshot of Best Friend campaign commercial.
Sharron Angle., 2010

In the campaign advertisement illustrated above, illegals are discursively framed in black-and-white as shadowy figures on the Other side of the border. They move in hordes at night, sneaking stealthily around an ineffective fence, a discursive precursor for today's calls to strengthen the southern border. In the same picture—but separated by lines—are the Americans whose safety purportedly at risk. They lead purposeful, color-filled lives: witness the mom by the open door of her home, tending happily to her three blond-haired kids. This part of the advertisement supports the comparison made today between the supposedly 'open door of immigration' and the open door of a personal property. Such understandings lean on the metaphor of the nation as a home, drawing comparisons between home-invaders and nation-invaders. Children are shown in this campaign advertisement to heighten the sense of threat that illegals bring to America's most vulnerable. The use of children reminds us of the cartoons and street protest signs of the late 1800s that speak of 'Our Boys and Girls' and likewise use children. Such discursive echoes tie the current 'problem' of immigration to the 'problems' of our national past, magnifying and making visceral the 'threat' of unchecked immigration, as well as giving a sense that such problems have a historical grounding. And then there are the skilled construction workers in their safety hats—workers all racialized as white—so content and secure in their jobs. The outcome of such representations is that the normative and racialized dichotomy of illegal migrant-workers versus American national-workers is upheld. The collective figure of the illegal can be seen as a potent symbol of Otherness that both co-constitutes ideas of the American, and also supports the hegemony of a system of immigration designed to hold everything in place. And so, while this visceral evocation of "Illegals sneaking across our border" (ibid) is deployed here by a Republican Senate nominee to promote herself as a candidate, it also amplifies the deviance of the migrant figure, and lends legitimacy to calls for augmenting the southern border.

If these discursive formations reify the sense that 'illegals' threaten the nation and 'its people', a distinct shift occurs in mid 2015 when a new moral entrepreneur enters the political scene. Trump's arrival as a presidential candidate heralds a renewed focus on 'criminal Mexicans' as a problematized collective subjectivity, and also shifts this subjectivity towards caricature mode. This represents a discursive shift not only because Trump stretches the bounds of what can be said, but also because such discursive formations create the conditions of possibility for migrant children to be separated from their families and caged for weeks in inhumane conditions at the border (Rubio and Dickerson 2019; Dickerson 2019).

And so, when Trump announces his candidacy for president in the summer of 2015, he throws the criminal Mexican subjectivity center stage. After starting his announcement speech by warning, "Our country is in serious trouble" (16 June 2015), Trump states:

> When Mexico sends its people, they're not sending their best. They're not sending you (gesturing to the audience). They're not sending you (pointing to audience). They're sending people that have lots of problems, and they're bringing those problems with us. They're bringing drugs. They're bringing crime. They're

> rapists. And some, I assume, are good people.

This speech constructs immigration as a 'broken' system that lets in Mexican criminals and rapists who 'cause trouble' for the US and risk the safety of its 'best' people. This is a characterization that amplifies the deviance of the collective figure of the Mexican, and also assigns Mexicans firmly to the 'them' side of a potential future 'us and them' confrontation. This is intensified by Trump's juxtaposition of deviant Mexicans in the same sentence that he evokes the 'best' people of the US. Such a juxtaposition suggests Mexicans—and the broken system of immigration that allows them in—threaten treasured, normative moral values of the US. Mexicans are thus produced in this speech as a collective figurative scapegoat, the articulation of racist and nationalist ideas about criminal bodily penetration and contamination of the national whole. Such iterations can be seen as blatant fear-mongering by a business entrepreneur as he launches his career as a moral entrepreneur. Such iterations can also be seen as the first step in the construction of a confrontation-producing immigration crisis.

While the speech is widely derided as both evidence of racism and proof that Trump is unfit for office, it nevertheless succeeds in rallying support for Trump. His ideas about criminal Mexicans, as well his promise later in the speech to, "make our country great again" (16 June 2015) resonate with large numbers of voters. And just as with the anti-immigrant discourse of the Know Nothings in the 1850s, there is political utility to be found in such an approach. Bernie Sanders notes as much on *The Late Show* a few months later (18 Sept 2015): "What Trump is doing is appealing to the baser instincts among us, xenophobia and frankly racism...that's the same old same old that's gone on in this country for a very long time...and you win votes like that".

Trump continues to amplify the deviance of 'criminal Mexicans' in subsequent speeches. In the third Presidential debate, for example, he refers to them in farcical faux-Spanish as, "bad hombres" (see *New York Times* 20 Oct 2016). This brings to mind Marx's comments in the *18th Brumaire* of *Louis Bonaparte* (1852), in which he reminisces that personages appear twice, "the first time as tragedy, the second time as farce" (1852/2010:5). Trump's creation and promotion of such farcical figures helps to mobilize support from voters and contributes to his election victory in 2016. Notes Corey Robin (2004:194) about the productive nature of such political fear-mongering:

> If fear is of the community-alien variety, elites still take the initiative and derive the greater benefit. Designated protectors of a community's safety, they determine which threats are most salient...They also mobilize the population against that threat. Because their success as protectors adds to their legitimacy and enhances their power, this kind of fear benefits them, politically, more than it does others.

In Trump's campaign announcement speech—and in many more speeches and tweets that follow—this idea of the US as under threat from criminal migrants helps to produce immigration as a crisis. The political and material effects are not just to amplify deviance and win votes, however. The discursive framing of migrant-as-illegal *necessarily* frames the response as a defensive one. In other words, such representations lend legitimacy to structures of enclosure such as 'the wall'.

Extreme Illegals

While criminal Mexicans are the focus of Trump in the run-up to his election, from 2017 onwards he shifts his attention to a new figurative subject that he associates with 'crisis' at the southern border: MS-13 gang members. Originally a Los Angeles gang started in the 1980s by Salvadorans escaping civil war, MS-13 has become a fixation for the current administration, and for Trump in particular, who discusses them as a danger to Americans in many of his claims about 'bad immigration laws'. Trump's characterizations of MS-13 gang members are stereotypical, homogenizing, and over-exaggerated: in other words, the stuff of moral panic. In an interview with TIME (Phippen 2017), for example, Trump lays out his claims about MS-13: "They come from Central America", he notes, thereby producing them as migrants from south of the border. Trump then amplifies their deviance and reiterates their migrant category: "They're tougher than any people you've ever met. They're killing and raping everybody out there. They're illegal" (ibid).

These 'animal' migrants are both new and familiar—to lean on Cohen's understanding (1972/2011:vii). They are demonized sub-humans bent on indiscriminate rape and murder. And their significance in terms of actual threat is exaggerated. Not only has the number of violent crimes due to any cause been declining since 1991, with only a small uptick in recent years (Statistica 2018), victims of MS-13 are far more likely to be migrants themselves (Blitzer 2018). However, when presented by Trump as a warning sign of the impending collapse of US communities, MS-13 make suitable scapegoats in the construction of immigration-as-crisis. And as with the figure of the witch, the veracity of such figurative subjects is irrelevant. As Bonnie Honig (2001) puts it: "Scapegoating is a social practice that finds or produces the objects it needs" (2000:34). In other words, once again we find the degraded migrant subjectivity as a 'truth' willed into being by power.

A month into his 'zero tolerance' policy that separates over 2,000 children from their families at the border, Trump amps up his rhetoric. Speaking at what the White House calls a "California Sanctuary State Roundtable" in May of 2018, Trump categorically dehumanizes such migrants. "These aren't people", Trump declares. "These are animals" (16 May 2018). While he is widely criticized for calling such people animals, he continues to dehumanize them, and does so using discursive crossover. In a 3am tweet from early July, for example, he notes: "we have an 'infestation' of MS-13 GANGS...rough criminal elelements [sic] that bad immigration laws allow into our country" (3 July 2018). Nobody wants an infestation of animals, and discursive crossover transfers the repulsiveness of this idea onto humans. What does not need to be said in this discursive formation is that an infestation can easily be 'solved'; and just as you might exterminate a bug infestation, so the logic goes, MS13 animals can also be exterminated. Perhaps buoyed by his own rhetoric, just two days later Trump uses discursive crossover to animalize migrants again, as well as presenting them as a threat to American safety and jobs:

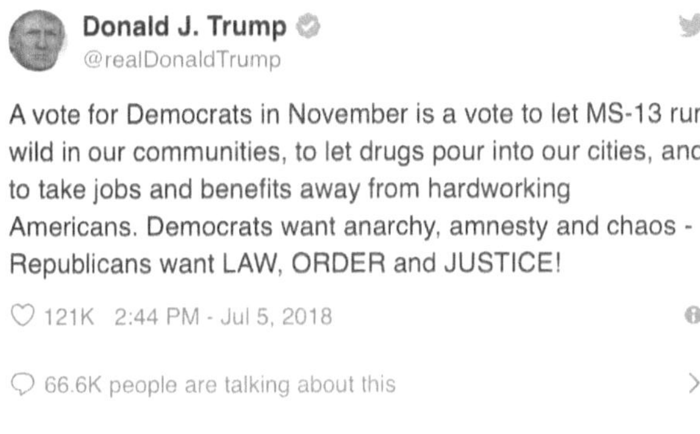

Image 19: @realDonaldTrump. 5:44pm - 5 July, 2018

This tweet not only animalizes MS-13 as 'running wild' but also deploys hydraulic metaphors to heighten the fear of drugs 'pouring' into cities. Finally, this tweet stakes Republicans as the party with the right moral values to provide solutions—and these solutions, it is emphasized—are legal ones that bring 'order' and promise control.

Mobile Homeless

There is one additional symbol that Trump employs just as his policy of zero tolerance becomes an actual practice at the border: the 'caravan'. This term used in the current immigration discourse most often as a collective noun (as in a 'caravan of migrants') and creates a vivid image of an unstoppable trajectory of the poor, the weak, and the out-of-place. Perhaps the term caravan is deployed as discursive crossover to evoke the most persecuted migrants in global history: so-called 'gypsies'. Certainly, there are negative connotations roused by the term, and these are amplified by the manner in which it is framed. In Trump's first use of the term in April 2018, for example, he implies caravans are the harbingers of imminent risk, and suggests that Republicans should override all opposition to promote immediate legal solutions: "Getting more dangerous. 'Caravans' coming. Republicans must go to Nuclear Option to pass tough laws NOW" (Trump @realDonaldTrump 1 April 2018). An article on *CNN* reprints this tweet, and explains what may have prompted Trump to use the term: "Trump appears to be referring to a migrant caravan assembled by the group *Pueblo Sin Fronteras* (Village without Borders), which is discussed on Fox News' *Fox & Friends* shortly before he published his tweet" (Dominguez 2018). In this manner, a sensationalist item on a morning news show gets promoted by Trump in his capacity as a moral entrepreneur. And this amplification of 'illegal migrant' deviance has almost immediate material effects.

Although many of the people approaching the southern border at this time may have been seeking a legal route to asylum, five days after Trump evokes the symbol of the 'dangerous caravan', the Attorney General Jeff Sessions announces they are enacting a practice of zero tolerance at the border. In a memo that accompanies the new practice, Sessions thanks Department of Justice (DOJ) prosecutors, stating: "I urge you: promoting and enforcing the rule of law is vital to protecting a nation, its borders, and its citizens" (DOJ 2018). But the policy is not just deployed in cases of, "illegal entry and illegal entry into the United States by an alien" (ibid), it is also deployed against people trying to seek asylum, many of whom are subsequently separated from their children. Perhaps to foster consent for this practice—all the while it draws criticism—both Trump and Sessions return to the symbol of the caravan throughout April and May of 2018. But unlike the solution to, "pass tough laws

NOW" (@realDonaldTrump 1 April 2018) that Trump tweets of at the beginning of April, by the end of the month he has started to use the caravan (or rather "large Caravans") to push hard for his border wall:

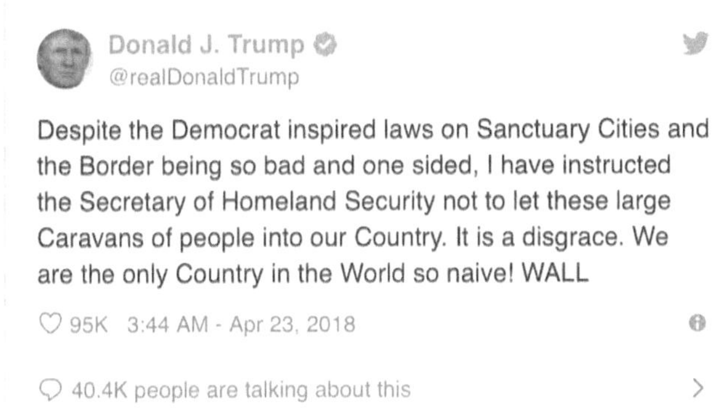

Image 20: Trump. 2018 @realDonaldTrump. 6:44am - 23 April.

In this tweet, Trump once again promotes Republicans as being the party with the solutions, and this time, it is the wall (all capitals) that he pushes as the solution. Note that in this tweet, when Trump states, "We are the only Country in the World so naive [to let people in]! WALL" (ibid), Trump evokes immigration exclusion as a *global* practice. Whether this statement holds any 'truth' is beside the point: such iterations are valuable because they add a global dimension to the *idea* of immigration exclusion, enabling Trump to advocate for his border wall.

Two weeks later, as criticism for the policy of zero tolerance becomes widespread, Sessions appeals to both a global and national audience and states that 'illegal aliens' make such a policy, "necessary" (US Department of Justice, 7 May 2018). In a speech that deploys both animalizing discursive crossover and caravan symbolism, Sessions evokes a visceral sense of threat to the nation and suggests that illegal entry on the southern border is triggering a crisis. Notes Sessions: "We are here to send a message to the world: we are not going to let this country be overwhelmed. People are not going to caravan or otherwise stampede our border" (ibid). In this speech, Sessions amplifies both a sense of crisis, and also amplifies the deviance of those said to be causing the crisis. Accordingly, the border is undergoing an animal "stampede" (ibid, para. 4), characterized by, "massive increases in illegal crossings in recent months" (ibid, para. 14). These are not individuals, but rather a homogenized collective people who "caravan" (ibid, para. 4). And then we have the co-constituted oppositional characters: "The American people [who] are right and just and decent" (ibid, para. 20).

The verbs Sessions uses to describe the movement of illegals reduces them to animalized sub-humans who in their illegality represent, "an affront to the American people and a threat to our very system of self-government" (ibid, para. 22). There is a subtle discursive echo between these iterations and those of the Chinese in the 1880s. Then, as now, migrants are represented as sub-human creatures who compromise the moral values of the US. Here, however, Sessions also presents them as threatening the very sovereignty of the US. And while immigration exclusion is seen as solving the 'Chinese crisis' in 1882, so here, increasing restriction and exclusion are promoted as solutions for the 'border crisis'. For Sessions, only a 'secure border' can solve a 'border stampede', and this he outlines in his concluding paragraph: "We will finally secure this border so that we can give the American people safety and peace of mind. That's what the people deserve" (ibid, para. 31). In his conclusion, Sessions shores up two co-constituting identities: "People around the world [who] have no right to demand entry in violation of our sovereignty" (ibid, para. 29); and "the American people" who deserve "safety and peace of mind" (ibid, para. 31). In this speech, Sessions thereby produces a unity of the American people against the fearful threat of illegals. Given the fearful subjects Sessions evokes in this speech—the animalized sub-humans who stampede the nation's borders—Trump's WALL solution is produced as commonsense.

THE WALL

Since emerging as a political candidate in 2015, Trump has steered the discourse on immigration in very particular ways. I posit that it is through Trump's continued emphasis on the migrant as a threatening and criminal subject-figure that the southern border wall is produced for many people as commonsense. For if 'Mexican rapists', 'bad hombres', the 'animals' of MS13, and the 'dangerous large caravans' enter the US by sneaking through the border, only a formidable physical structure can match their formidable physical threat.

There is also a sense put forward by both Trump and the Department of Homeland Security (DHS) that walls have worked in the past to contain formidable threats, work in other places around the world, and also work in the present in the many places along the southern border where a physical structure already exists (see figure 4). In the following depiction of these existing structures by the federal law enforcement arm of the DHS—the US Customs and Border Protection agency (US CBP 2017)—dark lines represent what they call, "Pedestrian Fencing" (ibid), and the light lines represent "Vehicle Fencing". In the original color image, blood red stains represent, "Increasing Apprehensions (Deportable)" (ibid), while darker stains indicate greater numbers of 'deportable apprehensions'.

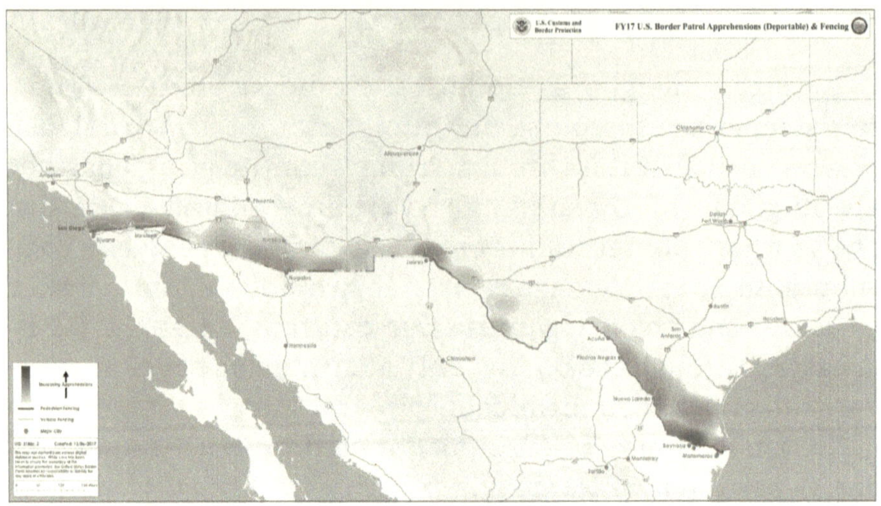

Figure 4: Southwest Border Apprehensions & Fencing, US Customs and Border Protection, 2017

While the term 'fencing' implies a light-weight structure such as one might use around one's home, some of the 'fences' depicted in the image above are over 20 feet high, are dug several feet into the ground, and are cemented into wide concrete trenches. The following image from the DHS illustrates the formidable nature of one of these 'fences' along the nearly 2,000-mile border with Mexico:

Image 21: Sand Dune Fence. nd. US Department of Homeland Security

This and many other structures are built as part of several 'operations' in the early 1990s that the CBP state are built, "in an effort to bring a level of control to the border" (US CPB 2018b). These operations are named in quasi-military terminology as, "Operation 'Hold the Line'" (ibid), and "Operation Gatekeeper" (ibid). Of these two operations, the CBP note the first, "proved an immediate success" (ibid), and the second, "reduced illegal entries in San Diego by more than 75%" (ibid). In other words, border fencing works. The extension of this logic is that the larger and more formidable the structure, the greater the chance of 'control' and 'success'. In a press release titled, "We Must Secure The Border And Build The Wall To Make America Safe Again" (15 Feb 2018), the DHS articulates this logic:

> Walls Work. When it comes to stopping drugs and illegal aliens across our borders, border walls have proven to be extremely effective... They have worked in Yuma, Arizona as a result of the 2006 Bipartisan Secure Border Act. They have also worked in San Diego. Both areas have seen 95 percent drops in attempted illegal border crossings.

What the DHS doesn't reveal is that the construction of walls in populated areas such as San Diego does not result in a drop in border crossings *in itself*, but rather drives migrants to cross the border in much more remote areas (Nevins 2010:174). One result of this material practice is to drastically increase the risk to migrants. A non-profit corporation called Humane Borders has recorded the deaths of 3,244 people who tried to cross the border between October 1999 and April of 2018, a majority of them in the remote and arid Sonoran Desert (Humane Borders 2018). A second result is a change in how migrants are perceived. Gone are the days in which migrants enter the US through urban areas during the day; now they cross at night, increasingly in groups, and for people who live and work in the area, the appearance is far more sinister (Nevins 2002, Williams 2013). In other words, such material practices and their ensuing outcomes have a negative effect on the generalized beliefs about migrants seen in border areas. This combined with alarmist and animalizing scapegoating by claims-makers such as Trump, Sessions, sensationalist news outlets, and others, has the effect of *producing the object that it needs*, to paraphrase Honig (2001). And this object, for Trump and others, is not just the scapegoat figure of the illegal migrant, it is also the proposed response to such a figurative threat: the wall.

Symbolic Structures

When Trump first mentions a border wall in his 2015 presidential announcement speech, he uses language that invokes the walls built in China for millennia: "I would build a great wall," Trump states in the speech (16 June 2015). "Nobody builds walls better than me, believe me, and I'll build them very inexpensively, I will build a great, great wall on our southern border" (ibid). Perhaps this language is used to legitimate the idea that 'great walls' work, much as they might have worked in

China. Two months later, at a New Hampshire town hall, Trump returns to China's wall. "We would like to have that wall," Trump states. "That wall, nobody gets through. That I can tell you" (Qiu 2015). But as Julia Lovell (2007) writes in *The Great Wall: China Against the World 1000BC – AC 2000*, not only did the Chinese wall (or, more accurately, walls) fail to prevent incursions of 'barbarians' from the northern steppe into the urban areas of the 'civilized', such walls are also seen as a sign of political weakness. Notes Lovell (2007:17):

> Over its 2,000-year history, Chinese wall-building was not invariably a symbol of national strength and prestige. It was often adopted as a defensive frontier strategy after all the other options for dealing with the barbarians—diplomacy, trade, punitive military expeditions—had been exhausted or discarded. It was a sign of military weakness, diplomatic failure and political paralysis, and a bankrupting polity that led the downfall of several once robust dynasties.

Trump, however, misses the valuable lessons that could be learned from China's history. He also appears to miss the antipathy to the wall that comes from both official and unofficial sources. In response to Trump declaring in a speech in Nashville, "in the end Mexico is paying for the wall...They're going to pay for the wall and they're going to enjoy it"[44] (29 May 2018), for example, Mexican President Enrique Peña tweets: "President @realDonaldTrump: NO. Mexico will NEVER pay for a wall. Not now, not ever. Sincerely, Mexico (all of us)" (Peña @EPN 2018)[45]. In an attempt to mock both Trump and his 'vision' of the 'great wall', a widely shared satirical web meme connects the Great Wall of China with Trump's great wall. The meme is framed by a mock Fox News screen shot and challenges Trump's logic by stretching it to its illogical ends. Accordingly, the meme points out that the Great Wall of China must be effective, because there are no 'illegal Mexicans' in China.

Image 22: Web meme. Bachmann fabricated as being quoted on Fox News, 2015

Despite these minor instances of discursive rebuttal, however, walls remain central to Trump's understanding of how to 'fix immigration'. In part this is because Trump constructs migrants as 'illegals aliens', fearful and animalized subject-figures who threaten the moral fabric of the nation. Trump's wall is also still a focus for him because it has proved so popular among his supporters. During the 2016 election, for example, "Build the Wall Vote TRUMP" yard signs, bumpers stickers, and pins appear across the US. "BUILD THE WALL" is a rousing and joyful chant that features at many of his campaign rallies both then and now, and the slogan is prominent once again as he prepares for a 2020 run:

Image 23: Build the Wall Trump 2020 Kit. TrumpStoreAmerica, 2019

Whether 'walls work' as actual structures of control as the DHS claim, is therefore somewhat irrelevant; walls certainly work to rally support for Trump. Notes Shapiro (2012:45):

> The discursive practices of a society are not a series of relatively accurate or inaccurate, coherent or incoherent assertions about something, but a historically produced economy of meaning and value. Statements have a currency insofar as they enable kinds of persons to act and allow various patterns of life to emerge.

In other words, the 'truth' of such discursive formations can be seen as a power effect of historically specific meaning-making structures that, in this case, enable Trump to call for further immigration restriction and exclusion.

△△△

I have spoken in this chapter about the figurative subjects of today's immigration discourse, subjects who are akin to Cohen's (1972) folk devils. I have argued that the criminalized alien figure who features in the contemporary discourse operates as a scapegoat, a stereotypical character whose deviance has been amplified by claims-makers such as Trump. A result of such scapegoating, I argue, is to lend legitimacy to calls for increased immigration restriction and exclusion, as well as to make commonsense of the idea of the wall.

In this chapter I have defined moral panics along the lines that Cohen (1972) does: as an overreaction to an exaggerated threat in which a stereotyped folk devil is presented by claims-makers as threatening the treasured values of a community. Positing that the contemporary immigration discourse is in crisis mode, I have focused on the material effects of such a construction. Chiefly, immigration-as-crisis is seen as producing consent for policies of detainment and family separation at the southern border, policies that have resulted in the inhumane treatment of migrants, many of whom are seeking asylum.

Central to current understandings of immigration-as-crisis is the figure of the migrant. This collective figurative subject is represented as an 'illegal alien', an animalized sub-human who 'caravans' and 'stampedes the border'. Because the existence, presence, and threat of the illegal alien has been exaggerated by Trump and others, the wall and associated policies of immigration restriction and exclusion become not only right, but also necessary, for those who uncritically accept the discourse.

EPILOGUE/IMAGINING A BETTER FUTURE

I began this study with the image of the schoolroom globe and by questioning how everyday cultural artifacts produce commonsense understandings of our world. Chief among these is the hegemonic understanding that the world is divided into separate units called nations. Break it down further, and the nation is understood as a specific geographic terrain with fixed borders. Within these borders are the people of the nation. But in order for a plurality of peoples to become *the* people of *the* nation, some inventive sleight of hand has to be deployed. This process is essential for nationalism, the rule of a specific terrain for a specific population. Beginning in 1787, when the words "We the People" are inserted into the preamble to the Constitution (US Congress 1787), an ever more specific biopolitical grouping of people are invoked both in discourse and through technologies of the state such as the census. Such practices shape ideas about the US as a nation, and shape ideas about who is seen as belonging, as well as who is seen as excluded. These are refined less than fifteen years later in the Naturalization Act as a place for the "free white person" (US Congress 1790). And within eight more years the oppositional figure of this free white space is also produced: the alien who poses an internal threat to the nation (US Congress 1798).

At first, these figurative subjects of the nation are produced through words alone. But in the mid 1880s by which time the process of chemical halftone engraving has been perfected, mass-printed photographs and illustrations also join the discourse. In the contemporary discourse we can add moving images, color, sound; a whole array of media that together help frame the figure of the migrant as a visceral threat to the nation. Imbued throughout these media are linguistic elements such as metonym and metaphor that magnify the sense of the migrant as a threat. Chief among these are the labels *alien* and *illegal* that work to invoke a range of unpleasant associations. Application of these labels is not just done to people who move from one nation-state to another, however. They are also applied to people who are racialized as being similar to the figure of the migrant, enabling agents of the nation-state such as Immigration and Customs Enforcement agents (ICE) to 'round up' people based on 'suspicion' of being an 'illegal alien'.

Today's discourse on the nation-state and its figurative subjects relates closely to the historical discourse. We are reminded of this through a series of discursive echoes that connect historical ideas about problematized migrants to contemporary ones. Chinese people who work on the railroads and in the mines in the nineteenth century, for example, are presented in a number of derogatory ways: as outcompeting American workers, as sojourner workers with no ties or allegiance to the US, and as animalized sub-humans who present a sexual threat. These figurative subjects resonate with contemporary iterations in which 'illegal Mexicans' are seen as out-competing American workers, as sending money 'home', and as being criminals and rapists. Such discursive echoes give a sense that such problems have a thorough grounding in the past. They also make 'sense' of the same 'solutions'.

One of the chief material effects of such negative discursive representations, I argue, is to lend legitimacy to practices and policies of immigration restriction and exclusion. Concomitant with the discourse that represents Chinese people in animalized and derogatory ways, for example, is the Page Act of 1875 that pivots on articulating ideas of race and nation in order to restrict the immigration of Chinese people. I argue that the stereotypical evocation of such people through media such as cartoons and songs legitimates the problematization of the Chinese migrant, and also fosters widespread consent for the Chinese Exclusion Act of 1882.

Metaphors used in the discourse on immigration amplify the sense that the migrant is a threat to the nation and also, I contend, provide a framework for restrictionist and exclusionary solutions. Centrally, metaphors in the discourse of immigration-as-crisis are those related to invasion and contamination, threat, and purity. So, we have the ubiquitous hydraulic metaphor to refer to how migrants move (flooding the border, or washing up on 'our' shores, for example). This hydraulic metaphor emerges in the 1850s when immigration is first problematized and gets used in increasingly forceful ways through the remainder of the nineteenth century, reaching 'full tide' after the First World War as Congress gears up to enact the restrictive and discriminatory quota acts of the 1920s.

Doing a genealogical analysis of metaphorical framing not only highlights shifts in the discourse, but also points to shifts in political and material practice. The metaphor of the US as a personal property or 'home' with walls and a gate or wall to keep it safe, for example, has been used since by US politicians and illustrators since at least the 1890s, and is also used today by Trump in order to promote consent for his plans for an augmented wall along the southern border. The metaphor of the US as a nation of immigrants conceals the historical actualities of how the nation is constructed. While it is frequently invoked in political speeches of the past—acting both to assuage fears of racism while constructing the US as a racially specific place—its removal from the US Customs and Immigration Service mission statement in 2018 is a hint at how the discourse of immigration-as-crisis is being redefined in the age of Trump. All such metaphors work to add to the perception that migrants are dangerous, lend legitimacy to fears that immigration is a pressing social problem, and frame restriction and exclusion as apposite solutions.

It has been shown in this study that discourse is an act of social constructionism that can be used as an efficient tool for ordering social relations. In this study I have explored discursive products such as television and print, films, novels, songs, web memes, tweets, press releases, speeches, illustrations, songs, and cartoons. Such discourses are seen as constructing the subject-figures who purportedly threaten the nation-state. Such discourses also construct the figurative subjects who are deemed desirable to the nation-state: the citizen who is structured in dichotomous opposition to the migrant. Such figures emerge through discourse as false binaries through a process of dialectics that pushes figurative ideas to oppositional ends.

When a discourse co-constitutes both the 'internal enemies' and desirable figures of the nation-state we can say that they are constitutive of the nation itself. Such discourses have the political and material effect of upholding the US as a prized geographic space being ruled for a specific people. Discursive formulations that create the figure of the migrant have the effect of creating the 'normal' figurative subject of the nation-state and can be seen as disciplinary tactics of the nation-state that is exercised over the whole population. Technologies of the state that count and categorize people into varying biopolitical groups turns people, literally, into figures, or what Foucault calls mere objects of knowledge (1995:28).

Articulating ideas about race and nation are central to the discourse of nationalism and to the discourse of immigration-as-crisis. The intersecting ideas of race and nation link the individual to a larger imagined collective. Central to this process of imagining are the use of collective symbolic markers for certain biopolitical groups. Symbols such as alcohol abuse that are tied discursively to German or Irish immigrants in the mid to late nineteenth century, for example, work to rally antipathy towards the entire collectivity. In this manner social problems are constructed as a, "part of a nexus of images, symbols, beliefs, and metaphors: a master problem" (Fine and Christoforides 1991:389).

One key way that immigration is constructed as a master problem is through what I term discursive crossover. This is deployed routinely in both historical and contemporary discourse to construct negative ideas about the migrant subjectivity by invoking negative ideas about out-of-place species as well as extra-terrestrial space creatures. All such figures are given the designation *alien*, and the result of discursive crossover is to amplify the sense that the out-of-place alien represents a threat to the nation and 'its people'.

The word *alien* has been as an official state category in the US since the Naturalization Act of 1790. Its pointed use by politicians and others to invoke a fearful and criminalized *figurative* subject, however, has powerful political and material effects. Chiefly, the outcome is to structure the alien subject-figure as the internal enemy of the nation-state. Such subject-making can be seen as a key part of what Cohen (1972) terms a moral panic: the alien is the exaggerated figure of an exaggerated problem that calls for extreme solutions. Such figures are constructed as dangerous in themselves, but also as heralding a new kind of future that must be avoided at all costs.

Discursive crossover is first deployed in the late 1800s in order to connect the 'problem' of English sparrow overpopulation to the nascent 'problem' of mass immigration. Such birds are anthropomorphized as invaders of national space, and the power effect of this crossover is to promote the idea that immigrants are also nation invaders, thereby both framing and legitimating aggressive state responses.

Discursive crossover works to invoke migrants as aggressive aliens, as lower-order animals, and as out-of-place species. Such crossovers are commonplace in the discourse on immigration, and work to degrade the migrant subjectivity in specific ways. In the 1860s, for example, Chinese workers are described as arriving or working in *swarms* (*New York Times* 1861, 1867). Such animalizing crossovers are used in the 1880s to promote the Chinese as extraneous to the national project, and following these crossovers comes violence, restriction, and then exclusion. In a discursive echo, migrants are described today as *infesting* the nation-state (Trump 19 June 2018). All such notions lend legitimacy to the sense that the alien migrant is out-of-place in the geography of the nation and, as such, a threat.

After the First World War there is a renewal of the animalizing discourse in order to frame the latest problematized migrant collective—southern and eastern European immigrants—as extraneous to the nation. Add to this an increase in hydraulic metaphor to describe problematized migrant movement, as well as deployment of the home and gate metaphors to describe the nation and its defenses, and we have all the conditions needed to support the racist and nationalist quota laws of the 1920s.

Discursive crossover animates shifts in the migrant subjectivity and a new shift occurs in the mid 1950s as the US grapples with Cold War tensions. Narratives of space alien invasion have become incredibly popular during this time frame and moral entrepreneurs make use of this new language to make sense of 'invasions' by unauthorized Mexican laborers along the southern border. Such discursive crossover modifies our understanding of 'invading Mexican aliens' such that the subjectivity is given renewed animation in a threatening and fearful direction.

Framing such migrations as militaristic incursions into national space doesn't just negatively impact the migrant subjectivity, however. By framing unauthorized Mexican migration as an assault on the nation and 'its people', militarization of the border is promoted as the appropriate response. Accordingly, throughout the seventies and increasingly after the Immigration Reform and Control Act (IRCA) is passed in 1986, the border is progressively buttressed with fences and walls and other physical structures of enclosure. This is done both to symbolize the nation as 'protected' from 'illegal aliens', as well as to symbolize the idea of 'control' over what is a vast and oftentimes desolate land space. Following this augmentation of the southern border comes a number of military-style 'operations' in the 1990s that again seek the control that IRCA has promised.

A final decisive shift in the discourse on the migrant occurs as Trump enters politics in 2015. Not only does Trump produce and reproduce a series of problematized subject-figures to animate the discussion on immigration, he also evokes a new symbol in order to frame himself as 'tough on immigration'. And so as he reinvents Mexicans as rapists—a collective problematized subjectivity that echoes discursively with other historical scapegoat figures such as the Chinese of the 1880s —he also promotes what he sees as logical solutions: "a great, great wall on our southern border" (Trump 16 June 2015).

Discursive crossover promotes 'differences' between the alien and the species who is seen as 'belonging' in particular nationalized spaces. In this way, discursive crossover functions to support the hegemony of a world divided into nation-states, a world in which each person and entity has their place. A power effect of discursive crossover is to legitimate aggressive state practices such as indefinite detention, militarized border controls, and family separation at the southern border. Discursive crossover also allows for discussion in one sphere that cannot easily or justifiably be discussed in another. We can talk freely about the need to contain and control so-called invasive alien species in a manner that serves, "as alibi, as a fertile allegory for making people and objects strange, thus to forge critical new social and political distinctions" (Comaroff and Comaroff 2001:234).

This study has shown that historical constructions of

difference that center on articulating notions of race and nation—as well as internal and supplementary ideas of poverty, gender, sexuality, and criminality—coalesce in the figure of the alien. Just as the alien is a symbolic figure, so too, the solution to the 'alien crisis' is seen as largely symbolic. Trump's border wall is envisioned as a vast, prophylactic structure, that will seal the nation at its most vulnerable point. 'Build the Wall' is a frequent rallying cry for pro-Trump supporters who accept this essentially nationalist vision of the US as a personal property in need of protection. If the alien is a figurative subject of invasion, a creature that causes panic, only a wall can stop this implicit threat.

IMAGINING A BETTER FUTURE

I began thinking about this project in 2012 when an older gentleman I was interviewing told me of his goals: "We need to not want to divide and subdivide and define and subdefine," he said. "That's my next project. A psychological one. I have to erase all of these things. I don't want to give them any kind of level...that limits your feeling about belonging". He died a few months later but I will never forget his words. They were a catalyst in my thinking about belonging, and about all the conceptual ways we limit the belonging of ourselves and of others.

As this study has shown, however, the figurative subjects of immigration are defined in a variety of ways. Immigration controls and practices, for example, are productive of certain migrant categories, as are commonsense discourses that reproduce migrants as 'alien' or 'illegal'. Both practices and discourses are productive of—and reinforce—generalized ideas about migrants, as well as related ideas about belonging and fixity. Given the diffuse nature of these practices and discourses, then, how do we start to imagine migrants and immigration in a more positive way?

One of the ways we can achieve this goal is to pay attention to migrants as individuals. If an effect of immigration practices and discourses is to homogenize the migrant—as well as to produce them as existing always in the collective—then giving attention to *individual* stories is one way we can counteract these constructions. The International Organization for Migration (IOM)—a related organization of the United Nations —employs just this tactic on its Instagram feed. Their daily posts feature both pictures and stories of individuals and includes the note: "Each migrant and refugee carries memories, traditions, history, and skills. That's why it is important that we recognize them as individuals" (IOM @unmigration 2019). They have over 45 thousand followers on Instagram, but this is tiny in comparison to the millions of followers that some celebrities have. By following the IOM's feed, however, and by sharing social media posts and other stories that individualize migrants widely, perhaps it is possible to broaden the reach of such messages.

In order to raise these conditions of possibility for migrants to be seen and imagined in more positive ways, it might also be necessary to broaden our media fields. Perhaps those who follow the IOM feed, for example, are already people interested in positive conceptions of migration. Following such a feed can thereby be seen as a feedback loop, one that affirms the things we already know, and think are important, rather than expanding our exposure to alternative realities. Encouraging ourselves and others to consume media widely, then, might help us find different ways of looking at the world. This is perhaps especially true of media that we find objectionable. If we have a liberal or textual media bias, then sitting through an hour of the TV show *Fox and Friends* sounds like an unbearable way to start the morning. But it will be productive in showing us the different conceptions people have of migrants. It will expose us to differential ideologies that lend legitimacy to Trump's calls to build the wall. And it will show us the representations of migrants that we may find objectionable. Seeing and listening to these representations is a necessary act in order that we can counteract them. Take screenshots, record video clips on your cellphones, and share them widely in order to explain the ideological reasoning behind such representations, and in order to explain the negative consequences that can arise from such articulations.

In analyzing the discourse on immigration, I am always conscious that discursive formations matter, that the ways we present and represent the things around us are far more than just symbolic expressions. This is because discursive formulations don't just construct and shape symbols and their meanings; they also have powerful political and material effects. In other words—as the old Haitian saying notes—*Words Have Wings*. And so, while it is easy to laugh at the farcical nature of expressions like 'bad hombres', or to feel relief when Trump's intended national emergency is rebutted by politicians on both sides of the party line, we have to remind ourselves of what is really at stake. And it is this: *everyday* expressions and ideas about migrants—as well as everyday practices of immigration that relate to these ideas—cause far-reaching misery for millions of people around the world. It is not just a question of the extremes. It is also a question of the commonplace.

BIBLIOGRAPHY

Adorno, Theodor W. 2005. *Minima Moralia: Reflections on a Damaged Life*. New York: Verso.

Allen, Theodore. 2012. *The Invention of the White Race*. New York: Verso.

Altheide, David L. 2002. *Creating Fear: News and the Construction of Crisis*. New York: Aldine de Gruyter.

Anderson, Benedict R. O'G. 1983. *Imagined Communities: Reflections on the Origin and Spread of Nationalism*. Rev. ed. New York: Verso.

Anderson, Bridget and Vanessa Hughes, eds. 2015. *Citizenship and Its others*. New York: Palgrave Macmillan.

Anderson, Bridget L. 2013. *Us and Them?: The Dangerous Politics of Immigration Control*. UK: Oxford University Press.

Angle, Sharron. 2010. "Best Friend". Campaign Commercial. Aired 14 Sept 2010. Retrieved 23 April 2013 (https://www.youtube.com/watch?gl=SN&hl=fr&v=oTbHwCDFfWg).

Anon. 1845. "The Annexation of Texas to the United States." *Martinsburg Gazette*, March 6. Retrieved 27 Oct 2017 (http://www.history.vt.edu/MxAmWar/MxAmNewspapers.pdf).

Anon. 1851a. "Later From California." *New York Times*, October 20, 1.

Anon. 1851b. "Mining Intelligence." *New York Times*, October 20, 1.

Anon. 1852a. "China-Men in America." *New York Times*, June 9, 2.

Anon. 1852b. "The Chinese in California". *New York Times*, September 27, 3.

Anon. 1852c. "Tide of Immigration". *New York Times*, December 3, 3.

Anon. 1853. "Affairs in Mexico." *New York Times*, September 23, 2.

Anon. 1855a. "From the Southwestern Frontier." *New York Times*, May 22, 2.

Anon. 1855b. "John Chinaman." *The California Songster*. San Francisco, CA: Appleton.

Anon. 1861a. "The Indian Nations." *New York Times*, May 24, 2.

Anon. 1861b. *The New England Historical and Genealogical Register*. Vol. XV. Newburyport, MA: Samuel G Drake.

Anon. 1874a. "A New Raid on the Chinese." *New York Times*, December 26, 4.

Anon. 1874b. "Nationality of Crime." *New York Times*, March 21, 9.

Anon. 1875. "Migration Westward." *New York Times*, April 15, 9.

Anon. 1882. "The Anti-Chinese Feeling." *New York Times*, March 5, 2.

Anon. 1883. "The English Sparrow in California." *New York Times*, March 11, 4.

Anon. 1886. "Citizenship in Indian Nations." *New York Times*, 18 August, 3.

Anon. 1896. "Must Guard Our Gates." *New York Times*, March 17, 3.

Anon. 1920. "Wants Immigration Facts." *New York Times*, May 12, 16.

Anon. 1921a. "Roused by Hawaiian Flood." *New York Times*, July 23, 1921, 2.

Anon. 1921b. "New Age of Migration." *New York Times*, Nov 13,

2.

Anon. 2015a. "Here's Donald Trump's Presidential Announcement Speech." *TIME*, June 16.

Anon. 2015b. "Time to Retire the Term 'Alien.'" *New York Times*, October 19, A24.

Anon. 2016. "Transcript of the Third Debate." *New York Times*, October 20.

Anon. 2017. "Trump's Immigrant Crime Hotline Trolled with Calls about Aliens and UFOs." *bbc.com*, April 27. Retrieved 08 June 2016 (https://www.bbc.com/news/world-us-canada-39731085).

Anon. 2018. "To Prosecute Migrants, 'You Have to Take the Children Away': Trump." *Agence France Presse*, June 19.

Arendt, Hannah. 1973. *The Origins of Totalitarianism*. New ed. New York: Harcourt Brace Jovanovich.

Armstrong, John. 1798. "To the Senate and Representatives of the United States, in Congress Assembled. It Is Equally Foreign from Our Wishes and Intentions to Criminate the Motives of the National Legislatures... Regarding the Alien and Sedition Laws. Poughkeepsie."

Baker, Peter. 2018. "'Use That Word!': Trump Embraces the 'Nationalist' Label." *New York Times*, October 23.

Bartlett, John Russell. 1854. *Personal Narrative of Explorations and Incidents in Texas, New Mexico, California, Sonora, and Chihuahua*. California: D. Appleton & Company.

Battaglia, Debbora, ed. 2005. *E.T. Culture: Anthropology in Outerspaces*. Durham [N.C.]: Duke University Press.

Bay, Michael. 2014. *Transformers: Age of Extinction*.

Becker, Howard. 1963. *The Outsiders: Studies in the Sociology of Deviance*. The Free Press.

Behdad, Ali. 2005. *A Forgetful Nation: On Immigration and Cultural Identity in the United States*. Durham, N.C: Duke University Press.

Berger, Peter L. and Thomas Luckmann. 1990. *The Social Construction of Reality: A Treatise in the Sociology of Knowledge*. New York: Anchor Books.

Billig, Michael. 1995. *Banal Nationalism*. London; Thousand Oaks, Calif: Sage.

Blitzer, Jonathan. 2018a. "The Teens Trapped Between a Gang and the Law." *The New Yorker*, January 1.

Blitzer, Jonathan. 2018b. "The Trump Administration Is Completely Unravelling the U.S. Asylum System." *The New Yorker*, June 11.

Blitt, Barry. 2008. "The Politics of Fear". *The New Yorker*. 21 July. Cover illustration.

Blomkamp, Neill. 2009. "District 9." *Sony Pictures*. Retrieved 18 July 2013 (http://www.sonypictures.com/movies/district9/).

Bremer, Thomas S. 2004. *Blessed with Tourists: The Borderlands of Religion and Tourism in San Antonio*. Chapel Hill: University of North Carolina Press.

Broedel, Hans Peter. 2004. *The "Malleus Maleficarum" and the Construction of Witchcraft: Theology and Popular Belief*. Manchester University Press.

Brown, Christopher L. 1999. "Empire without Slaves: British Concepts of Emancipation in the Age of the American Revolution." *The William and Mary Quarterly* 56(2):273.

Brubaker, Rogers and Frederick Cooper. 2000. "Beyond 'Identity'." *Theory and Society* 29:1–47.

Bulmus, Birsen. 2012. *Plague, Quarantines and Geopolitics in the Ottoman Empire*. Edinburgh: Edinburgh Univ. Press.

Burton, Tim. 1996. *Mars Attacks!* Warner Bros.

Bustamante, Jorge. 1983. "The Mexicans Are Coming: From Ideology to Labor Relations." *International Migration Review* 17(2):323–41.

Butler, Judith. 1997. "Merely Cultural." *Social Text* 52/53(Autumn/Winter).

Cambrensis, Giraldus. 1982. *Topographia Hibernica*. rev. ed. Harmondsworth, Middlesex, England; New York, N.Y: Penguin Books.

Central London Recruiting Depot. 1914. *Friendly Aliens and the British Army*.

Chapman, Leonard F. Jr. 1975. Speech by the Commissioner of the Immigration and Naturalization Service to the Executives Club of Chicago, 21 March 1975. Retrieved 09 June 2019 (https://www.fordlibrarymuseum.gov/library/document/0110/1181029.pdf).

Chen, Yong. 2002. *Chinese San Francisco, 1850 - 1943: A Trans-Pacific Community*. Stanford, Calif: Stanford Univ. Press.

Cisneros, Natalie. 2013. "Alien Sexuality: Race, Maternity, and Citizenship." *Hypatia* 28(2):290–306.

Cohen, Stanley. 1967. "Mods, Rockers and the Rest: Community Reactions to Juvenile Delinquency". Lecture given to Howard League, 6 Dec 1966. https://doi.org/10.1111/j.1468-2311.1967.tb00231.x

Cohen, Stanley. 1972. *Folk Devils and Moral Panics: The Creation of the Mods and Rockers*. Abingdon, Oxon; New York: Routledge.

Coleman-Norton, Paul Robinson, Frank Card Bourne, and Allan Chester Johnson. 1961. *Ancient Roman Statutes*. Austin, TX: University of Texas Press.

Comaroff, Jean and John L. Comaroff. 2001. "Naturing the Nation: Aliens, Apocalypse, and the Postcolonial State." *Social Identities* 7(2):233–65.

Coogan, Tim Pat. 2012. The Famine Plot: England's Role in Ireland's Greatest Tragedy. 1st ed. New York, NY: Palgrave Macmillan.

Cox, Alex. 1989. *Mars Attacks*. Never Distributed. Retrieved 13 July 2016 (http://www.alexcox.com/pdfs/MARS_ATTACKS_3.pdf).

CQ Almanac. 1954. "State, Justice, Commerce". Washington, DC: Congressional Quarterly, 1955. Retrieved 12 July 2018 (http://library.cqpress.com/cqalmanac/cqal54-1361159).

culturestrike. nd. "Migration is Beautiful". Retrieved 21 Feb 2019 (https://www.culturestrike.org/project/migration-is-beautiful).

Custred, Glynn. 2000. "Alien Crossings". *The American Specta-*

tor. October. Retrieved 25 June 2019 (https://vdare.com/articles/alien-crossings).

Daley, Jason. 2018. "People Were Messing Around In Texas at Least 2,500 Years Earlier Than Previously Thought". Retrieved 18 Oct 2018 (https://www.Smithsonianmag.com/Smart-News/People-Were-Texas-3000-Years-Earlier-Previously-Thought). *Smithsonian*, July 25.

Davies, C. S. L. 1966. "Slavery and Protector Somerset; The Vagrancy Act of 1547." *The Economic History Review* 19(3):533.

Dean, Jodi. 1998. *Aliens in America: Conspiracy Cultures from Outerspace to Cyberspace*. Ithaca, N.Y: Cornell University Press.

Deleuze, Gilles. 1981. *Francis Bacon: The Logic of Sensation*. London: Continuum.

Department of Justice. 2018. "Attorney General Announces Zero-Tolerance Policy for Criminal Illegal Entry."

Diamond, Jeremy. 2015. "Donald Trump: Birthright Babies Not Citizens." *CNN.Com*. Retrieved 18 July 2017 (http://www.cnn.com/2015/08/19/politics/donald-trump-birthright-american-citizenship/index.html).

Diamond, Jeremy. 2016. "Donald Trump: Ted Cruz Is an 'Anchor Baby.'" *CNN*, January 29.

Dickerson, Caitlin. 2019. "'There Is a Stench': Soiled Clothes and No Baths for Migrant Children at a Texas Center." *New York Times*. 21 June. Retrieved 25 June 2019(https://www.nytimes.com/2019/06/21/us/migrant-children-border-soap.html?searchResultPosition=5).

Dominguez, Claudia. 2018. "Immigrant 'caravan' Heading to US-Mexico Border Sparks Trump's Concern." *CNN Politics*, April 2.

Doty, Roxanne Lynn. 1993. "Foreign Policy as Social Construction: A Post-Positivist Analysis of U.S. Counterinsurgency Policy in the Philippines." *International Studies Quarterly*

37(3):297–320.

Doty, Roxanne Lynn. 1996. "Immigration and National Identity: Constructing the Nation." *Review of International Studies* 22(3):235–55.

Doty, Roxanne Lynn. 2003. *Anti-Immigrantism in Western Democracies: Statecraft, Desire, and the Politics of Exclusion.* London: Routledge.

Doty, Roxanne Lynn. 2009. *The Law into Their Own Hands: Immigration and the Politics of Exceptionalism.* Tucson: University of Arizona Press.

Du Bois, W. E. B. 1903. *The Souls of Black Folk.* The Project Gutenberg EBook. Retrieved 2 Jan 2019 (https://www.gutenberg.org/files/408/408-h/408-h.htm).

Dueben, Alex. 2014. "Puck Magazine and the Birth of Modern Political Cartooning." *Vulture*, September 10.

Dunn, Timothy J. 2009. *Blockading the Border and Human Rights: The El Paso Operation That Remade Immigration Enforcement.* 1st ed. Austin: University of Texas Press.

Egelko, Bob. 2018. "Justice's Use of Term Illegal Alien Sends Message." *San Francisco Chronicle*, March 29.

Elliott, Robert C. 2019. "Satire." Encyclopedia Britannica.

Evon, Dan. 2015. Fabricated web meme. "No Illegal Mexicans in China Thanks to the Great Wall." Retrieved 2 July 2016 (https://www.snopes.com/fact-check/bachmann-trump-overdrive/).

Executive Order 13768. 2017. "Enhancing Public Safety in the Interior of the United States". Issued 25 Jan. Retrieved 14 Feb 2017 (https://www.whitehouse.gov/presidential-actions/executive-order-enhancing-public-safety-interior-united-states/).

Fairclough, Norman. 1995. *Critical Discourse Analysis: The Critical Study of Language.* London; New York: Longman.

Federici, Silvia Beatriz. 2014. *Caliban and the Witch.* 2., rev. ed. New York, NY: Autonomedia.

Fenn, Elizabeth A. 2001. *Pox Americana: The Great Smallpox Epi-*

demic of 1775-82. 1st ed. New York: Hill and Wang.

Fine, Gary Alan and Lazaros Christoforides. 1991. "Dirty Birds, Filthy Immigrants, and the English Sparrow War: Metaphorical Linkage in Constructing Social Problems." *Symbolic Interaction* 14(4):375–93.

Fine, Michelle. 1998. *Working the Hyphens: Reinventing Self and other in Qualitative Research.*

Fishman, Mark. 1978. "Crime Waves as Ideology." *Social Problems* 25(5):531–43.

Fletcher, Michael A. 1997. "Police in Arizona Accused of Civil Rights Violations." *The Washington Post*, August 20.

Field, Margaret A. 1993. "Genocide and the Indians of California, 1769-1873". Graduate Masters Theses, University of Massachusetts, Boston. Paper 141.

Foucault, Michel. 1970. *The Order of Things: An Archaeology of the Human Sciences*. Vintage books edition. New York NY: Vintage Books.

Foucault, Michel. 1976. *Society Must Be Defended: Lectures at the Collège de France, 1975-76*. 1st Picador pbk. ed. New York: Picador.

Foucault, Michel. 1978. *The History of Sexuality*. Vintage Books ed. New York: Vintage Books.

Foucault, Michel. 1980. *Power/Knowledge: Selected Interviews and other Writings, 1972-1977*. 1st American ed. edited by C. Gordon. New York: Pantheon Books.

Foucault, Michel. 1982. "The Subject and Power." *Critical Inquiry* 8(4):777–95.

Foucault, Michel. 1984. *The Foucault Reader*. 1st ed. edited by P. Rabinow. New York: Pantheon Books.

Foucault, Michel. 1987. *The Use of Pleasure*. Vintage Books ed. New York: Vintage Books.

Foucault, Michel. 1991. *Remarks on Marx*. Conversation with Duccio Trombadori. Semiotext(E). New York: Columbia University Press

Foucault, Michel. 1995. *Discipline and Punish: The Birth of the Prison*. 2nd Vintage Books ed. New York: Vintage Books.

Foucault, Michel. 2007. *Security, Territory, Population: Lectures at the Collège de France, 1977-1978*. New York: Palgrave Macmillan.

Foucault, Michel and Colin Gordon. 1980. *Power/Knowledge: Selected Interviews and other Writings, 1972-1977*. 1st American ed. New York: Pantheon Books.

Franklin, Benjamin. 1755. "Observations Concerning the Increase of Mankind, People of Countries, Etc."

Garcia, Juan R. 2003. *Mexicans in the Midwest: 1900-1932*. Tucson: Univ. of Arizona Press.

Goode, Erich and Nachman Ben-Yehuda. 1994. *Moral Panics: The Social Construction of Deviance*. Oxford, UK; Cambridge, USA: Blackwell.

Grandin, Greg. 2019. *The End of the Myth: From the Frontier to the Border Wall in the Mind of America*. NY: Metropolitan Books.

Gramsci, Antonio. 1971. *Selections From The Prison Notebooks Of Antonio Gramsci*. edited by Q. Hoare and G. N. Smith. London: ElecBook.

Grinnell, Joseph. 1919. "The English Sparrow Has Arrived in Death Valley: An Experiment in Nature." *The American Naturalist* 53(628):468–72.

Guardino, Peter. 2017. *The Dead March: A History of the Mexican-American War*. Cambridge, Massachusetts: Harvard University Press.

Gusfield, Joseph R. 1963. *Symbolic Crusade: Status Politics and the American Temperance Movement*. 2nd ed. Urbana: University of Illinois Press.

Habermas, Jürgen. 1979. *Communication and the Evolution of Society*. Boston: Beacon Press.

Habermas, Jürgen and Frederick Lawrence. 2004. *The Philosophical Discourse of Modernity*. 14. Nachdr. Cambridge, Mass: MIT Pr.

Hall, Stuart. 1988. "The Rediscovery of 'Ideology': Return of the Repressed in Media Studies." in *Culture, society, and the media*. London; New York: Routledge.

Hall, Stuart. 1993. "Which Public, Whose Service?" in *All our futures: the changing role and purpose of the BBC*, edited by W. Stevenson. London: BFI Publishing.

Hall, Stuart, Chas Critcher, Tony Jefferson, John Clarke, and Brian Roberts. 1978/2002. *Policing the Crisis: Mugging, the State, and Law and Order*. edited by J. Young and P. Walton. London: Macmillan.

Hall, Stuart and Paul Du Gay, eds. 1996. *Questions of Cultural Identity*. London; Thousand Oaks, Calif: Sage.

Hallahan. 1921. "The Only Way to Handle It". 7 May, p. 13, reprinting of a cartoon for the Providence *Evening Bulletin* in *The Literary Digest*. Retrieved 04 March 2015 (http://www.loc.gov/pictures/item/2007680185/).

Hernandez, Richard. 2018. "The fall of employment in the manufacturing sector." US Department of Labor, Bureau of Labor Statistics. *Monthly Labor Review*. August. Retrieved 13 Jan 2019 (https://www.bls.gov/opub/mlr/2018/beyond-bls/the-fall-of-employment-in-the-manufacturing-sector.htm).

Hildreth, Richard. 2012. *The History of the United States of America: John Adams and Jefferson*. Ulan Press.

Horsey, David. 2015. "Europe's migrant crisis dwarfs U.S. problems on the Mexican border." *Los Angeles Times*. Retrieved 19 June 2016 (https://www.latimes.com/opinion/topoftheticket/la-na-tt-europe-migrant-crisis-20150902-story.html).

Hughes, Everett Cherrington. 1945. "Dilemmas and Contradictions of Status." *American Journal of Sociology* 50(5):353–59.

Humane Borders, Inc. 2018. "Migrant Death Mapping." *Humane Borders*. Retrieved 21 August 2018 (https://humaneborders.org/migrant-death-mapping/).

International Organization for Migration (@unmigration). 2019. Instagram post of 1 March 2019. Retrieved 2 March 2019 from Instagram.

Jäger, Siegfried. 2001. "Discourse and Knowledge: Theoretical and Methodological Aspects of a Critical Discourse and Dispositive Analysis." in *Methods of Critical Discourse Analysis*. London: SAGE.

Jerolmack, Colin. 2008. "How Pigeons Became Rats: The Cultural-Spatial Logic of Problem Animals." *Social Problems* 55(2):72–94.

Johnson-Cartee, Karen S. 2005. *News Narratives and News Framing: Constructing Political Reality*. Oxford, UK: Rowman and Littlefield Publishers, Inc.

Jordan, Miriam. 2018. "8-Year-Old Migrant Child From Guatemala Dies in U.S. Custody." *New York Times*, December 25. Retrieved 05 Jan 2019 (https://www.nytimes.com/2018/12/25/us/guatemalan-boy-dies-border-patrol.html).

Jørgensen, Marianne and Louise Phillips. 2011. *Discourse Analysis as Theory and Method*. Los Angeles, Calif: Sage.

Keller, George Frederick. 1882. "What Shall We Do With Our Boys?", *The San Francisco Illustrated Wasp*. 3 March. Retrieved 19 June 2013 (https://thomasnastcartoons.com/2014/02/14/what-shall-we-do-with-our-boys-3-march-1882/).

Kelly, John F. 2017. Written Testimony of DHS Secretary John F. Kelly for a Senate Committee on Homeland Security and Governmental Affairs Hearing Titled, "The Department of Homeland Security Fiscal Year 2018 Budget Request." 342 Dirksen Senate Office Bldg.: DHS.

Kendall, Brent. 2016. "Trump Says Judge's Mexican Heritage Presents 'Absolute Conflict.'" *Wall Street Journal*, 3 June. Retrieved 18 July 2016 (https://www.wsj.com/articles/donald-trump-keeps-up-attacks-on-judge-gonzalo-curiel-1464911442).

Kennedy, John F. 1958. *A Nation of Immigrants*. Harper Perennial.

Keppler, Joseph Ferdinand. 1880. "The Chinese Invasion." *Puck*, 7.158:24–25.

Kramer, Heinrich and Jacob Sprenger. 1487. *Malleus maleficarum, or: the hammer of witches*. Place of publication not identified: ReadaClassic.com.

Kraus, George. 1969. "Chinese Laborers and the Construction of the Central Pacific." *Utah Historical Quarterly* 37(1):41–57.

Kristeva, Julia and Toril Moi. 1986. *The Kristeva Reader*. New York: Columbia University Press.

Lancaster, Roger N. 2011. *Sex Panic and the Punitive State*. 1st ed. University of California Press.

Lee, John. 2013. "What Do Butterflies Have to Do with Open Borders? Migration Is Beautiful." *Open Borders*. Retrieved 4 July 2016 (https://openborders.info/blog/what-do-butterflies-have-to-do-with-open-borders-migration-is-beautiful/).

Lewis, Danny. 2015. "Reagan and Gorbachev Agreed to Pause the Cold War in Case of an Alien Invasion". *Smithsonian Magazine*. Retrieved 05 June 2017 (https://www.smithsonianmag.com/smart-news/reagan-and-gorbachev-agreed-pause-cold-war-case-alien-invasion-180957402/).

Linebaugh, Peter and Marcus Rediker. 2013. *The Many-Headed Hydra: Sailors, Slaves, Commoners, and the Hidden History of the Revolutionary Atlantic*. Second edition. Boston: Beacon Press.

Lovell, Julia. 2007. *The Great Wall: China Against the World, 1000 BC - AD 2000*. NY: Grove Press.

Lucian. 160-190/1902. *True History*. London: A.H. Bullen.

Madley, Benjamin. 2017. *An American Genocide: The United States and the California Indian Catastrophe, 1846-1873*. New Haven: Yale University Press.

Mamdani, Mahmood. 2012. *Define and Rule: Native as Political Identity*. 1st edition. Cambridge, Mass: Harvard University Press.

Mann, Charles C. 2006. *1491: New Revelations of the Americas before Columbus*. 1st Vintage Books ed. New York: Vintage.

Marchetti, Gina. 1994. *Romance and the Yellow Peril: Race, Sex, and Discursive Strategies in Hollywood Fiction*. University of California Press.

Markle, Meghan. 2015. "I'm More Than An 'Other.'" *ELLE Magazine*, 22 December. Retrieved 6 Dec 2017 (http://www.elleuk.com/life-and-culture/news/a26855/more-than-an-other/).

Marrapodi, Michele, ed. 2004. *Shakespeare, Italy, and Intertextuality*. Manchester; New York: New York: Manchester University Press; Distributed exclusively in the USA by Palgrave.

Martin, F. X. and Giraldus Cambrensis. 1978. "Giraldus as Historian." Pp. 267–84 in *Expugnatio Hibernica*. Vol. 3, *Conquest of Ireland*. Royal Irish Academy.

Marx, Karl. 1852. *The Eighteenth Brumaire of Louis Bonaparte*. Marx/Engels Internet Archive.

Marx, Karl. 1867. *Capital: A Critique Of Political Economy*. edited by F. Engels. Moscow, USSR: Progress Publishers.

Marx, Karl and Friedrich Engels. 1845. *The German Ideology*. London: Electric Book Co.

Marx, Karl and Friedrich Engels. 2010. *Marx & Engels Collected Works Volume 5 (1845-47)*. London: Lawrence & Wishart Electric Book.

McKeown, Adam. 2008. *Melancholy Order: Asian Migration and the Globalization of Borders*. New York: Columbia University Press.

Merchant, Nomaan. 2018. "Hundreds of Children Wait in Border Patrol Facility in Texas." *AP*, 17 June. Retrieved 18 June 2018 (https://www.apnews.com/9794de32d39d4c6f89fbe-faea3780769).

Miles, Jack. 1995. "The Coming Immigration Debate." *The Atlantic Monthly,* digital ed. April. Retrieved 24 May 2018 (https://www.theatlantic.com/past/docs/politics/immigrat/miles2f.htm).

Miroff, Nick. 2018. "Homeland Security Says Surge in Illegal Border Crossings Is a 'Crisis,' Warrants Military Deployment." *The Washington Post*. 5 April. Retrieved 23 March

2018 (https://www.washingtonpost.com/world/national-security/homeland-security-says-surge-in-illegal-border-crossings-is-a-crisis-warrants-military-deployment/2018/04/05/de4a496c-3903-11e8-b57c-9445cc4dfa5e_story.html?noredirect=on&utm_term=.49d86273efb1).

Mirzoeff, Nicholas. 1999. *An Introduction to Visual Culture.* London; New York: Routledge.

Model, Suzanne W. 1990. "Work and Family: Blacks and Immigrants from South and East Europe." Pp. 130–59 in *Immigration Reconsidered: History, Sociology, and Politics*, edited by V. Yans-McLaughlin. New York: Oxford University Press.

Mohney, Gillian. 2016. "Zika Virus: President Obama Urges Congress to Pass Full Funding to Fight Virus." *ABC News*, 20 May. Retrieved 29 May 2016 (http://abcnews.go.com/Health/zika-virus-cdc-dramatically-ups-number-infected-pregnant/story?id=39253562).

Morawska, Ewa. 1990. "The Sociology and Historiography of Immigration." Pp. 187–240 in *Immigration Reconsidered: History, Sociology, and Politics*, edited by V. Yans-McLaughlin. New York: Oxford University Press.

Nast, Thomas. 1882. "Which Color is to be Tabooed Next?", *Harper's Weekly.* 25 March p.192. Retrieved 29 June 2015 (https://thomasnastcartoons.com/tag/thomas-nast/).

Nast, Thomas. 1879. "'Every Dog' (No Distinction Of Color) 'Has His Day'". *Harper's Weekly*, p.1, 8 Feb. Retrieved 18 Jan 2016 (https://thomasnastcartoons.com/2014/04/01/every-dog-no-distinction-of-color-has-his-da/).

National Congress of American Indians. n.d. "Tribal Nations and the United States: An Introduction". Retrieved 5 Feb 2019 (http://www.ncai.org/about-tribes).

Nevins, Joseph. 2010. *Operation Gatekeeper and beyond: The War on "Illegals" and the Remaking of the U.S.-Mexico Boundary.* 2nd ed. New York: Routledge.

Newport, Frank. 2018. "Immigration Surges to Top of Most

Important Problem List." *GALLUP*, July 18. Retrieved 10 Sept 2018 (https://news.gallup.com/poll/237389/immigration-surges-top-important-problem-list.aspx).

Nossiter, Adam and Tyler Hicks. 2016. "Inside France's 'Jungle': Desperate Migrants Keep Coming to Calais." *New York Times.* 26 Sept.

Obama, Barack. 2004. *Dreams from My Father: A Story of Race and Inheritance.* 1st pbk. ed. New York: Three Rivers Press.

obeygiant. 2017. "Welcome Visitor Diptych Avail. 05/05!". Retrieved 21 Feb 2019 (https://obeygiant.com/welcome-visitor-diptych-avail-05-09/).

O'Brien, Gerald V. 2003. "Indigestible Food, Conquering Hordes, and Waste Materials: Metaphors of Immigrants and the Early Immigration Restriction Debate in the United States." *Metaphor and Symbol* 18(1):33–47.

Office of Inspector General. 2019. *Separated Children Placed in Office of Refugee Resettlement Care.* OEI-BL-18-00511. Retrieved 20 Jan 2019 (https://www.oig.hhs.gov/oei/reports/oei-BL-18-00511.asp).

Omi, Michael and Howard Winant. 1986. *Racial Formation in the United States from the 1960s to the 1980s.* Routledge & Kegan Paul Inc., NY.

O'Sullivan, John. 1845. "Annexation." *The United States Magazine and Democratic Review*, 5–10.

Oxford English Dictionary. All dictionary entries retrieved from the following dated versions at (http://www.oed.com.eres.library.manoa.hawaii.edu/).

1989. "Invasion." Noun.

1989. "Loophole." Noun.

2003. "Nation." Noun.

2008. "Race." Noun.

2008b. "Discourse." Adjective.

2011. "Homeland." Noun.

2012a. "Alien." Adjective and Noun.

2012b. "Autochthon." Noun.

2018. "Catch-and-release." Adjective and Noun.

Peffer, George Anthony. 1999. *If They Don't Bring Their Women Here: Chinese Female Immigration before Exclusion*. Urbana: University of Illinois Press.

Peña, Enrique (@EPN). 2018. 6:25 PM - 29 May 2018. "President @realDonaldTrump: NO. Mexico will NEVER pay for a wall. Not now, not ever. Sincerely, Mexico (all of us)". Retrieved 4 June 2018 (https://twitter.com/EPN/status/1001635649550663680).

Phippen, J. Weston. 2017. "What Trump Doesn't Understand About MS-13." *The Atlantic*, 26 June. Retrieved 24 July 2017 (https://www.theatlantic.com/news/archive/2017/06/trump-ms-13/528453/).

Poff, Jeremiah. 2018. "An Army of Illegal Aliens Is About to Storm Our Border." *Todd Starnes.Com*, April 3. Retrieved 4 May 2018 (https://www.toddstarnes.com/show/an-army-of-illegal-aliens-is-about-to-storm-our-border/).

Portes, Alejandro and John Walton. 1981. *Labor, Class, and the International System*. NY: Academic Press.

Portes, Alejandro and Rubén G. Rumbaut. 2014. *Immigrant America: A Portrait*. Fourth edition, revised, updated, and expanded. Berkeley and Los Angeles, California: University of California Press.

Qiu, Linda. 2015. "No, Michele Bachmann Did Not Say There Are No 'illegal Mexicans in China' Thanks to the Great Wall." *Politifact*, August 20. Retrieved 23 Sept 2017 (https://www.politifact.com/punditfact/statements/2015/aug/20/facebook-posts/no-michele-bachmann-did-not-say-there-are-no-illeg/).

Reagan, Ronald. 1986. "Statement on Signing the Immigration Reform and Control Act of 1986". Retrieved 15 June 2019 (https://www.reaganlibrary.gov/research/speeches/110686b).

Rezaian, Jason. 2018. "USCIS Director Who Eliminated nation of immigrants Is the Son of an Immigrant." *The Washington Post*, February 23. Retrieved 23 March 2018 (https://www.washingtonpost.com/news/worldviews/

wp/2018/02/23/uscis-director-who-eliminated-nation-of-immigrants-is-the-son-of-an-immigrant/?utm_term=.3fecd8294ed6).

Rieder, John. 2008. *Colonialism and the Emergence of Science Fiction*. Middletown, Conn: Wesleyan University Press.

Robin, Corey. 2004. *Fear: The History of a Political Idea*. Oxford: Oxford Univ. Press.

Rodriquez, Favianna. 2012. tumbler post. Retrieved 24 Jan 2018 (http://favianna.tumblr.com/post/40508094090/the-monarch-butterfly-has-come-to-represent-the).

Rogers, W. A. c.1918. "The Breath of the Hun." *New York Herald*, 28 March 1918, p.5. Retrieved 12 Nov 2014 (http://www.loc.gov/pictures/item/2010717783/).

Rubio, Arturo and Caitlin Dickerson. 2019. "Migrant Children Moved Back to Troubled Texas Border Facility." *New York Times*. 25 June. Retrieved 25 June 2019 (https://www.nytimes.com/2019/06/25/us/john-sanders-cbp.html?module=inline).

Sack, Kevin. 2001. "Far From Mexico, Making a Place Like Home." *New York Times*, July 30, 1.

Said, Edward W. 1978. *Orientalism*. 1st Vintage Books ed. New York: Vintage Books.

Sassen-Koob, Saskia. 1981. "Towards a Conceptualization of Immigrant Labor." *Social Problems* 29(1):65–85.

Sassen, Saskia. 1988. *The Mobility of Labor and Capital: A Study in International Investment and Labor Flow*. Transferred to digital printing. Cambridge: Cambridge Univ. Press.

Shaire Productions 2009. District 9 Viral Marketing Campaign by Sherrie Thai. Retrieved 18 Aug 2018 (http://shaireproductions.blogspot.com/2009/07/).

Schirato, Tony and Jen Webb. 2004. *Reading the Visual*. Crows Nest, NSW: Allen & Unwin.

Shapiro, Michael J. 1985. "Metaphor in the Philosophy of the Social Sciences." *Cultural Critique* (2):191.

Shapiro, Michael J. 1997a. Violent Cartographies: Mapping Cultures of War. Minneapolis: University of Minnesota Press.

Shapiro, Michael J. 1997b. "Narrating the Nation, Unwelcoming the Stranger: Anti-Immigration Policy in Contemporary 'America.'" *Alternatives: Global, Local, Political* 22(1):1–34.

Shapiro, Michael J. 2008. *Cinematic Geopolitics*. Florence, US: Routledge.

Shapiro, Michael J. 2012. *Discourse, Culture, Violence*. NY: Routledge.

Sharma, Nandita. 2006. *Home Economics*. Toronto, Canada: University of Toronto Press Incorporated.

Sloan, Bill. 2017. *Their Backs against the Sea: The Battle of Saipan and the Largest Banzai Attack of World War II*. Boston, MA: Da Capo Press.

Smith, Adam. 1776. *An Inquiry into the Nature and Causes of the Wealth of Nations*. 1st edition. London, England: W. Strahan; and T. Cadell.

Smith, Dorothy E. 1996. "The Relations of Ruling: A Feminist Inquiry." *Culture and Organization* 2(2):171–91.

Sony Pictures. 2014. "About District 9". *Sony Pictures*. Retrieved 12 July 2015 (http://www.sonypictures.com/movies/district9/).

Spector, Malcolm and John I. Kitsuse. 1977. *Constructing Social Problems*. Menlo Park, CA: Cummings Publishing Company.

Spencer, Herbert. 1981. *The Man versus the State: With Six Essays on Government, Society, and Freedom*. Indianapolis, Ind: Liberty Classics.

State of California. 1876. *The Social, Moral, and Political Effect of Chinese Immigration*. Testimony Taken Before a Committee of the Senate of the State of California. Sacramento, CA: State Printing Office. Retrieved 14 Jan 2017 (https://archive.org/details/chineseimmigrati00cali/page/n5).

Starnes, Todd. 2019. facebook page authenticated as belonging to Todd Starnes. Retrieved 12 Jan 2019 (https://www.facebook.com/pg/ToddStarnesFNC/about/?ref=page_internal).

Statistica. 2018. "Reported Violent Crime Rate in the

United States from 1990 to 2017." Retrieved 12 Oct 2018 (https://www.statista.com/statistics/191219/reported-violent-crime-rate-in-the-usa-since-1990/).

Steinfeld, Robert J. 1991. *The Invention of Free Labor: The Employment Relation in English and American Law and Culture, 1350-1870*. Chapel Hill: Univ. of North Carolina Press.

Stoler, Ann Laura. 1995. *Race and the Education of Desire: Foucault's History of Sexuality and the Colonial Order of Things*. Durham: Duke University Press.

Stoler, Ann Laura. 2017. "Introduction: The Dark Logic of Invasive Others." *Social Research: An International Quarterly* 84(1):3–5.

Surette, Ray. 1998. *Media, Crime, and Criminal Justice*. Wadsworth Publishing.

Swift, Jonathan. 1726. *Gulliver's Travels*. Bookbyte Digital Edition.

Takaki, Ronald T. 1998. *Strangers from a Different Shore: A History of Asian Americans*. Updated and rev. ed., 1st Back Bay ed. Boston: Little, Brown.

Tannenbaum, Frank. 1938. *Crime and the Community*. Columbia University Press.

Thomas and Anton C. Pegis. 1259. *Summa Contra Gentiles*. Notre Dame, IN: University of Notre Dame Press.

timbergsp. 2007. *Michigan Sportsman*. General Michigan Hunting forum. Post started by TheBigEasy, Oct 20. "English Sparrow Are Game?". "my grandpa used to tell me about when he was a kid they would get 2 cents a bird for them just took them up to the court house and give them to the clerk. this was somthing to do with keeping the kids out of trouble. he said the clerk would toss them out the window and he would go pick them up and take them back in about 1 hour later. then they started cutting the heads off first before they tossed them out the window". Retrieved 12 July 2016 (https://www.michigan-sportsman.com/forum/threads/english-sparrow-are-game.205788/page-2).

Trauner, Joan B. 1978. "Chinese as Medical Scapegoats, 1870 – 1905." *California History Magazine.* Retrieved 13 June 2019 (http://www.foundsf.org/index.php?title=Chinese_as_Medical_Scapegoats,_1870-1905).

Trollope, Frances. 1839. *Domestic Manners of the Americans.* 5th ed. London, England: Richard Bentley.

Trump, Donald J. (@realDonaldTrump). 2014. 12:24pm – 10 Jul 2014. "Mexico is allowing many thousands to go thru their country & to our very stupid open door. The Mexicans are laughing at us as the buses pass by." Retrieved 24 Jun 2016 (https://twitter.com/realDonaldTrump/status/487316499208896512).

Trump, Donald J. 2015. "Announcement of Candidacy." Trump Tower, New York. 16 June. Retrieved 18 June 2015 (http://www.p2016.org/trump/trump061615sp.html).

Trump, Donald J. 2016. "Donald Trump's Contract with the American Voter." Retrieved 2 July 2017 (https://assets.donaldjtrump.com/_landings/contract/O-TRU-102316-Contractv02.pdf).

Trump, Donald J. (@realDonaldTrump). 2018a. 6:56 AM - 1 Apr 2018. "Border Patrol Agents are not allowed to properly do their job at the Border because of ridiculous liberal (Democrat) laws like Catch & Release. Getting more dangerous. "Caravans" coming. Republicans must go to Nuclear Option to pass tough laws NOW. NO MORE DACA DEAL!". Retrieved 4 April 2018 (https://twitter.com/realDonaldTrump/status/980443810529533952?ref_src=twsrc%5Etfw%7Ctwcamp%5Etweetembed%7Ctwterm%5E980443810529533952&ref_url=https%3A%2F%2Fwww.cnn.com%2F2018%2F04%2F01%2Fpolitics%2Ftrump-mexico-caravan-tweet%2Findex.html).

Trump, Donald J. (@realDonaldTrump). 2018b. 6:44 AM - 23 Apr 2018. "Despite the Democrat inspired laws on Sanctuary Cities and the Border being so bad and one sided, I have instructed the Secretary of Homeland Security not to let these large Caravans of people into our Country. It is a disgrace. We are the only Country in the World so naive! WALL". Retrieved 5 May 2018 (https://twitter.com/realDonaldTrump/status/988413372298416128?ref_src=twsrc%5Etfw%7Ctwcamp%5Etweetembed%7Ctwterm%5E988413372298416128&ref_url=https%3A%2F%2Fwww.voanews.com%2Fa%2Ftrickle-of-caravan-migrants-arrives-at-us-border-not-welcome-tweets-trump%2F4362090.html).

Trump, Donald J. 2018c."Remarks by President Trump at a California Sanctuary State Roundtable," 16 May, California. Retrieved 18 Sept 2018 (https://www.whitehouse.gov/briefings-statements/remarks-president-trump-california-sanctuary-state-roundtable/).

Trump, Donald J. 2018d. May 29, Speech in Nashville, TN. Retrieved 18 July 2018 (https://www.cnn.com/2018/05/30/politics/trump-nashville-speech/index.html).

Trump, Donald J. (@realDonaldTrump). 2018e. 3:49am – 2 Jul 2018. "When we have an 'infestation' of MS-13 GANGS in certain parts of our country, who do we sent to get them out? ICE! They are tougher and smarter than these rough criminal elelments that bad immigration laws allow into our country. Dems do not appreciate the great job they do! Nov." Retrieved 23 Aug 2018 (https://twitter.com/realDonaldTrump/status/1014098721460686849).

Trump, Donald J. (@realDonaldTrump). 2018f. 5:44pm – 5 Jul 2018. "A vote for Democrats in November is a vote to let MS-13 run wild in our communities, to let drugs pour into our cities, and to take jobs and benefits away from hard-working Americans. Democrats want anarchy, amnesty and chaos – Republicans want LAW, ORDER AND JUSTICE!". Retrieved 13 Jul 2018 (https://twitter.com/realDonaldTrump/status/1015033658548207616).

Trump, Donald J. (@realDonaldTrump). 2018g. 4:41am – 29 Oct 2018. "Many Gang Members and some very bad people are mixed into the Caravan heading to our Southern Border Please go back, you will not be admitted into the United States unless you go through the legal process. This is an invasion of our Country and our Military is waiting for you!". Retrieved 18 April 2019 (https://www.nytimes.com/2018/10/29/us/politics/caravan-trump-shooting-elections.html?searchResultPosition=4).

Trump, Donald J. 2019. "President Donald J. Trump's Address to the Nation on the Crisis at the Border." The White House, 8 January. Retrieved 17 Jan 2019 (https://www.whitehouse.gov/briefings-statements/president-donald-j-trumps-address-nation-crisis-border/).

Trump, Donald J. 2019b. "Presidential Proclamation on Declaring a National Emergency Concerning the Southern Border of the United States." The White House, 15 February. Accessed 21 Feb 2019 (https://www.whitehouse.gov/presidential-actions/presidential-proclamation-declaring-national-emergency-concerning-southern-border-united-states/).

Trump Jr., Donald. 2018. (@DonaldJTrumpJr). 5:57 AM - 26 Jun 2018. "We are a nation of laws. And yes, of immigrants… LEGAL immigrants. Don't equate those that wait in line and do it the right way to those that break our laws and expect special treatment". Retrieved (https://twitter.com/donaldjtrumpjr/status/1011594389502783495?lang=en).

TrumpStoreAmerica. 2019. "Build the Wall – Trump Kit 2020". Retrieved 12 Jan 2019 (https://trumpstoreamerica.com/products/build-the-wall-trump-2020-kit?variant=12963298738239).

Tucker, Spencer, James R. Arnold, Roberta Wiener, Paul G. Pierpaoli, Thomas W. Cutrer, and Pedro Santoni, eds. 2013. *The Encyclopedia of the Mexican-American War: A Political, Social, and Military History*. Santa Barbara, Calif: ABC-CLIO.

Turner, Ralph J. and Samuel J. Surace. 1956. "Zoot-Suiters and Mexicans: Symbols in Crowd Behavior." *American Journal of Sociology* 62(1):14–20.

UNESCO. 1950. *Four Statements on the Race Question.* United Nations Educational, Scientific and Cultural Organizations. Retrieved 18 April 2013 (http://unesdoc.unesco.org/images/0012/001282/128291eo.pdf).

UNESCO. 1951. *Four Statements on the Race Question.* United Nations Educational, Scientific and Cultural Organizations. Retrieved 18 April 2013 (http://unesdoc.unesco.org/images/0017/001789/178908eb.pdf).

Urry, John. 2000. *Sociology beyond Societies: Mobilities for the Twenty-First Century.* London; New York: Routledge.

US Census Bureau. 1870. "Compendium of the Ninth Census: Population. With Race."

US Census Bureau. 1949. "Historical Statistics of the United States 1789-1945." Retrieved 14 Jan 2014 (https://www2.census.gov/prod2/statcomp/documents/HistoricalStatisticsoftheUnitedStates1789-1945.pdf).

US Census Bureau. 1999. "Nativity of the Population for Urban Places Ever Among the 50 Largest Urban Places Since 1870: 1850 to 1990."

US Census Bureau. 2011. "CSPAN Presentation December 2, 2011_11-30-11". Retrieved 9 March 2015 (https://www.census.gov/newsroom/pdf/cspan_fb_slides.pdf).

US Census Bureau. n.d. "1930". Retrieved 13 Jan 2014 (https://www.census.gov/history/www/through_the_decades/index_of_questions/1930_1.html)

US Congress. 1776. "Declaration of Independence."

US Congress. 1790. "An Act to Establish an Uniform Rule of Naturalization."

US Congress. 1862. "An Act to prohibit the 'Coolie Trade' by American Citizens in American Vessels." 19 Feb. Chap. XXVII.

US Congress. 1864. "An Act to Encourage Immigration."

US Congress. 1875. "An Act Supplementary to the Acts in Relation to Immigration."

US Congress. 1917. "An Act to Regulate the Immigration of Aliens to, and the Residence of Aliens in, the United States." 5 Feb. Chap. 29.

US Congress. 1921. "An Act to Limit the Immigration of Aliens into the United States." 19 May. Chap. 8.

US Congress. 1986. "Immigration Reform and Control Act."

US Customs and Border Protection. 2017. "BP Southwest Border Apps Fencing FY17." Retrieved 18 April 2018 (https://www.cbp.gov/sites/default/files/assets/documents/2017-Dec/BP%20Southwest%20Border%20Apps%20Fencing%20FY17.pdf).

US Customs and Border Protection. 2018a. "El Centro Sector California." Retrieved 15 June 2018 (https://www.cbp.gov/border-security/along-us-borders/border-patrol-sectors/el-centro-sector-california).

US Customs and Border Protection. 2018b. "Southwest Border Migration FY2018." Retrieved 18 April 2018 (https://www.cbp.gov/newsroom/stats/sw-border-migration).

US Customs and Border Protection. 2018. "Border Patrol History". 5 October. Retrieved 03 Dec 2018 (https://www.cbp.gov/border-security/along-us-borders/history#).

US Department of Homeland Security. nd. Image retrieved 07 Feb 2019 (https://www.dhs.gov/xlibrary/photos/sand-dune-fence.jpg).

US Department of Homeland Security. 2016. "Mission". Retrieved 18 Oct 2018 (https://www.dhs.gov/mission).

US Department of Homeland Security. 2018. *We Must Secure The Border And Build The Wall To Make America Safe Again.* Retrieved 18 Oct 2018 (https://www.dhs.gov/news/2018/02/15/we-must-secure-border-and-build-wall-make-america-safe-again).

US Department of Justice. 2018. "Attorney General Sessions Delivers Remarks Discussing the Immigration Enforcement

Actions of the Trump Administration." Retrieved 18 Oct 2018 (https://www.justice.gov/opa/speech/attorney-general-sessions-delivers-remarks-discussing-immigration-enforcement-actions).

US Holocaust Museum. nd. "Refugees." *US Holocaust Memorial Museum*. Retrieved 10 Jan 2018 (https://encyclopedia.ushmm.org/content/en/article/refugees).

US Government. 2017. "O-1 Visa: Individuals with Extraordinary Ability or Achievement." *US Citizenship and Immigration Services*. Retrieved 8 Jan 2018 (https://www.uscis.gov/working-united-states/temporary-workers/o-1-visa-individuals-extraordinary-ability-or-achievement).

US Government Publishing Office, Congressional Record. 14 June 1954. Retrieved 25 April 2019 (https://www.govinfo.gov/content/pkg/GPO-CRECB-1954-pt6/pdf/GPO-CRECB-1954-pt6-13-1.pdf).

US Immigration and Customs Enforcement. 2018. "Victims Of Immigration Crime Engagement (VOICE) Office." *US Immigration and Customs Enforcement*. Retrieved 18 Oct 2018 (https://www.ice.gov/voice).

US State of Arizona. 2010. *Support Our Law Enforcement and Safe Neighborhoods Act*. (Arizona SB 1070). Retrieved 13 June 2014 (https://www.azleg.gov/legtext/49leg/2r/bills/sb1070s.pdf).

Van Hollen, Chris (@ChrisVanHollen). 2018. 8:24pm - Jun 17. "Just left Border Patrol Processing Center in McAllen—aka 'the dog kennel.' Witnessed loads of kids massed together in large pens of chain-linked fence separated from their moms and dads. @realDonaldTrump, change your shameful policy today! #FamiliesBelongTogether." Retrieved 13 Feb 2019 (https://www.bbc.com/news/world-us-canada-44518942).

Volti, Rudi. 2017. *Society and Technological Change*. 8th Ed. New York: Worth Publishers.

Von Spakovsky, Hans A. 2016. "Sorry, but the Accurate Legal Term Is 'Illegal Alien.'" *National Review*, November 4.

Wallace, Chris. 2013. *Fox News* "Special Report". 19 September.

Watts, Sheldon J. 1999. *Epidemics and History: Disease, Power and Imperialism*. New Haven: Yale Univ. Press.

Weldes, Jutta, ed. 2003. *To Seek out New Worlds: Science Fiction and World Politics*. 1st Palgrave Macmillan ed. New York: Palgrave Macmillan.

Wells, H. G. 1898. *The War of the Worlds*. The Pennsylvania State University.

West, Richard Samuel. 2004. *The San Francisco Wasp: An Illustrated History*. Easthampton, Mass: Periodyssey Press.

Wheeler, Keith. 1976. *The Chroniclers*. Ed. Daniels, George G. Part of the *Time-Life Books* series on *The Old West*. NY: Time-Life Books.

White House. 2018a. "What You Need To Know About Loopholes Allowing Unaccompanied Alien Children To Stay In The Country". White House Press release. Retrieved 18 May 2018 (https://www.whitehouse.gov/briefings-statements/need-know-loopholes-allowing-unaccompanied-alien-children-stay-country/).

White House. 2018b. "President Donald J. Trump Stands with the Victims of Illegal Alien Crime." June 22. Retrieved 18 May (https://www.whitehouse.gov/briefings-statements/president-donald-j-trump-stands-victims-illegal-alien-crime/).

Williams, Jill. 2013. "When Arrest Becomes Rescue," October 31, Presentation at UH Mānoa Geography Department, Honolulu, HI.

Wimmer, Andreas and Nina Glick Schiller. 2003. "Methodological Nationalism, the Social Sciences, and the Study of Migration: An Essay in Historical Epistemology." *The International Migration Review* 37(3):576–610.

Wodak, Ruth and Michael Meyer, eds. 2001. *Methods of Critical Discourse Analysis*. London: SAGE.

Wodak, Ruth and Michael Meyer, eds. 2009. *Methods of Crit-*

ical Discourse Analysis. 2nd ed. London; Thousand Oaks [Calif.]: SAGE.

Wood, Ellen Meiksins. 2002. *The Origin of Capitalism: A Longer View*. Verso: London.

Yans-McLaughlin, Virginia, ed. 1990. *Immigration Reconsidered: History, Sociology, and Politics*. New York: Oxford University Press.

Zangwill, Israel. 1909. *The Melting-Pot*. Project Gutenberg Ebook.

Žižek, Slavoj. 1993. *Tarrying with the Negative: Kant, Hegel, and the Critique of Ideology*. Durham: Duke University Press.

---

[1] In this study I routinely use scare quotes in an attempt to denaturalize ideas and state categorizations such as 'nation', 'race', 'alien', and 'migrant', as well as to alert us to the political nature of concepts such as 'knowledge', 'belonging', and 'crisis'. This stylistic device is intended to disrupt the known, and to remind us that such terms are habitually used to organize social relations. For the purposes of readability, however, I will only employ scare quotes at the first instance of using them.

[2] Also known as the Trump travel ban, the Muslim ban is the commonly used term that refers to actions by the Trump administration—including Executive Orders 13769 and 13790 from January and March of 2017—that restrict entry to the US from eight nation-states with predominantly Muslim populations.

[3] Henceforth, the term *subject* (in its noun form) is used in this study to refer to official legal state categories such as alien and citizen, while the term *figurative subject* is used to denote the imaginative ways people are constructed as subject-figures.

[4] For clarification, the terms immigrant, emigrant, and migrant are interchangeable, with each being a popular term for the same thing in different historical periods.

[5] A detailed account of systematic changes to policy and practice during this time frame can be found in Massey, Durand, and Malone (2002).

[6] Ali Behdad calls this, "amnesia in the founding of the nation" (2005:29).

[7] An alternative perspective might consider such articulations indicative of the *conflation* between colonialism and immigration.

[8] Also commonly translated as "rule of thoughts" (1845/2016:1)

[9] W.E.B. Du Bois discusses a similar process in what he terms double-consciousness, a, "sense of always looking at one's self through the eyes of others, of measuring one's soul by the tape of a world that looks on in amused contempt and pity" (1903/2008:4).

[10] See Keppler's 1880 political cartoon titled, "The Chinese Invasion" on p.162, for example.

[11] It should be noted, however, that all of the September 11th hijackers were issued visas and entered the US through official ports of entry.

[12] I employ the noun 'subject' in this study to refer to official state categories such as alien and citizen, while I use the term 'figurative subject' to denote the imaginative ways people are constructed as subject-figures.

[13] The law also prescribes that 'vagrants' be branded with the letter V, and allows for their sale into slavery for a period of two years (Davies 1966:533).

[14] See Nevins 2002:59-75 for a historical account of transformations to practices and subjectivities along what he calls, "the San Diego-Tijuana Divide" (2002:59).

[15] There is no question determining citizenship status on the current US census, although the Trump administration proposes to add one to 2020 census forms.

[16] Although both African-origin slaves and people of Indian tribes are considered Other to the US national project, they are never considered 'immigrants'. For this reason, their appearance in this study is limited except as they relate to and impact upon US national and immigrant subjectivities.

[17] Anderson notes that one of the ways imagined national communities legitimize their existence is by, "always regard[ing] themselves as somehow ancient" (1983:109).

[18] In the UK during the interwar period of 1918-1939, Hall (1993) finds that BBC radio broadcasts helped construct the nation. Notes Hall: "It produced the nation which it addressed: it constructed its audience by the ways it represented them" (1993:32).

[19] Women are not imagined as part of "all men" either, and do not gain voting rights throughout the US until 1920.

[20] This iteration of people as 'property' extends back to the Roman Empire. After the Edict of Caracalla is issued in 212 CE, all free inhab-

itants of the Roman empire are granted citizenship; slaves, however, are thought of as 'property', thereby lacking the legal personhood that would have afforded them citizenship (in Coleman-Norton, Bourne, and Johnson 1961:225).

[21] Although the work is commonly referred to as a history of Ireland, the title in Latin is *Topographia Hibernica,* and Cambrensis himself always referred to it as his *Topography* (O'Meara 1982:14). Perhaps this also is indicative of the conflation between 'a people' and the particular geography or topography to which 'a people' are seen as belonging.

[22] In the 1920s the estimates had been reduced to 40 or 50 million for the entire hemisphere, but contemporary estimates are higher. Notes Mann: "The High Counters seem to be winning the argument, at least for now. No definitive data exist, but the majority of the extant evidentiary scraps indicate it: (2006:151).

[23] As Fine and Christoforides (1991) point out, conjoining an old 'problem' with a new one is a productive way to magnify 'problems' and make sense of them.

[24] Although it is important to be mindful that ideas of race and nationality have an impact on who is enumerated at the census in any historical period.

[25] And again we must be mindful that idea about class and gender, as well as race and nationality, have an impact on who is counted as 'immigrant'.

[26] Which at the time meant Turkey, Armenia, Persia and Arabia, according to the US Census Bureau (1949:21).

[27] Such laws emerged in colonial America in the 1660s and are not repealed nationwide until 1967, three years after the Civil Rights Act of 1964.

[28] Bearing in mind that the census is as much productive of identity as a reflection of it.

[29] Because of the discriminatory nature of the term 'alien migrant', I only use it when clarity requires. Ideas of alien-ness, however, are seen as intrinsic to the term 'migrant'.

[30] 'Rounding up' in itself is a polyvalent term. It is a term used on farms to refer to the practice of herding docile animals like sheep. 'Roundup' is also the name of a popular toxic chemical used on out-of-place plants.

[31] These two ideas—being a lowly animal who is also capable of invading—seem paradoxical in exactly the same manner as the 'Indian native' subjectivity is produced as both 'lazy' *and* 'barbaric'.

[32] In other words, discursive crossover works to modify the animal subjectivity too, in this case giving them human motives of imposition and invasion as if they are privy to human ideologies about frontiers, boundaries, and 'races'. The power effects of this are to legitimate aggressive 'solutions' such as species extermination. For the purposes of this study, however, my focus is how discursive crossover affects the *human* migrant subjectivity.

[33] Although far-right and fascist regimes (among others) do stretch the bounds of possibility when it comes to talking about humans in this manner.

[34] This might also explain why some people insist on using the archaic term 'alien' to refer to out-of-place humans: the space alien crossover that this term evokes jars the senses, or prompts an interior giggle, but either way detracts from the seriousness of what is happening to the actual people being labeled this way.

[35] Of course the same could be said of unauthorized migrants: they don't go through customs, and neither do walls prevent their migrations.

[36] A full index of works that Deleuze considers is listed in *Francis Bacon: The Logic of Sensation* 1981:162-171.

[37] An early draft of *Mars Attacks* from 1989 features a dystopian nightmare in which Martians have claimed earth as a dumping ground for consumer products, and Donald Trump is President (Cox 1989:3).

[38] During the 1985 Geneva Summit, legend has it that Reagan and Gorbachev go on a private walk in which they informally agree to help each other in the event of a space alien invasion (Lewis 2015).

[39] In the nature of discursive crossover, *True History* can be seen as an allegory that questions the political and material practices of the Roman empire without specifically mentioning it.

[40] For an analysis of the discourse on the anchor baby and problematized 'alien' sexuality, see Cisneros (2013).

[41] Or as Mexican history books call it, the Invasión Estadounidense a México, or the United States' Invasion of Mexico (Sandoval 2000). Such naming practices remind us of the quote attributed to Jawaharlal Nehru (1946), that "history is almost always written by the victors".

[42] This paradox could be indicative of how the process of stereotype construction tends to push figurative subjects into false binaries (we saw this with the trope of the 'lazy barbarian'). It could equally herald a shift in the Mexican subjectivity from lazy to increasingly threatening in the period leading up to the signing of the Gadsden Treaty in 1854.

[43] Immigration reached 19% of mentions as the top problem of the nation in April 2006, as Congress considered a comprehensive immigration bill. It also hit 17% in the summer of 2014, as news cautioned about large numbers of migrants attempting to enter the US from Central America (Newport 2018).

[44] It is hard to miss the rape-like trope here, that Mexicans—like those being raped—'are going to enjoy it'.

[45] Perhaps Peña's inclusion of "all of us" is indicative of how divisive rhetoric can serve a unifying function.